Fort Bridger, Wyoming

FORT BRIDGER, WYOMING

Trading Post for Indians, Mountain Men and Westward Migrants

by

Hunt Janin

McFarland & Company, Inc., Publishers
Jefferson, North Carolina, and London

Library of Congress Cataloguing-in-Publication Data

Janin, Hunt, 1940–
    Fort Bridger, Wyoming : trading post for Indians, mountain men
and westward migrants / by Hunt Janin.
       p.   cm.
    Includes bibliographical references (p.) and index.   ∞
    ISBN 0-7864-0884-7 (illustrated case binding : 50# alkaline paper)
    1. Fort Bridger (Wyo.) — History.   2. Frontier and pioneer life —
Wyoming — Fort Bridger Region.   3. Pioneers — Wyoming — Fort
Bridger Region — History — 19th century.   4. Pioneers — West (U.S.) —
History — 19th century.   5. Frontier and pioneer life — West (U.S.)
6. Overland journeys to the Pacific.   I. Title.
F769.F54J36   2001
978.7'84 — dc21   00-51133

British Library cataloguing data are available

On the cover: Log cabin at Fort Bridger. (Photograph by the author.)

Manufactured in the United States of America

McFarland & Company, Inc., Publishers
Box 611, Jefferson, North Carolina 28640
www.mcfarlandpub.com

Table of Contents

List of Illustrations

List of Maps

Preface

My interest in the frontier was encouraged by my late father-in-law, Professor Omer Call Stewart (1908–1991). He was a specialist on the Indians of the trans–Mississippi West and chronicled the use of peyote — a small, spineless cactus with psychedelic properties — which was consumed for religious purposes by some of these Indians. A readable account of Stewart's life and work can be found in Carol L. Howell's *Cannibalism Is an Acquired Taste, and Other Notes: Conversations with Anthropologist Omer C. Stewart* (1998).

I must thank Stephen and Kyra Kuhn, who via the Internet helped me find sources for many of the 19th century illustrations used in this book. These pictures and photos are among the very best representations of the American frontier; my only regret is that they cannot be reproduced here in the full color and large format which they deserve.

Special thanks are also due to Linda N. Byers, the superintendent at Fort Bridger, and to the local residents there.

Mrs. Byers gave me a hands-on tour of the post, as well as half a day of her valuable time, when I visited Fort Bridger in April 1999. Some of the local residents were kind enough to let me interview them about conditions in the Fort Bridger area today. From them I learned the important fact that the local economy is no longer based chiefly on ranching but on a naturally occurring raw material known as "trona." Trona, whose chemical name is sodium sesquicarbonate, is mined near the Green River and is used to make soda ash and other sodium chemicals; these in turn are used for making glass, paper and detergents.

"Larry" Syversen, an expert on the frontier West, gave me detailed information on some of the weapons of that era. Petronella van Gorkom read an earlier draft of this book and corrected a number of editorial and substantive mistakes. Any errors or misjudgments remaining here, however, are my responsibility alone.

Hunt Janin

When his trading post flourished at Fort Bridger, he [Jim Bridger] was supposed to have a large amount of money in his possession. Some desperadoes entered his house one night for the purpose of robbing him.

Bridger, awakening from his sleep, quickly said, "What are you lookin' for?"

One of the desperadoes answered, "We are looking for your money." Bridger replied, "Wait jest a minute and I'll git up and help you." This disconcerted the robbers, and knowing their man they concluded not to wait until he "got up," but quickly departed.

J. Lee Humfreville,
Twenty Years Among Our Savage Indians
(1897)

Introduction

I have wanted to write this book for a long time. The seminal idea for *Fort Bridger, Wyoming* came from Holling Clancy Holling's *Tree in the Trail* (1942), an illustrated book for children which I read and reread when I was growing up in San Francisco. Holling tells the story of an ancient cottonwood tree growing near the border between Kansas and Colorado. A full cast of characters from the Great Plains and the Rocky Mountain West passed close by this tree at one point or another, from the time it sprouted in 1610 until it was felled in 1834 by the combination of old age, lightning and a tornado.

Remarkably, however, the tree's adventures did not end there. A wagon master on the Santa Fe Trail who knew its history carved an ornate yoke out of the fallen trunk. He then hitched his prime pair of oxen to the new yoke and, working together with five other pairs of oxen, these sturdy beasts hauled trade goods and supplies along the Santa Fe Trail.[1] I was immensely pleased to be able to buy a reprinted copy of *Tree in the Trail* in Santa Fe in 1985.

The book you now have in your hands is the final result of that purchase.

It draws heavily on primary sources and, retaining the original spelling and punctuation of these documents, lets the participants tell the story of the frontier in their own words. It tries to recapture three qualities which were key factors in the exploration and settlement of the West from the late 1700s until 1890 — *the spirit of adventure, the hopes for a new start in life*, and *the dream of unbounded personal freedom*. These are the same factors we use today to create and re-create the mythic West — that is, the West as we imagine it to have been, not as history tells us it really was.

Although a great deal has been written about other aspects of frontier life, no author writing for adult readers has used a trading post–frontier fort as a peg on which to hang a description of the Rocky Mountain West and its formidable cast of characters — the explorers, Indians, mountain men (beaver trappers), emigrants, soldiers, stagecoach drivers, Pony Express riders, Forty-niners (California gold miners), cowboys, outlaws, sheepmen, soldiers and professional buffalo hunters. (Professional buffalo hunters were well-organized and in the 1870s and 1880s shot millions of

1

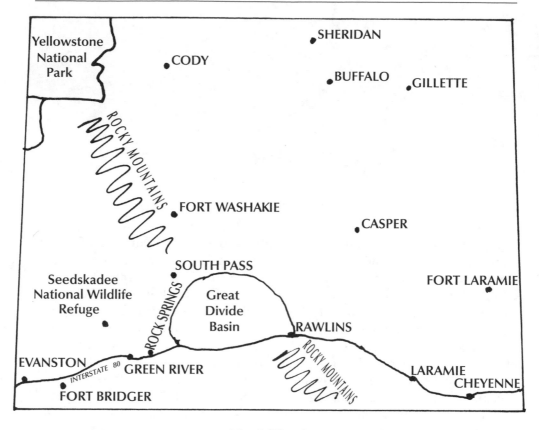

Map 1: Wyoming

buffalo on a commercial basis for their hides alone, rather than for food or sport.[2])

This book tries to be a brief, factually accurate, informal account of the frontier experience as a whole, as reflected in events which took place at or near Fort Bridger or are otherwise relevant to the history of the fort. Because the book deals with both the real West and the mythic West, it is more of a primer for the layman than a narrowly focused work for the professional academician. Even the scholar, however, may find something of interest in the extensive quotes which are taken from primary sources. What the reader will find, I believe, is that these direct quotes convey the flavor of frontier times much better than any modern paraphrases possibly can.

One word of warning: this is not a politically correct book. For the reasons outlined in Appendix I, it does not give equal time to women. It also contains some strong language, some racial epithets and some violent scenes. But all of these come directly from 19th century sources. I have used them not to shock the reader but to give a truthful report of these important aspects of frontier life.

A Road Map for This Book

Topics are approached here in roughly chronological order but with some intentional overlaps. In Chapter II we will look at Jim Bridger as a prime example of Westering and then at the historical process of Westering itself, from the days of Daniel Boone to the closing of the frontier. Chapter III discusses the Indians of the Northern Rockies, particularly the Shoshoni, in the 1820s, which was the high point of their nomadic culture. By that time the horse had fundamentally improved the Indians' way of life, and the numbers, rifles, alcohol, diseases and broken treaties of the white man had not yet overwhelmed it.

It is important to remember here that not everyone on the frontier was "white"; that is, of Caucasian descent. There were also large numbers of Mexicans, Chinese, Afro-Americans, Europeans and a host of other ethnic groups and nationalities. Whites were in the majority, however, so this term will be used here as a literary shorthand, referring to the majority of newcomers on the frontier.

Chapter IV deals with the mountain men and the fur trade in the 1830s. Chapter V takes up the story of the movement of men, women and children across the Great Plains by covered wagon in the 1840s and 1850s. Chapter VI shows how in the middle of the 19th century Fort Bridger helped to forge military, transportation and communications links on the frontier by serving as a U.S. Army base and as a supply point for stagecoaches, the Pony Express, the telegraph line and the Union Pacific Railroad.

Chapter VII looks at the 1867 gold rush near South Pass in the Wind River mountains of Wyoming, and then at the Great Diamond Hoax of 1872, which involved crooked prospectors, greedy financiers, dedicated geologists and my own grandfather, a Western mining engineer named Henry Janin. Chapter VIII recounts the ways of life of different kinds of frontiersmen from about 1875, when barbed wire began to close off the open range, to about 1890, when the Indian Wars were over and the U.S. Army closed Fort Bridger for the last time.

Chapter IX tries to clear up some common misperceptions about the shotguns, rifles, pistols and knives used on the frontier. Finally, Chapter X explores how the real West of the 19th century has been transformed into the mythic West of our own imagination. The five appendices and the chronology are self-explanatory. Readers are encouraged to consult the endnotes, which have been used freely here not only for attribution but also to elaborate on points which are historically relevant but which might break up the flow of the text itself.

A Note on Sources

Nearly all the Indians and many of the fur trappers, including Jim Bridger himself, were illiterate. But in retrospect it seems that nearly everybody else living west of the Missouri River in the 19th century could hardly wait to set pen to paper to record their experiences in the Great Plains, the Rockies, the Great Basin (the desert area between the Wasatch mountains of Utah and the Sierra Nevada mountains of California) or in California itself.

This formidable literary output means there is no shortage of primary and secondary sources about the West. To take but one example, the Bancroft Library at the University of California at Berkeley is one of the largest and most

"Arizona Cowboy," an image of the mythic West (Frederic Remington, Prints and Photographs Division, Library of Congress)

heavily used libraries of manuscripts, rare books, and special collections in the United States.[3] It has over 400,000 volumes on Western Americana and Latin Americana, 90 percent of which deal with the American West. It also has 32,000 linear feet of manuscripts; 2.3 million photographs and other pictorial materials; 67,000 microforms; and 21,000 maps. Many of these items, too, focus on the American West. Faced with such an embarrassment of literary and illustrative riches, I have had to be selective about the topics and sources chosen here. So if any reader finds that his or her favorite topic or source has been overlooked, this is the reason.

One of the goals of this book is to encourage a new generation of readers to learn more about the West. The works of Ray Allen Billington, Bernard DeVoto and William H. Goetzmann are good starting points. Even better are three "I-was-there" primary sources: Francis Parkman's *The Oregon Trail* (1847), Captain Randolph B. Marcy's *The Prairie Traveler* (1859), and Mark Twain's *Roughing It* (1872). Two modern anthologies of 19th century writing can be highly recommended as well: Tony Hillerman's *The Best of the West* (1991) and James H. Maguire's *A Rendezvous Reader* (1997), both of which I have drawn upon heavily.

Those who believe a picture is worth a thousand words will find the widest range of contemporary illustrations and photographs in the 26 volumes of Time-Life's outstanding series *The Old West*. If these books are not available, then Time-Life's one-volume distillation of the series, also entitled *The Old West* (1990), is a partial substitute.

So many works of fiction have been written about the West that it is difficult to choose among them, but for a hefty dose of humor about the frontier it is hard to beat Thomas Berger's meticulously researched story, *Little Big Man*, which upon publication in 1964 was praised by the *New York Times Book Review* as "the very best novel ever written about the American West."[4]

Geographic Placenames

Some of the Western states, national parks and other geographic entities were formally named only after the events described here. However, to avoid constantly having to specify that a given event occurred in "the area now known as Wyoming" or "in present-day Utah," I will simply say that it occurred "in Wyoming" or "in Utah," even if these places technically may not have existed at that time.

Chapter I

Looking for the Frontier West

What an experience it must have been to come into southwestern Wyoming in 1850 via the Oregon Trail, on horseback or plodding on foot alongside a covered wagon drawn by a team of oxen, and to cross the Continental Divide at South Pass, 7,550 feet high! From South Pass, the Oregon Trail followed the Big Sandy River down the western slope of the Rocky Mountains, heading for the Pacific Ocean. It crossed the Green River, called at Fort Bridger and then continued on its way toward the promised lands of the 19th century West — Utah, California or Oregon.

Southwestern Wyoming is one of the best places in the United States today to come to grips with the frontier West. In the language of the Delaware Indians, *Mecheweami-ing* meant "at the big plains" or "on the great plain." This is the origin of our own word "Wyoming" and is still a good description of the region now, even though the high plains of Wyoming are not in fact table-top flat but are studded with hills and buttes and are riven by occasional streams. To get a good feel for what large parts of the West must have been like in the mid–19th century, all you have to do is to get off Interstate 80 and follow one of Wyoming's rural roads across these high plains.

Beginning the search for the frontier West at Fort Bridger itself, however, is not necessarily recommended because this outpost is simply too well situated to convey the inhospitable nature of southwestern Wyoming. The New York editor Horace Greeley spelled out the reasons why during a stagecoach journey to San Francisco in the summer of 1859. "Fort Bridger," he reported to his readers,

> may be regarded as the terminus ... of the Great American Desert [the 19th century's name for the Great Plains]. Not that the intervening country is fertile or productive, for it is neither; but at Bridger its character visibly changes. The hills we here approach are thinly covered with a straggling growth of low, scraggy cedar; the sagebrush continues even into this valley, but it is no longer universal and almost alone; grass is more frequent and far more abundant ... Black's Fork ... is here a clearly, sparkling mountain torrent, divided into half a dozen streams by the flat, pebbly islets on which the little village [of Fort Bridger] — or rather post — is located....[5]

Fort Bridger still has good grass and water (Photograph by the author)

A Hard Country

To find the frontier West today one must get off the beaten track, that is, off Interstate 80. But where to go? A good destination for a side trip is the remote, little-known Seedskadee National Wildlife Refuge, a wildlife habitat and breeding ground which runs along a 35-mile segment of the Green River and which is located on Highway 327, about 50 miles northeast of Fort Bridger itself.

This 22,000-acre refuge lies in the very heart of a high, wild, lonesome region — an arid, empty landscape of desolate, flat, sagebrush-covered uplands whipped by the wind, fringed on the far horizons not by towns or cities but by the Bad Lands Hills and the snow-covered peaks of the Wind River Mountains. This is in big-sky country, without any of the familiar landmarks which in other parts of the United States give the viewer a sense of scale. There are, for example, hardly any trees here. The few cottonwoods and the willow thickets marking the course of the shallow, fast-flowing Green River are stunted and offer no shelter or visual relief.

Distances, too, are deceiving. On a clear day you can see for 50 miles, but the scenery varies so little that even when driving over the speed limit at 85 miles per hour along one of the arrow-straight roads bordering Seedskadee, you have the feeling that you are standing still. Off-road travel here can never be taken for granted: after heavy rains or a good snowfall, the dirt roads of the region are impassable, even for four-wheel-drive vehicles with high ground clearance.

The entrance to the Seedskadee National Wildlife Refuge (Photograph by the author)

The land is still virtually deserted. Because it is high (the average elevation is about 6,300 feet), it is cold much of the year. Summers are warm, dry and dusty. Except for a handful of cattle ranchers, trona miners and employees of the Refuge itself, very few people live here. The nearest center of civilization is a combined store and service station 15 miles northwest of the Refuge; the next closest facilities are clustered in the small town of Green River, 37 miles to the southeast. The Refuge itself is closed to camping. The U.S. Fish and Wildlife Service warns visitors to bring enough water, food, and fuel for their entire visit.

A Microcosm of the West

Despite its isolation and its lack of people, Seedskadee has a feeling of history about it. This Refuge can be seen, in fact, as a kind of microcosm of the 19th century West as a whole.

Like other parts of the frontier, Seedskadee had a great diversity of wildlife and is still a prime habitat for Canada geese, ducks, herons and birds of prey. During the dry summer months, flocks of "prairie chickens" (sage grouse) can be seen making their way to water. Pronghorn antelope are common on the desert uplands, as are mule deer. A few moose feed in the brushy or forested river bottoms. A host of smaller mammals — coyotes, red fox, beavers, muskrats, badgers and rabbits — live in the Refuge as well.

The Shoshoni Indians spread into the Seedskadee area about 700 years ago and found good hunting here. Indeed, "sisk-a-die-agie" meant "river of the prairie chicken" in their language; later

Storm, southwestern Wyoming (Photograph by the author)

on, fur trappers corrupted the Indian name to "seedskadee." The Shoshonis hunted not only sage grouse but also buffalo, deer, elk, mountain sheep, pronghorn antelope, eagles and the waterfowl of the Green River itself. But eventually the Indians' monopoly of the land came to an end.

In 1811 a group of American trappers representing John Jacob Astor's Pacific Fur Company penetrated the Green River basin in search of beaver. One of these men, Donald Mackenzie, later joined the British Northwest Company and led trapping expeditions into this area. By 1820 Mackenzie's men had found the places where the Green River could be crossed most safely. The first wagon train, led by the independent fur trader Captain Bonneville, came over South Pass in 1832 and followed the Big

Sandy down to the Green River. Correctly foreseeing that many others would follow the wagon trail Bonneville had blazed, two mountain men — Jim Bridger and Henry Fraeb — set up a trading post near the confluence of the Green and the Big Sandy in 1839.

Fraeb was killed by Indians in 1841; the circumstances of his death remind us of just how dangerous the frontier could be. Jim Baker, a mountain man who saw Fraeb's body, said that Fraeb was the ugliest dead man he had ever seen: "His face was all covered with blood, and he had rotten front teeth and a terrible grin. When he was killed he never fell, but sat braced against a stump, a sight to behold."[6]

The surviving mountain men did not scare easily, however, and a few enterprising trappers built and operated a

"Indians Hunting the Bison" (Karl Bodmer, courtesy of Alecto Historical Editions, London)

ferry across the Green River in 1843, catering to the thousands of pioneers who arrived at the river in their covered wagons, bound for Utah, Oregon or California. Pioneer diaries often mention the dangers and difficulties of crossing the Green River: ferries were swept away and lives and possessions were lost. Also in 1843, Jim Bridger founded Fort Bridger, about 50 miles southwest of Seedskadee. Many of the emigrants who crossed the Green River rested their oxen, bought supplies and repaired their wagons at Fort Bridger before pushing on farther west.

For many years no one settled in Seedskadee because of its remote location and cold, arid climate. Indian uprisings along the Oregon Trail in the 1860s deterred would-be settlers, too, but in 1867 gold was discovered near South Pass and the next year the Union Pacific Railroad line was built just 20 miles south of Seedskadee. With the coming of the railroad, Wyoming cattlemen had access to eastern markets for the first time and therefore began to settle in the Seedskadee region.

The ranchers pastured their herds on Seedskadee's nutritious grasses. The cattle industry prospered here (and in other parts of the state) to such an extent that by the 1870s it was the biggest business in Wyoming. Sheep moved into the area, too, and friction between cattlemen and sheepmen became common as both sides competed for ever scarcer forage. By the late 1880s, Seedskadee's long-term prospects were grim. The range was overstocked and in poor condition; there was a drought; beef prices were low; and the terrible winter of 1886-1887 killed about half of the big herds of cattle pastured on the open range. The combination of these factors, together with the growing availability of a new, cheap form of fencing (barbed wire) spelled the end of open range grazing and of the open range itself.

The cattlemen's and sheepmen's loss, however, was wildlife's gain. Remedial measures were gradually taken at Seedskadee to restore the habitat for wildlife. Fencing and controlled burning of sagebrush helped bring back the native grasses; the Refuge itself was established in 1965 to offset the loss of wildlife habitat caused by the construction of the Fontenelle and Flaming Gorge Dams on the Green River.[7]

The Old and the New Frontier

Because of its own history, Seedskadee is a good jumping-off place for a look at the 19th century frontier as a whole. This is a period of American history which offers a remarkably rich cascade of people and events. The fact that by historical standards the American frontier had a short life span — only about 115 years — does not detract from its uniqueness.[8]

Other dates could be used to calculate how long the frontier lasted but here we will use a continuum beginning in 1775. This was when the explorer and backwoodsman Daniel Boone opened up the old trans–Appalachian frontier by blazing a trail, known as the Wilderness Road, across the Appalachian Mountains. It was over this track that Boone led the first contingent of settlers through the Cumberland Gap and into Kentucky.[9] At first the Wilderness Road was only a narrow trail but later on it

was improved; ultimately, it became one of the primary routes from Virginia to the Ohio River.

At the other end of this continuum, we will note that the new trans–Mississippi frontier, which the Louisiana Purchase had opened up in 1803, closed in 1890, when the superintendent of the U.S. Census proclaimed that,

> Up to and including 1880 the country [the continental United States] had a frontier of settlement, but at present the unsettled area has been so broken up by isolated bodies of settlement that there can hardly be said to be a frontier line. In the discussion of its extent, its westward movement, etc., it can not, therefore, any longer have a place in the census reports.

What is so striking about the frontier West is that even though it only lasted from about 1775 to 1890, it still exerts a powerful tug on the imagination of urban Americans today and, indeed, on the imagination of people in many other countries of the world.[10]

The Importance of Fort Bridger

Our first focus here will be on the uniquely American tradition of *Westering*, that is, the process of constantly moving westward. We will look at three often-overlapping regions — the sunlit uplands of the northern Rockies; what the cattlemen called "the northern range"; and the area around Fort Bridger, which was a trading post and frontier fort located in the southwestern corner of Wyoming.

Jim Bridger, one of the most famous of the beaver trappers and outdoorsmen of the frontier, built this post

Map 2: The Wilderness Road and the Louisiana Purchase

in 1843, and from the outset it was a success. For example, Fort Bridger became a popular trading post and campground for the Shoshoni Indians, who were also known as the Snake Indians, probably because of their skill at eluding pursuit by hiding themselves.[11] When Edwin Bryant, a California-bound emigrant, stopped at Fort Bridger in 1846, he found 500 Shoshonis camped there.[12]

Jim Bridger traded with other tribes (the Bannocks and the Utes) as well and, more importantly and more profitably, he also provided supplies and services both for the mountain men and especially for the emigrants heading West. Later on, Fort Bridger did two tours of duty as a military base until it was closed by the U.S. Army for the second and last time in 1890.

This was not the end of the story, however, because in 1929 Fort Bridger

was acquired by the Historical Landmark Commission of Wyoming and in 1933 it was dedicated as a Wyoming Historical Landmark and Museum. Now known as the Fort Bridger State Historic Site, it has been tastefully restored and is staffed by helpful, knowledgeable people. Half a day at Fort Bridger and half a day at Seedskadee is time well spent.

Seedskadee is the best introduction to the geography and climate of southwestern Wyoming but Fort Bridger is the best reference point for historical purposes because from 1843 to 1890 it was involved, directly or indirectly, in almost all of the important events of the lands which lay, as the 19th century ballad "Shenandoah" puts it, "across the wide Missouri." The history of the fort is well-documented and helps us understand the chronological sequence of events on the 19th century frontier.

Chapter II

Westering

In a skirmish in 1832 at the Battle of Pierre's Hole, a valley on the Gallatin River in Idaho northwest of Yellowstone National Park, a Blackfoot Indian shot an arrow into Jim Bridger's back. The wooden shaft of the arrow broke off but the iron arrowhead, which was three inches long, remained lodged in the muscles. It stayed there for three years. Finally, at a rendezvous on the Green River in southwestern Wyoming (a rendezvous was an annual gathering of mountain men), Marcus Whitman, a missionary doctor en route to Oregon, where he and his wife would later be killed by Indians, dug out the arrowhead without benefit of anesthesia.[13]

One of Dr. Whitman's traveling companions, Samuel Parker, witnessed this frontier surgery. "The doctor pursued the operation with great self-possession and perseverance," Parker reported, "and his patient manifested equal firmness."[14] It is said that when the doctor expressed his astonishment that the wound made by the arrowhead had not become septic, Bridger replied cheerfully, "In the mountains, doctor, meat don't spoil!"

Old Gabe

Known to his friends as "Old Gabe" (probably a reference to the archangel Gabriel, a Biblical messenger), Jim Bridger was a Westering man.[15] He was born in Richmond, Virginia, on 17 March 1804. His father was a surveyor and innkeeper. In 1812 the Bridger family decided to seek their fortunes in the West and moved to a little town on the Illinois River variously called Six Mile Prairie and the American Bottoms. His mother and father died not long after; from then on, Bridger had to support himself and his only sister. Since St. Louis, Missouri, was just across the river from his home, Bridger got his first job running a flatbed ferryboat to and from that city. He then tried his hand as an apprentice blacksmith but did not like the work.

At the age of 18 he was just coming into his prime. David L. Brown, a mountain man who later joined Bridger's fur trapping brigade, described him as, "Tall — six feet at least — muscular, without an ounce of superfluous flesh." He was too adventuresome to settle down in St. Louis or anywhere else.

Bridger could neither read nor write: Brown said that "he was perfectly ignorant of all knowledge contained in books, not even knowing the letters of the alphabet." But he was alert, intelligent and knew what was going on around him. So it would not have been long before he heard about the following advertisement, which appeared in the *Missouri Gazette & Public Advertiser* on 13 February 1822:

TO

Enterprising Young Men

The subscriber wishes to engage ONE HUNDRED MEN, to ascend the river Missouri to its source, there to be employed for one, two, or three years — For particulars, enquire of Major Andrew Henry ... (who will ascend with, and command the party) or to the subscriber at St. Louis.

Wm. H. Ashley

Bridger joined the Ashley-Henry expedition in 1822 and set off for the Rockies.[16] There his adventures began in earnest. When another mountain man, Hugh Glass, was critically wounded by a grizzly in 1823, two of Henry's men — John S. Fitzgerald and young Jim Bridger — volunteered to stay with him until he died. The story of how Fitzgerald and Bridger abandoned Glass but how Glass still managed to survive, is recounted in Chapter IV.

Bridger then took part in the 1824 campaign against the Arikara Indians. To settle a bet, late in 1824 or early in 1825 he built a bullboat (a small round boat made of deer or buffalo skin stretched over a wooden frame), floated down the Bear River in southeastern Idaho and became the first white man to see the Great Salt Lake. However, another account asserts that he must have been on horse-

Jim Bridger in his later years (Wyoming Division of Cultural Resources)

back, not in a boat, because he discovered the water to be salty "when he, with some other trappers, dismounted to get a drink."[17]

Bridger then trapped for the fur-trading firm of Smith, Jackson, and Sublette. In 1825 or 1826, alone on a raft on the Big Horn River in southern Montana, he ran a narrow canyon with walls that soared 1,000 feet above him. He trapped in the lands of the Crow Indians in 1828–29. Between 1830 and 1834 he was a partner of the Rocky Mountain Fur Company and, as mentioned before, was wounded at the Battle of Pierre's Hole in 1832.

Old Gabe was certainly the only mountain man who ever had a suit of armor. This "armor," which was in fact the plumed steel helmet and the polished

"Jim Bridger, in a Suit of English Armor" (Alfred Jacob Miller, Joslyn Art Museum, Omaha)

steel cuirass (breastplate) of a crack British regiment, was presented to Bridger at the rendezvous of 1837 by Sir William Drummond Stewart, an English nobleman making his second hunting expedition to the West. Bridger lost no time riding around the camp to show off his new possessions to his fellow mountain men and bemused Indians — a lighthearted episode which was recorded for posterity by the artist Alfred Jacob Miller.

Bridger attended nearly every rendezvous. Sarah Smith, an Oregon-bound missionary, met Bridger's party at the 1838 rendezvous. It consisted, she wrote,

> [of about] 100 men & perhaps 60 Indian females & a great number of guns & noisy shouts. Thought perhaps that we would be interested, therefore came & saluted us with firing, drumming,

singing & dancing. Their appearance was rude & savage, were painted in a most hideous manner. One carried a scalp of a Black Foot in his hand…. The Indians made no attack on B's [Bridger's] party but this party attacked them & shot 15 of them dead without excuse but to please their wicked passions.[18]

In 1840 Bridger led a party of 30 traders and trappers to the Columbia River on the border between Oregon and Washington. Old Gabe then pressed on to Los Angeles, reaching it early in 1841. Returning to the Rockies and with Louis Vasquez as a partner, he built Fort Bridger in 1843 and then led another party of men to California in 1844–45. As the outstanding guide of his time (the historian Bernard DeVoto called him "an atlas of the West"), Bridger had no shortage of important clients[19]:

Year	Clients
1847	Mormon leader Brigham Young[20]
1850	Captain Howard Stansbury's survey
1855–57	Sir St. George Gore's hunting party
1857–58	Colonel Albert Sidney Johnston's military deployment during the Mormon War
1859–60	Captain William V. Raymond's Yellowstone expedition
1861	Captain E.I. Berthoud's exploring party, seeking a direct route from Denver to Salt Lake
1865–66	Powder River expedition
late 1860s	Major General Grenville M. Dodge's Union Pacific Railroad survey[21]

Captain Randolph B. Marcy, whom we shall meet often in this book, spent most of his military career in the American West and was an excellent writer. The War Department therefore asked him to write a guidebook for Westering pioneers; the result was *The Prairie Traveler* (1859), which soon became a bible for the emigrants. Marcy first met Bridger at Fort Laramie in 1857 and praised him as "one who occupies an exalted position among his confrères [colleagues] as a successful trapper and hunter, and who has no superior as a reliable guide and bold Indian fighter." Bridger, then 53 years old, was tall, thin and wiry; his face was "well bronzed by toil and exposure, with an independent, generous, and open cast of countenance indicating brave and noble impulses."[22]

Even in his middle years Bridger's eyesight was incredibly acute. In 1865, when he was guiding a U.S. Army expedition near the Tongue River in northeastern Wyoming, he called the attention of one officer, Captain Palmer, to what he said was a thin wisp of smoke in a saddle-shaped depression nearly 50 miles away. Palmer could not see the smoke even with his binoculars. But his scouts, who had been sent forward to reconnoiter, reported that the smoke was rising from an Indian village where campfires were burning. (In the clear air of the northeastern Rockies it was possible to see small objects at great distances. In a letter written in 1884 Mary Ella Inderwick, the wife of a rancher in Alberta, Canada, reported that she was able to see rooftops 22 miles away.[23])

Only when Old Gabe's eyesight began to fail at the age of 64 did he leave his beloved mountains and settle down in 1868 on a farm near a Missouri town with the fitting name of Westport, which was close to the city with an equally appropriate name — Independence. He died on his farm on 17 July 1881, just nine years before Westering itself came to an end.

In addition to loving the wilderness, Bridger also seems to have loved women and children. He was married three times to Indian women and had seven children by them, whom he sent to school in Missouri when their mothers died. His first wife seems to have been a Flathead Indian, who became the mother of two girls and a boy. After she died in 1846, Bridger married a Shoshoni, who bore a son but died giving birth to a daughter in 1849. The third wife, whose tribal affiliation is not recorded, bore Bridger a daughter and a son and lived with him on his Missouri farm.

A monument to Bridger was unveiled at the Kansas City Cemetery in 1904. The epitaph on it gives a good summary of his adventuresome life:

1804 — James Bridger — 1881

Celebrated as a Hunter, Trapper, Fur Trader and Guide. Discovered Salt Lake, 1824; the South Pass [a broad gateway

"Laramie's Fort" (Alfred Jacob Miller, Walters Art Gallery, Baltimore). The buffalo-hide teepees of the Plains Indians were strong, portable, comfortable and handsome.

through the Rockies, used by Indians, mountain men and wagon trains], 1827; visited Yellowstone Lake and Geysers, 1830; Founded Fort Bridger, 1843; Opened Overland Route by Bridger's Pass to Salt Lake. Was Guide for Exploring Expeditions, Albert Sidney Johnston's Army in 1857, and G.M. Dodge in U.P. [Union Pacific Railroad] Surveys and Indian Campaigns in 1865–66.[24]

A sign now hanging at the entrance to Fort Bridger is even more explicit about Bridger's abilities:

His unerring judgment regarding problems of trappers, traders, soldiers, emigrants and gold-seekers bordered on the miraculous, and his advice was universally in demand in the early history of this state. Bridger has been

prominently recognized as America's greatest frontiersman and the West's most gifted scout.

For these reasons, memories of Jim Bridger are not likely to fade soon, especially in Wyoming. Not only is the Fort Bridger State Historic Site there but so is the Bridger-Teton National Forest and the 11,007-foot Bridger Peak. A small town near the Yellowstone River in south-central Montana is named after him, too.

Westering: An American Tradition

The exploits of Old Gabe are only one small part of the long American tradition of Westering. The first permanent colonists, of course, sailed west from Europe to get to the New World. Jamestown, the earliest English settlement on the American mainland, was founded in 1607. But the early settlers, there and elsewhere along the east coast of the United States, did not at first stray far from the flat and relatively safe coastal plains. In the 1780s the vast lands lying to the west of the Appalachian mountains were little known. Writing in 1833, one chronicler remarked that in the late 18th century this western region was still considered by the inhabitants of the long-settled eastern states as having "something of the same obscurity which lay over the American continent after its first discovery by Columbus."[25] Easterners feared and avoided this frontier because they felt it contained only ferocious Indians and dangerous beasts.

The Old Trans-Appalachian Frontier: Daniel Boone

One of the earliest and arguably the greatest of the first trailblazers to explore this unknown region was Daniel Boone, who visited Kentucky twice in 1767 and after a third visit decided to move his family there. In 1775 he led his wife, daughter and a group of about 80 other settlers through the Cumberland Gap — a natural opening in the mountains, located near the borders of Kentucky, Virginia and Tennessee — and blazed a trail to Kentucky known as the Wilderness Road.

Boone's achievements as an explorer, hunter, trapper, expert rifleman and soldier were quite extraordinary. His memory and his sense of direction were uncanny. He never lost his bearings in the wilderness, although he candidly admitted that he was "*bewildered* once for three days."[26]

In about 1799 in Kentucky, Boone managed to escape at night from some Indians who had captured him. Much later, while on a hunting trip with John James Audubon (the great painter of the birds of North America) Boone told him that to mark the spot of his escape he had paused just long enough to cut three large chips out of an ash sapling before running off. Boone added that a boundary line was later drawn in Kentucky which used as one of its corners "an ash marked by three distinct notches of the tomahawk [hatchet] of a white man." Twenty years after his nighttime escape, to help settle a lawsuit involving this boundary line Boone agreed to go back to the area to see if he could still find the tree. While watched by four witnesses, he did indeed find it: they reported that he "scraped away at the wood with care, until three hacks, as plain as any three notches ever were, could be seen."[27]

Daniel Boone probably did more than any other man to open up for American settlement the territory west of the Appalachians. More than 20,000 settlers flocked to Kentucky after Boone led the way; in 1792 it became the fifteenth state. But by then it was getting too crowded for Boone, who had once joked to his wife that it was time to move on because another family had settled 70 miles away. So, Westering once more, Boone took his family to Missouri in 1799. In his old age and on his own he continued to explore even further west, possibly reaching the Yellowstone River in northwestern Wyoming in 1816.

Daniel Boone died back in Missouri in 1820 at the age of 85 but his pioneering spirit and his descendants lived on in the new frontier of the trans–Mississippi West. His grandson, Albert Gallatin Boone, became a mountain man in the Rockies and was praised by the famous trapper, guide and Indian fighter Kit Carson as "a man who isn't afraid of anything."[28]

The Trans-Mississippi West: The Lewis and Clark Expedition

By one master stroke in 1803, President Thomas Jefferson virtually doubled the size of the United States. He did this by buying the French possessions in North America from Napoleon Bonaparte, the ruler of France, who needed money urgently to pay for his foreign wars. Neither Napoleon nor his foreign minister, Talleyrand, knew much about the huge chunk of real estate they were selling to Jefferson. What fragmentary information was available suggested that somewhere in these possessions was a long chain of high mountains, which were variously described as "the Stoney Mountains" or as mountains of pure crystal. These mountains ran north and south — or then again, perhaps east and west. From these snowcapped pinnacles, shallow rivers trickled down into an endless plain referred to as "a great prairie ocean." All that was known as a fact was that one enormous river, the Missouri, ran north across the prairies and then west toward the mountains.[29]

The Louisiana Purchase, as Jefferson's bargain came to be called, consisted of 800,000 square miles of virgin land between the Mississippi River and the Rocky Mountains. The western boundaries of this vast tract were not defined.

Albert Gallatin Boone, grandson of Daniel Boone (State Historical Society of Missouri, Columbia)

Somewhere far to the northwest lay the Oregon country (the Columbia River Basin) which the United States had claimed since 1792. To the west and southwest were the Spanish possessions in North America, which became Mexican possessions after 1821, when Mexico won its independence from Spain, and which would not become part of the United States until after its war with Mexico in 1848.

To explore his new acquisitions, Jefferson sent out an expedition in 1804 under the joint leadership of his secretary, Captain Meriwether Lewis, and another able Army officer, Second Lieutenant William Clark. In a letter of 1813, Jefferson recounted why he had decided to put Lewis in charge of this expedition:

Of courage undaunted, possessing a firmness & perseverance of purpose which nothing but impossibilities could divert from its direction, careful as a father of those committed to his charge, yet steady in the maintenance of order & discipline.... I could have no hesitation in confiding the enterprise to him.[30]

Known at the time as the Corps of Discovery, the Lewis and Clark expedition was an unqualified success. By the time Lewis, Clark and their men returned to St. Louis in 1806, they had traveled more than 7,600 miles through trackless country — all the way to the Pacific Ocean and back. This great adventure had taken two exhausting years and involved enormous risks to life and limb.

For example, Lewis once had to dive into a river to escape from a grizzly bear. In another and more lethal encounter, he and his men ran into a band of eight young Blackfoot warriors. One of the Indians tried to steal the expedition's rifles, which were essential for its survival. Two of Lewis' men chased the Indian for 50 yards, wrestled the rifles away from him and plunged a knife into his chest, killing him instantly. In the meantime, however, the other Indians were trying to steal the expedition's horses, which were also essential for its survival. Lewis still had his own rifle and when one Indian, who was armed with a British rifle, turned toward him with hostile intent, Lewis shot him through the belly, wounding him seriously and probably fatally. (The unrelenting hostility of the Blackfeet towards the mountain men of the 1820s and 1830s is thought to have stemmed from this one incident.[31]) Later, on a hunting trip in the woods, Lewis himself was painfully wounded in the buttocks when one of his companions, who was blind in one eye, mistook him for an elk or bear and opened fire.[32]

But Lewis and Clark managed to overcome all these setbacks and returned with meticulously detailed and carefully illustrated reports on the geography, geology, climate, Indians, animals, birds and plants of the northwestern United States. These reports became the keystones of later explorations and were also indirectly responsible for the creation of Fort Bridger itself.

This came about because Lewis and Clark reported that there were large numbers of fur-bearing animals, especially beavers, in the lands recently bought from France. Beavers had few natural predators in the mountains and the Indians usually did not hunt them. With unlimited supplies of food and water, these industrious animals flourished along the tree-lined streams and tributaries of western rivers. This was a fact worth knowing because at that time beaver pelts were in great demand in Europe and the eastern United States because they could be turned into felt for gentlemen's top hats. The reports of the Lewis and Clark expedition contributed to a boom in fur trapping and led to an increase in the number of mountain men engaged in this perilous calling.

Jim Bridger himself began as a beaver trapper but, as we shall see, when the market for beaver pelts began to decline in the late 1830s (because men started to wear top hats made of silk), Old Gabe saw that he would either have to find other work in the Rockies or leave them altogether. With remarkable foresight, he then set up Fort Bridger to cater to the waves of emigrants coming West in the 1840s.

A more immediate and perhaps ultimately more important result of the Lewis and Clark expedition was that it had established an excellent relationship with the Shoshoni Indians. While camped on the upper reaches of the Missouri, Lewis and Clark had hired a French-Canadian, Toussaint Charbonneau, to serve as their interpreter with the Indians. Charbonneau lived with the Minnetaree tribe and spoke their language. His greatest asset, however, turned out to be his 16-year old wife, a courageous and intelligent Shoshoni woman named Sacajawea. She had been captured by the Minnetarees when she was a child and now wanted to go west with the Lewis and Clark expedition in hopes of meeting up with her own tribe once again.

So Sacajawea joined the expedition. Near the headwaters of the Missouri she recognized some landmarks and guided Lewis and Clark over the Continental Divide. This is the ridgeline of the Rocky Mountains which separates the streams flowing toward the Gulf of California and the Pacific Ocean from those flowing toward the Gulf of Mexico and Canada. Tongue in cheek, Osborne Russell, a mountain man who crossed the Continental Divide near Yellowstone National Park in 1836, solemnly assured his readers that a river flowing off this ridgeline divided equally, one-half running west and the other east, thus bidding adieu to each other, one bound for the Pacific and the other for the Atlantic ocean. Here a trout twelve inches in length may cross the mountains in safety.[33]

Humor aside, this was Shoshoni territory and Sacajawea again proved her worth. The expedition desperately needed horses but the local Indians were distrustful and refused to trade. Suddenly, a Shoshoni woman saw Sacajawea and rushed forward to hug her, recognizing her as a girlhood friend. Even more remarkably, when the Shoshonis finally did agree to trade with Lewis and Clark, their chief, Cameahwait, turned out to be none other than Sacajawea's long-lost brother. Lewis and Clark recorded in their journals that when she recognized Cameahwait, "She instantly jumped up, and ran and embraced him, throwing over him her blanket and weeping profusely."[34]

As we will see, the resulting friendship between the Shoshonis and the explorers paid very high dividends over the years. Unlike the Blackfeet, who for decades thereafter would make unremitting war on the mountain men and the emigrants, most Shoshonis would be friendly, offering good advice and helping them reach their destinations.

Chapter III

Indians of the Northern Rockies

In the early decades of the 19th century there were surprisingly few Indians living in the enormous sweep of territory (about 2.5 million square miles) between the Mississippi River and the shores of the Pacific Ocean. The best guess is that there were only about 300,000 Indians there — roughly the same number of people who were then living in New York City.

In addition to being so few in number when compared to the whites, these Indians also lacked any centralized organization, whether military, political, economic, religious or social, which might have acted as a breakwater to the rising tide of newcomers. Instead, the Indians were loosely grouped into about 30 different tribes, which differed greatly in size, in wealth, in language, in the way of life they followed and in their responses — hostile, friendly or neutral — to this rising tide. These tribes, moreover, were often at war with one another.

Given the numbers, organizational skills, wealth and firepower of the whites, the Plains Indians had virtually no chance of preserving their nomadic culture, which was based on free and unrestricted access to huge chunks of territory which the whites now wanted for themselves.

Indeed, with the benefit of hindsight it is clear that the nomadic way of life was doomed as soon as Lewis and Clark returned to St. Louis in 1806 with their glowing reports about the West. In the 1830s, however, by what was for posterity an extraordinary stroke of good luck, three sensitive and talented artists — Karl Bodmer, Alfred Jacob Miller and George Catlin — each made vivid paintings of the Indian way of life.[35]

Since the Indian way of life in the Great Plains and Rockies had not changed significantly over the previous decade, we can assume that the scenes these artists recorded would have been much the same in the 1820s as well. This period was probably the high point of Plains Indian culture: the Shoshonis and other Indians had mastered the horse and had learned to use firearms but they were not yet bearing the full brunt of the white influx which would eventually destroy their way of life.

The Indian Way of Life

Tribal boundaries were not fixed but fluctuated according to buffalo hunting

"Bison-Dance of the Mandan Indians in Front of Their Medicine Lodge" (Karl Bodmer, courtesy of Alecto Historical Editions, London). This painting is arguably the best representation of the culture of the Plains Indians before the coming of the whites.

or other seasonal activities. Whole tribes moved permanently, too: the Sioux and the Cheyenne initially lived in the woods around the upper Mississippi and the Great Lakes but then moved west onto the Great Plains. Rather than trying to list all the tribes and their approximate locations, it seems more useful to give here only those tribes which at one time or another violently resisted white incursions[36]:

Regions	Tribes
Indian Territory (Oklahoma)	Cheyenne, Arapaho, Kiowa, Comanche, Osage, Cado
Texas	Comanche
Nebraska	Sioux, Pawnee
North and South Dakota	Sioux, Cheyenne, Arikara
Montana and Canadian Rockies	Blackfoot
Wyoming	Crow, Sioux, Arapaho, Shoshoni[37]
Colorado	Ute
Idaho	Nez Percé ("pierced nose" in French)
Arizona and New Mexico	Apache, Navaho
California	Modoc

The Coming of the Horse

The "god dog" or "big dog"—two of the names by which the horse was known—changed trans–Mississippi Indian society as radically as the telecommunications revolution is changing our own. The first horses in the Americas were ten stallions and six mares brought to Mexico by Hernando Cortes in 1519. As more Spanish settlers came to Mexico and to the American Southwest, they brought more horses with them. As the horses multiplied, many of them escaped or were captured by the Indians. In the 18th century, horses continued to spread north, thanks to intertribal trading and livestock raids.

A map outlining this process of equine diffusion would show that, on the eastern side of the Rockies, it started in the San Antonio area and gradually spread north to the Canadian border, bringing the horse to all the tribes along the way — the Apache, Comanche, Kiowa, Cheyenne, Dakota, Arikara, Mandan-Hidatsa and at last to the Assiniboin and Plains Cree in southern Canada. A separate path of diffusion threaded its way northwards along the western side of the Rockies, beginning near Santa Fe and sequentially bringing the horse to the Ute, Shoshoni, Nez Percé, Cayuse, Flathead and, finally, to the Blackfoot along the Canadian border. The Shoshonis living in the Fort Bridger area played a key role in intertribal trade; the Crows of northeastern Wyoming, for example, probably got their horses from Shoshoni traders.[38]

It must be remembered that before the coming of the horse, many Indians lived close to the subsistence level. Hunting had to be done on foot, which was time consuming, exhausting and did not produce much of a food surplus. Their only beast of burden was the wolf-like dog, which could carry 50 pounds on its back or could pull a travois loaded with 75 pounds. (A travois was a drag shaped like an inverted V, made from two long wooden poles.) But this means of transport was not enough to permit a far-ranging nomadic lifestyle.

A horse, on the other hand, could carry 200 pounds on its back or could pull 300 pounds on a travois; so laden, it could easily travel ten or twelve miles a day, compared to only five or six miles per day for a train of dogs. With horses, an Indian family could have a more comfortable teepee (a Sioux word for tent): the horse could carry longer poles for the frame of the teepee and a bigger buffalo-skin cover to fit over it. Horses also facilitated trade with other Indians and with the whites. Most dramatically, however, possession of horses encouraged some Indians to raid enemy tribes for more horses, personal glory and scalps. The nomadic Indian warrior whom we know from 19th century illustrations and books (and whom we have re-created in film and television) was truly the child of the horse.[39]

The Indians were not only superb horsemen but superb trackers of horses as well. This was an important skill because it helped them know what other, potentially hostile, Indians had crossed the prairie. Captain Marcy gives a good example:

> Upon one occasion, as I was riding with a Delaware upon the prairies, we crossed the track of a large party of Indians traveling with lodges [teepees]. The tracks appeared to be quite fresh, and I remarked to the Indian that we must be near the party. "Oh no," said he, "the trail was made two days before, in the morning," [and] at the same time pointed with his finger to where the sun would have been at about 8 o'clock.
>
> Then, seeing that my curiosity was excited to know by what means he had arrived at this conclusion, he called my attention to the fact that

Corpse of a scalped hunter (Seaver Center for Western History Research, Los Angeles County Museum of Natural History)

there had been no dew for the last two nights, but that on the previous morning it had been heavy. He then pointed out to me some spears of grass that had been pressed down into the earth by the horses' hoofs, upon which the sand still adhered, having dried on, thus clearly showing that the grass was wet when the tracks were made.[40]

Thus, as part of their necessary survival skills, the Indians could "read sign" (that is, follow and interpret a trail) with remarkably accuracy. Captain Marcy remembered that on one occasion when he was riding on the prairies with an Indian, Marcy saw on the ground what seemed to be a distinct bear track. The Indian, however, said "Oh no, captain,

may be so he not bear-track." To show what he meant, the Indian then dismounted and, using the ramrod of his rifle, demonstrated to Marcy how that when wind bent over the long grass until it touched the ground, the grass would move in an oscillating motion, thereby scooping the loose sand into indentations which resembled a bear track.[41]

Mastering the horse also meant the Indians of the Plains and Rockies could move their camps over great distances to hunt buffalo, which existed in such staggering numbers (estimated at up to 50 million in 1800) that a surplus of food was guaranteed. The Indians used virtually every part of the buffalo and rarely killed purely for sport. Perishable parts were eaten immediately. For example, a U.S. Army officer reported in 1876 that,

> The Indians ate the buffalo liver raw, sometimes sprinkling a pinch of gall up it; the warm liver alone is not bad for a hungry man, tasting very much like a raw oyster. The entrails are also much in favor with the aborigines; they are cleaned, wound around a ramrod or something akin to it ... and held in the hot ashes until cooked through; they make a palatable dish.[42]

Whatever was not eaten on the spot or dried in the sun to make jerky or pemmican (powdered jerky mixed with berries and fat) was transformed into clothing, teepees and furnishings for them, recreational equipment, riding and transportation gear, weapons and tools or utensils. Buffalo dung was burned in place of wood on the treeless plains. So great was the Indians' dependence on the buffalo that when the great herds were finally killed off in the early 1880s (a slaughter which is described in Chapter VIII), the nomadic way of life was irrevocably ended.

"Counting Coup"

Physical endurance, freedom and independence were the hallmarks of men in these fighting societies. Chiefs usually had to lead by personal example because their warriors were reluctant to accept discipline and obey orders. A man's worth was measured by how many enemies he had killed or how many times he had "counted coup." (*Coup* is French for "a blow.") This often-lethal adventure involved riding into battle unarmed or carrying only a light wooden coup-stick. If a warrior managed to strike an enemy with his hand or with his coup-stick and then escape unharmed, this was a glorious achievement indeed.

Indians of the Fort Bridger Area

The Shoshonis were the dominant tribe in the regions lying north and west of Fort Bridger. Local placenames still reflect this fact: a modern atlas shows Shoshone Falls and the Snake River Plain, both in eastern Idaho; the town of Shoshoni in central Wyoming; Fort Washakie in western Wyoming, named after Washakie, the chief of the Eastern Band of the Wyoming Shoshonis, sometimes called Washakie's Band; the 12,238-foot peaks known as the Washakie Needles, east of Grand Teton National Park; and the Little Snake River in northwestern Colorado. But a great many other Indians passed through the Fort Bridger region, too.

These included the Indians who traded with the whites at Fort Bridger and with each other; Indian buffalo hunters from north, south and west (Shoshonis, Utes, Flatheads, Nez Percé and sometimes Crows); the Navahos, who followed an old Indian and Spanish trail up the Green River; the Taugudika, whose name meant "eaters of white tailed deer"; the Haivodika, or "dove-eaters," so named because they behaved timidly on buffalo hunts; the Tukudika, or "sheep eaters," who hunted bighorn sheep in the Rockies; and many Shoshoni half-breeds, the offspring of white trappers and Indian mothers. Male "breeds," as they were called, usually became buffalo hunters and traders, just like their full-blooded kinsmen.[43]

It is not easy for us today to get an unbiased idea of what Indian life in the West was like in the 1820s, particularly how men, women and children in a given tribe treated themselves and each other. Most of the Indians were illiterate. Even when they could read and write, they were not trained to produce anthropological studies of their own societies. It is risky to generalize about the white authors who were writing about Indians because their own views varied from genocidal to romantic. Some whites, usually those living on the frontier itself, felt that "the only good Indian is a dead one." Others, generally those in the settled parts of the United States, were more inclined to praise the Indians as the "noble savages" conjured up by the 18th century French philosopher and author, Jean Jacques Rousseau.

For its part, the pictorial record left by Miller, Bodmer, Catlin and other contemporary artists is immensely valuable but it tends, understandably, to depict Indians in the most dramatic and most favorable light. This romantic bias was recognized even at the time: a mountain man once joked that he had never seen a real Indian who looked like one of Catlin's models. Beginning in the 1860s, the early photographs taken of Western Indians give us a more balanced look at Indian culture because they reveal, if only inadvertently, the squalid as well as the noble side of Indian life. By that time, however, Western tribes had been in contact with the whites for 40 years, so these photographs cannot tell us very much about what tribal culture was like in the 1820s.

The Cult of Violence—and How to Deal with It

What is certain, however, is that for the males of many nomadic Western tribes, warfare was a totally consuming way of life. Boys were trained under the most rigorous conditions to become superb riders, trackers, hunters, scalp-takers and horse thieves. Violence was encouraged and rewarded so systematically in the culture of the Plains Indians that it was recorded even by the most sympathetic observers. One of these was Prince Maximilian of Wied-Neuwied, a Prussian scholar-aristocrat who made an epic journey up the Missouri in 1833, accompanied by a young Swiss artist named Karl Bodmer.[44]

During their extensive travels they had a good introduction to intertribal violence. On 28 August 1833, for example, Maximilian made the following entry in his journal when staying at Fort Mackenzie near Great Falls, Montana:

> At break of day, we were awakened by musket-shot, and Doucette [their interpreter] entered our room crying, "Levez-vous, il faut nous battre" ["Get up: we have to fight!"] on which we rose in haste, dressed ourselves, and loaded our fowling-pieces with ball [that is, loaded their guns with solid bullets rather than with less-lethal birdshot].[45]

Maximilian and Bodmer survived this day only because the attack was not on the fort, as the interpreter had feared, but was instead a bloody struggle between the Indians themselves. Apparently without provocation, a joint force of nearly 600 Assiniboins and 100 Crees had attacked a small group of Blackfeet who had pitched 18 to 20 tents just outside the fort. The Blackfoot warriors, about 30 in number, fired a few shots when their enemies attacked and then sought refuge inside the fort, where they ran up to the roofs and began shooting again. The defenders of the fort, including

"When Sioux and Blackfeet Meet" (Charles M. Russell, from the collection of Gilcrease Museum, Tulsa, no. 0237.1448). Violence was an essential component of the culture of the Plains Indians.

some of Maximilian's men, opened fire, too, until it became clear that the attack was not directed against them. Despite all the gunfire, casualties were lighter than Maximilian had expected. The reason was, he says, that "the Indians had fired quite at random, otherwise the loss would have been much greater on both sides." As it was, more than 14 Blackfeet were killed and many others were hurt in this clash. Assiniboin losses were put at three killed and more than 20 seriously wounded.

Maximilian himself retained his composure during this fight and even found time to admire the Blackfoot warriors who were riding to the fort to help their companions:

> From the place where the range of hills turns to the Missouri, more and more Blackfeet continued to arrive. They came galloping in groups, from three to twenty together, their horses covered with foam, and they themselves in their finest apparel, with all kinds of ornaments and arms, bows and quivers on their backs, guns in their hands, furnished with their medicines [ritual objects carried into battle to help assure victory], with feathers on their heads; some had splendid crowns of black and white eagles' feathers, and a large hood of feathers hanging down behind, sitting on fine panther [mountain lion] skins lined with red; the upper part of their bodies partly naked, with a long strip of wolf's skin thrown across the shoulder, and carrying shields adorned with feathers and pieces of cloth. A truly original sight![46]

Cruelty as well as violence was commonplace in Indian culture. Francis Parkman, accompanied by his friend and relative Quincy Adams Shaw, left St. Louis in 1846 "on a tour of curiosity and amusement to the Rocky Mountains."

"Fort Mackenzie, August 28th 1833" (Karl Bodmer, 1833, courtesy of Alecto Historical Editions, London). Bodmer and his patron Prince Maximilian watched this fight from inside the fort. The two figures standing on the palisade of the fort, visible between the two teepees, probably represent Bodmer and Maximilian.

(Parkman followed the Oregon Trail as far as Fort Laramie in eastern Wyoming and then rode southwest with a Sioux war party. He returned to Fort Laramie, rode south to the Arkansas River in southeastern Colorado, and then east along the Santa Fe Trail back to Missouri.) A famous warrior named Kongra-Tonga boasted to Parkman that he himself had killed 14 men in battle. As this warrior recounted tale after tale of his prowess, Parkman tells us "there was one among the rest illustrating the worst features of Indian character too well for me to omit it." This is the story:

> Pointing out of the opening of the lodge towards the Medicine Bow Mountain [in southeastern Wyoming], not many miles distant, [Kongra-Tonga] said that

he was there a few summers ago with a war-party of his young men. Here they found two Snake Indians, hunting. They shot one of them with arrows, and chased the other up the side of the mountain till they surrounded him, and Kongra-Tonga himself, jumping forward among the trees, seized him by the arm. Two of his young men then ran up and held him fast while he scalped him alive. They then built a great fire, and cutting the tendons of their captive's wrists and feet, threw him in, and held him down with long poles until he was burnt to death. [Kongra-Tonga] garnished his story with descriptive particulars much too revolting to mention.[47]

This unpredictable readiness to resort to violence and cruelty to settle disputes or to win glory forced many whites to conclude that the only way to deal with Indians was to intimidate them. Although later generations would deplore the whites' treatment of the Indians — and, indeed, the story of broken promises and broken treaties is not a pretty one — the most experienced pioneers of the time saw the Indians as a real threat.

Osborne Russell, an intelligent, energetic man who trapped and hunted in the Rockies from 1834 to 1843 and then went into Oregon politics, has left us one of the most vivid, most thorough and best-written accounts of a mountain man's life. Here is what he said happened when Bannock Indians tried to recapture some horses from Jim Bridger and his men. The Bannocks were described as "lawless banditti, frequently infesting the routes of travel and causing trouble to the emigrants."[48] They had originally stolen the horses from a party of French trappers.

> Mr. Bridger was holding one of the stolen horses by the bridle when one of the Bannocks rushed through the crowd, seized the bridle and attempted to drag it from Mr. Bridger by force, without heeding the cocked rifles that surrounded him any more than if they had been so many reeds in the hands of children. He was a brave Indian, but his bravery proved fatal to himself, for the moment he seized the bridle two rifle balls whistled through his body. The others wheeled to run, but twelve of them we shot from their horses before they were out of reach of rifles. We then mounted horses and pursued them, destroyed and plundered their village, and followed and fought them for three days, when they begged us to let them go and promised to be good Indians in the future. We granted their request and returned to our camp,

satisfied that the best way to negotiate and settle dispute[s] with hostile Indians is with the rifle, for that is the only pen that can write a treaty they will not forget. Two days after we had left them three white trappers, ignorant of what had taken place, went into their village and were treated in the most friendly manner.[49]

A similar view of Indians and how to deal with them was expressed by Captain Marcy, who may have shared the prejudices of his times but was not given to overstatement. This was his stern advice:

> The Indians of the Plains ... have not, so far as I have observed, the most distant conception of [gratitude]. You may confer numberless benefits upon them for years, and the more that is done for them the more they will expect.... The only way to make these merciless freebooters fear or respect the authority of our government is, when they misbehave, first of all to chastise them well by striking such a blow as will be felt for a long time, and thus show them that we are superior to them in war. They will then respect us much more than when their good-will is purchased with presents.[50]

To add a touch of humor to his dry, matter-of-fact guidebook, Marcy added that a mountain man who was a close friend of his and who had spent 25 years among the Indians of the Rocky Mountains had once told him:

> [The Indians] are the most onsartainest varmints in all creation, and I reckon tha'r not mor'n half human; for you never seed a human, arter you'd fed and treated him to the best fixins in your lodge, jist turn round and steal all your horses, or ary other thing he could lay hands on.... Tain't no use to talk about honor with them, Cap. [Captain]; they hain't got no such

thing in um; and they won't show fair fight, any way you can fix it. Don't they kill and sculp a white man when-ar they can get the better on him? The mean varmints, they'll never behave themselves until you give um a clean out and out licking ... ef you treat um decently, they think you ar afeard. You may depend on't, Cap., the only way to treat Injuns is to thrash them well at first, then the balance will sorter take to you and behave themselves.[51]

The story of how Jim Bridger rescued his fellow mountain man Joe Meek from certain death at the hands of the Crow Indians also makes the point about the importance of taking a firm stand.[52] Meek was a member of Bridger's fur trapping brigade but set off from camp by himself. Five days later, at Rocky Fork on the Yellowstone River, he was captured by a Crow war party which numbered 187 men, nine boys and three women. Meek understood their language well enough to be able to respond when the chief, who was named "The Bold," said to him: "I have known the whites for a long time, and I know them to be great liars, deserving death; but if *you* will tell the truth, you shall live."

The Bold then asked Meek who his leader was and how many men he had. Although there were in fact 240 men in Bridger's brigade, Meek decided to lie and said there were only 40. At this answer The Bold laughed and said, "We will make them poor, and you shall live, but they shall die." With Meek afoot and under close guard, the Indians made their way to Bridger's camp. When they got near it, The Bold ordered Meek to get one of Bridger's sentries to come close to them. Instead, he shouted to the sentry to stay away because the Indians would kill him if he approached.

The sentry ran to warn Jim Bridger,

who appeared a few minutes later on a big white horse. Halting 300 yards away and using Meek as an interpreter, Bridger said that The Bold should send one of his lieutenants to smoke a peace pipe with the mountain men. The Bold reflected on this for a moment and then ordered his second-in-command, a chief named Little Gun, to ride forward and smoke with Bridger. In the meantime, however, the rest of the war party got ready to attack, putting on paint and feathers, arranging the scalps at their belts, choosing their best arrows and checking their ammunition.

Little Gun went forward but stopped about 100 yards from Bridger because, as Meek explains, "according to the Crow laws of war, each war [was] forced to strip himself, and proceed the remaining distance in a state of nudity, and kiss and embrace." When this ceremony was going on, five of Bridger's men, hidden in a ravine, moved toward the Indians and cut off Little Gun's line of retreat. With Little Gun suddenly a captive, Bridger proposed to The Bold that they exchange their respective prisoners. The Bold sullenly consented to their trade because, he said, "he could not afford to give a chief for one white dog's scalp." Meek and Little Gun then were released and went back to their own sides.

Remarkably, though, that very evening, The Bold, of his own volition and accompanied by an honor guard of 40 warriors, came to see Bridger and agreed to a three-month treaty. The Crows said they formerly had been at war with the whites but now they wanted to be friendly with them so that, together, they could fight their common enemy, the Blackfeet. In a spirit of good-fellowship, the Indians gave Meek's mule, rifle and beaver pelts back to him. Moreover, they even gave him a name in their own language: *Shiam Shaspusia*, which meant "He who can out-lie the Crows."

The Shoshonis

Linguistically, the Shoshoni family was a broad grouping which included a number of related tribes. These were the Northern Shoshonis encountered by the Lewis and Clark expedition; the Western Shoshonis, who lived in the desert areas of Nevada, Utah and Idaho and were called "Digger Indians" by the whites; and the Eastern or Wind River Shoshonis, who had horses, hunted buffalo and lived in the valleys of the Wind, Green and Big Horn Rivers.[53]

Not all these Indians were colorful nomadic warriors. The harsh environment of the deserts severely limited cultural development for the tribes of the Great Basin.[54] They had no horses or teepees. The lack of horses forced them to hunt rabbits and other small game on foot or get their nourishment from fish, roots, seeds and berries. For this reason they were called "Diggers." They were pitied and derided by the whites and considered a separate race of Indians.

Zenas Leonard, a mountain man who traveled widely in the West from 1831 to 1835, commented that these Indians were "the most indolent and have the least ambition of any tribe we had yet discovered. They are lazy and dirty; and only strive to get as much as will keep them from starving."[55] Joseph Goldsborough Bruff, who led a party of 63 men and 13 wagons to California during the 1849 gold rush, was of the same mind:

> While breakfasting this morning, two miserable, half clad, shivering indians came into camp. They were armed with full quivers and bows, and very different and inferior to any indians I had before seen; and was confident that they were the "Diggers".... I said to one of them, "*Digger?*"—he replied with a shake of the head, and downcast look, "*Shoshonee*"—but I knew he lied.[56]

In contrast, the Wind River Shoshoni (also known as the Eastern Shoshoni) had a much richer culture because they could draw on the natural resources of the Rockies and, since they had horses, they could ride out to pursue the buffalo herds on the Great Plains. One of the best first-hand accounts of the Shoshonis was written by trapper and mountain man Osborne Russell; excerpts can be found in Appendix II. The visual record is impressive, too. Pictures of the Shoshonis painted on the spot by Alfred Jacob Miller, a Baltimore artist who came West in 1837 with a group of mountain men, show them to have been numerous (Miller's estimate was 2,000 warriors), in superb physical condition, well-mounted, well-armed (with rifles or muskets, bows and arrows, and spears) and living in spacious teepees made of well-tanned buffalo skins. A Jesuit missionary, Father Pierre Jean De Smet, was also quite taken with the Shoshonis he saw at the 1837 rendezvous:

> Three hundred of their warriors came up in good order and at full gallop into the midst of our camp. They were hideously painted, armed with war clubs and covered all over with feathers, pearls, wolves' tails, teeth and claws of animals.... Those who had wounds received in war, and those who had killed the enemies of their tribe, displayed their scars ostentatiously and waved the scalps, they had taken on the ends of poles.... [T]hey

A "Digger" Indian home in the Uinta Basin, northeastern Utah, 1873 (Smithsonian Institution, photograph no. 1547)

dismounted, and all came to shake hands with the whites in sign of friendship.[57]

The difference in appearance and in self-esteem between the Indians of the Great Basin and those of the northern Rockies was striking. On the same day he met the "Digger" Indians, Bruff also tells us that,

"Cavalcade" (Alfred Jacob Miller, Walters Art Gallery, Baltimore)

At dinner another indian rode in to us: — neatly clad, and on a fine little yellow mare; he was armed with a long old fashioned flint rifle, quiver of arrows, bow, &c. I at once perceived that the smiling, good looking fellow, was one of our old friends, — a Shoshonee. — He readily permitted us to examine his arms, and gave several arrows to the men, they were pointed with yellow quartz. He dined with us.

Indian Buffalo Hunts

The most dangerous aspect of a warrior's life was raiding other tribes for horses and scalps. But hunting buffalo was a close second. Writing in 1847, Francis Parkman described how lightly equipped an Indian hunting party was:

There was not a saddle or a bridle in the whole party. A piece of buffalo-robe, girthed over the horse's back, served in the place of the one, and a cord of twisted hair, lashed round his lower jaw, answered for the other. Eagle feathers dangled from every mane and tail, as marks of courage and speed. As for the rider, he wore no other clothing than a light cincture [loin cloth] at his waist, and a pair of moccasins. He had a heavy whip, with a handle of solid elk-horn, and a lash of knotted bull-hide, fastened to his wrist by a band. His bow was in his hand, and his quiver of otter or panther skin hung at his shoulder.[58]

The biggest buffalo herds were those of the Great Plains. The Shoshoni, however, did not have to go all the way to Kansas in order to hunt. Osborne Russell

Shoshoni Indian Chief Washakie. (Denver Public Library, Western History Collection). Because he was such a good friend to the emigrants, Washakie was photographed often. This picture was taken toward the end of the 19th century by the Denver photographers Rose and Hopkins.

Ironically, this peace-loving Washakie was a famous warrior in his own right. On one occasion, when young Shoshoni braves began to criticize him for being too friendly with the whites and for being unwilling to approve raids against neighboring tribes, Washakie slipped out of camp by himself and came back several days later with seven fresh scalps. He had encountered a war party of hostile Indians and had killed seven of them. "Let him who can do a greater feat than this claim the chieftainship," he told his followers. "Let him who would take my place count as many scalps." No one challenged his authority after this.[66]

Washakie won the affection, respect and thanks of the whites. Nine thousand grateful settlers once signed a document expressing their gratitude to him and his men for all their assistance. Washakie welcomed the wagon trains and there are many anecdotes about how the Shoshonis helped the emigrants in crossing dangerous rivers and recovering stray livestock. Bruff recounts that in 1849 a member of an emigrant party went into the Bear River mountains, not far from Fort Bridger, to hunt. The man became lost. He then met some Shoshonis and gave them his rifle in return for then guiding him back to his camp. When he got there, however, he found that his companions had gone on without him, so he asked the Indians to take him all the way to Salt Lake, which they did.

Bruff also tells us that another emigrant went out hunting near the Green River, also in the general vicinity of Fort Bridger, and was attacked by a party of Shoshonis who took his rifle, tied him to a tree, shot him in the back and killed him. When his comrades found the corpse, they tracked the Indians back to Washakie's camp and demanded redress. Washakie identified the murderer, had him tied to a tree and told the emigrants to do what they liked with him. The emigrants replied that it was up to the Indians to inflict an appropriate punishment. Washakie then called the brother of the culprit and ordered him to cut the offender's throat, which he instantly did. The emigrants returned to their own camp, fully satisfied with the chief's brand of justice.

Washakie also welcomed the Pony Express, the telegraph and the Union Pacific Railroad. He counted Jim Bridger and Kit Carson among his close friends. In 1868 he persuaded the U.S. Government to give the Shoshonis a reservation in the Wind River valley, about 130 miles northeast of Fort Bridger. In 1876, fighting alongside General George Crook, he led his warriors against the Sioux at the battle of Rosebud Creek. One of Crook's staff officers, Lieutenant John Gregory Bourke, who saw Washakie in action there, remembered how, "The chief of the Shoshones appeared to great advantage, mounted on a fiery pony, he himself naked to the waist and wearing one of the gorgeous headdresses of eagle feathers sweeping far along the ground behind his pony's tail."[67]

In recognition of the courageous role the Shoshonis had played in this battle — together with their allies, the Crows, they held their ground against Sioux attacks which otherwise would have overwhelmed Crook — Washakie was pre-sented with a handsome silver-trimmed saddle, a gift from President Ulysses S. Grant. In 1878 Washakie received another tribute — Camp Brown, a military post on the Shoshoni reservation, was renamed Fort Washakie. President Chester Arthur, en route to Yellowstone National Park for some trout fishing, called on Washakie at his lodge at Fort Washakie in 1883. Seven years later, Washakie died in his nineties. His last words to his family are said to have been: "You now have that for which we so long and bravely fought. Keep it forever in peace and honor. Go now and rest. I shall speak to you no more."[68] He was buried with full military honors at Fort Washakie.

Chapter IV

Mountain Men
and the Fur Trade

It was purely for the sake of men's fashions that John Colter and other mountain men risked and often lost their lives. From the 17th century to about 1840, a well-dressed European or American gentleman simply could not appear in public without a top hat made of beaver fur. In 1760 alone, enough beaver pelts to make 576,000 hats were exported to England from the river valleys of North America.[69] Although the fur was turned into felt by using mercury, which could poison the hatters and make them crazed (hence the expression "mad as a hatter"), there was such a demand for beaver hats that high prices were paid for prime pelts. A shortage of pelts sparked the early 19th century fur rush into the Rockies, especially after Lewis and Clark brought back word in 1806 of the multitude of beavers and other fur-bearing animals which were there for the taking. The men who became fur trappers were the best outdoorsmen in North America. Their endurance and their wilderness skills are not likely ever to be equaled again, let alone surpassed. Take the case of John Colter, for example.

Colter's Run

John Colter was a member of the Lewis and Clark expedition but decided to stay on in the mountains near the headwaters of the Missouri because of the "abundance of beaver being there," rather than returning to St. Louis. In 1808 his trapping companion was a mountain man named Potts. Both of them were aware of the hostility of the Blackfoot Indians, at least one and probably two of whom, as we have seen, had been killed by the Lewis and Clark expedition.

Colter and Potts were in their canoe one morning, checking their traps in a narrow creek near Jefferson's Fork in southwestern Montana, when a party of 500 to 600 Blackfoot Indians discovered them. The Indians beckoned them to come ashore. Retreat was impossible, so Colter turned the bow of the canoe toward the shore. As soon as it touched, an Indian seized Potts' rifle but Colter, a remarkably strong man, wrested the rifle away and gave it back to Potts. The two men pushed the canoe off the bank but Potts was immediately wounded by an

"Carson's Men" (Charles M. Russell, from the collection of Gilcrease Museum, Tulsa, no. 0137.2245). When this picture is reproduced in color and in a larger format, it is arguably the best image of the mountain men.

arrow. Colter tried to persuade him that they should beach the canoe again because he knew they could not escape. But as Bradbury relates in *Travels in the Interior of America*, Potts "instantly leveled his rifle at an Indian and shot him dead on the spot…. [Potts] was instantly pierced with arrows so numerous, that, to use the language of Colter, '*he was made a riddle of*.'"

The Indians then seized Colter, stripped him completely naked and began to argue among themselves about how he should die. Colter had lived with the Crow Indians, where he had also learned the language of the Blackfeet, so when the chief asked him if he was a good runner, he knew the only chance he would have was to run for his life. Colter therefore told the chief that he was a very bad runner, although in point of fact he was

remarkably fast. Ordering the other Indians to stay where they were, the chief led Colter out onto the open prairie for 300 to 400 yards and then released him, "bidding him *to save himself if he could* (Bradbury 19)."

Running barefoot at top speed over a plain where the prickly pear cactus spiked his feet, Colter made for Jefferson's Fork, which was about six miles away. The Indians gave a shout and started off in pursuit. After about three miles he looked over his shoulder and saw that although he outdistanced most of the Indians, one warrior, armed with a spear and carrying a light blanket, was only 100 yards behind him. For the first time, Colter felt he might be able to escape after all and redoubled his efforts, blood pouring from his nose because of his exertions.

Within a mile of the river, he heard footsteps behind and saw that the warrior had gained on him and was now only 20 yards away. Suddenly, Colter stopped, wheeled around and spread his arms wide. The Indian, surprised by this unexpected action and by Colter's bloody appearance, tried to stop, too. But he was exhausted from running and fell while trying to throw his spear. The point stuck in the ground and broke off. Colter instantly seized the spearpoint and killed the Indian with it. He then picked up the blanket as well and began to run again. The rest of the Indians halted briefly at the corpse of their fallen comrade, but they soon resumed the chase.

Their brief stop gave Colter just enough time to reach Jefferson's Fork. He plunged into the river and saw that a large amount of driftwood had washed up against a small island nearby, forming a kind of raft. He dove under the raft and succeeded in wriggling upwards through it until his head was above water but he was well-hidden thanks to the intertwined branches above him. Moments later, "the Indians arrived on the river, screeching and yelling, as Colter expressed it, 'like so many devils.'" (Bradbury 20) The Indians searched diligently for him, often climbing onto the raft itself, but could not find him.

When night came, Colter slipped out from under the raft, swam a long way downstream and then started toward Lisa's Fort on the Bighorn River in southeastern Montana, which was about 300 miles away. Despite his escape from the Blackfeet, his situation was still perilous: he was completely naked except for the blanket, barefoot, hungry and with no means of killing game (the spearpoint was useless for this purpose). Nevertheless, he managed to reach Lisa's

Fort in 11 days, having survived on edible roots and the bark of trees. When he reached the fort, "his beard was long, his face and whole [body] were thin and emaciated by hunger, and his limbs and feet swollen and sore." Indeed, the men at the fort did not recognize him until he told them his name.[70]

Masters of Their Universe

Lightly armed and even more lightly equipped, the mountain men roamed at will throughout the Rockies, living off the land, beholden to no one. George Frederick Ruxton, an English traveler who met some of them when he passed through New Mexico in 1846, said they were men who "with the sky for a roof and their rifles to supply them with food and clothing, call no man lord or master, and are free as the game they follow."[71]

The trappers have been variously described as heroic wilderness-taming pathfinders; as murderous pathological loners who could not tolerate the normal restraints of civilized life; and, more academically, even as "expectant capitalists"—that is, as ambitious working-class men who wanted to accumulate a little bit of capital quickly so they could move into more permanent and less dangerous lines of work, such as owning their own farms.[72] It seems easier to conclude, though, that most of them were adventuresome young men in their twenties and thirties who liked the outdoors and were simply trying to earn a living.

A few of them, like Jim Bridger, were admirable in almost all respects. Bridger himself made friends easily and was "a very companionable man ... expression mild and manners agreeable.

"'I TOOK YE FOR AN INJIN.'"

"I Took Ye for an Injun" (Frederic Remington, Buffalo Bill Historical Center, Cody, Wyoming)

He was hospitable and generous, and was always trusted and respected."[73] But many other mountain men were, according to another contemporary account, "a desperate set of men, more outlandish and brutal than the traders, and more than half-Indian in appearance and habits."[74] No matter how we choose to categorize the mountain men, however, it is clear there were never very many of them. At the high point of the beaver trade around 1832, for example, there were only about 1,000 trappers on the upper Missouri and in the Rockies, plus another 600 working in Canada for the Hudson's Bay Company, plus a small number of free trappers (men working for themselves rather than for a fur trading company) in northern New Mexico.[75]

The Beaver—and How to Trap It[76]

The trapper Osborne Russell tells us that, "The beaver, as almost every one knows, is an amphibious animal, but the instinct with which it is possessed surpasses the reason of no small portion of the human race." The beaver is about two and one-half feet long and weighs between 30 and 60 pounds. Its broad, flat tail propels it and steers it through the mountain rivers where it thrived in the early 19th century and to which it now has in many places returned. For mountain men, the beaver tail was a great delicacy: it was first charred in the flames of a campfire to get the skin off and then roasted over the coals. The rest of the beaver was discarded except, of course, for the pelt, which weighed about 1½ pounds when dressed (prepared for market).

Beavers themselves eat the bark of trees and branches they cut with their chisel-like teeth. The inedible parts of this diet are turned into dams and lodges. From their preputial glands near the anus they secrete a gummy, musky substance known as "castorium," which the mountain men extracted from dead beavers and carried in a small wooden box or plugged horn bottle on their belts. Osborne Russell explains why this was done:

It is this deposit [castorium] which causes the destruction of the beaver by the hunters. When a beaver, male or female, leaves the lodge [a rounded structure they make from the branches of trees] to swim about the pond, they go to the bottom and fetch up some mud between their forepaws and breast, carry it to the bank and emit upon it a small quantity of castorium.... [The trapper] sets his trap in the water near the bank about one foot from it and puts a small portion of the castorium thereon. After night the beaver comes out of his lodge, smells the fatal bait 200 or 300 yards distant, and steers his course directly for it. He hastens to ascend the bank, but the trap grasps his foot and soon drowns him in the struggle to escape, for the beaver, though termed an amphibious animal, cannot respire beneath the water.[77]

A dressed beaver pelt, the object of the long hours spent by mountain men standing knee-deep in icy water to set and retrieve their traps, was a valuable commodity. At the first rendezvous, held at Henry's Fork, Wyoming (about 25 miles southeast of Fort Bridger), in 1825, traders bought pelts from the mountain men at prices ranging from $2.00 to $5.00 per pound. That year the trapper Jedediah Smith had 668 pelts to sell, which was probably a record for a single man. The average mountain man had only 300 to 400 pelts but this would still net him between $1,000 and $2,000. But often these riches evaporated then and there at the rendezvous, making it necessary for him to go back to the mountains again to trap more beaver. In effect, the mountain men were working 11 months of the year for a one-month debauch at the rendezvous.[78]

One reason for this rapid return to

poverty (in addition to drinking, gambling and buying trinkets for their squaws) was that the mountain men had to buy their own supplies from traders who were peddling goods bought for low prices in St. Louis and sold for very high prices in the Rockies. In fairness to the traders, it must be noted that it took 70 days of hard travel to bring these goods from St. Louis to the mountains. Still, they made good money.

St. Louis was the prosperous pivot-point of the fur trade: between 1807 and 1840, about $200,000 to $300,000 worth of furs passed through there each year en route to the east coast of the United States and Western Europe. The value of the return flow of trade goods through the town was about the same.[79] Examples of what the traders sold to the mountain men include knives at $2.50 each, lead for casting into bullets at $1.00 per pound, tobacco at $2.00 to $3.00 per pound, and coffee and sugar at $1.50 per pound.[80] The traders' real profits, however, came from marketing the furs: in St. Louis, a beaver pelt purchased at $2.00 to $5.00 a pound could be resold for $6.00 to $8.00 a pound.

To get an idea of what a dollar was worth in 1825, in the settled parts of the United States a skilled worker — say, a carpenter or a mason — earned about $1.50 per day. A semi-skilled member of a flatboat (raft) crew on the Mississippi River made $1.25 per day, plus his room and board. Indeed, flatboating is precisely the kind of job a mountain man might have had before Westering took possession of him: the trapper "Pegleg" Smith, whom we shall meet again later in this book, had in fact worked on Mississippi River flatboats before signing up in St. Louis in 1824 for a journey to Santa Fe.[81]

Surviving in the Rockies

In April 1838, Osborne Russell and about 30 trappers who were also working with Jim Bridger got their gear ready and set off into the wilderness on a spring beaver hunt along the Big Horn River in southeastern Montana. By modern standards a trapper was singularly ill-equipped to spend six months or more in the Rockies. This is all he usually had[82]:

• A riding horse with saddle, bridle and saddlebags.
• A pack horse or mule to carry his gear.
• A sack containing five or six beaver traps.
• A blanket.
• An extra pair of moccasins.
• A single-shot .53 caliber Hawken rifle (see Chapter IX), which he carried in front of him across the pommel of the saddle, sometimes in a skin casing to protect it from bad weather.
• One or two single-shot pistols of about .45 caliber, to serve as emergency backup weapons after the rifle had been fired.
• A horn to carry gunpowder and a leather pouch to carry bullets.
• A broad leather belt, to which was strapped a buffalo-hide sheath holding a Bowie knife or a Green River knife, a container for castorium, a "possibles" sack containing a pipe, tobacco and flint and steel to make a fire.[83]
• A tomahawk, fastened to the saddle horn.

A trapper's hair, usually long and unwashed, fell loosely over his shoulders. His clothes consisted of the following:

"Free Trappers" (Charles M. Russell, courtesy of the Montana Historical Society, Mackay Collection). A free trapper was one who worked on his own account rather than as an employee of a fur trading company.

- A cotton or flannel shirt if he had one; if not, a shirt made of antelope skin.
- A pair of leather pants which in cold weather could be covered with leggings made of a blanket or smoked buffalo skin.
- A coat made of a blanket or buffalo robe.
- A broad-brimmed, low-crowned hat.
- Stockings consisting of pieces of blanket wrapped around his feet.
- Moccasins made of dressed deer, elk or buffalo skin.

If the trappers were poor in terms of worldly goods, they were rich in their use of the English language. Their jargon was so remarkable that it is worthwhile listening to a little of it. Here are some excerpts from a first-hand account of a conversation with John L. ("Long") Hatcher, a Westering mountain man who was born in Virginia, moved to southeastern Colorado, drove sheep from New Mexico to California and eventually settled in Oregon.[84] Hatcher explains why he has risen so early despite the cold weather and why he does not want to go back to civilized life. He also asks where his listener is going:

> This hos is no b'ar to stick his nose under cover all the robe season, an' lay round camp.... This chil' hates an American what hasn't seen Injuns skulped, or doesn't know a Yute from a Kian mok'sin.... This chil' says — "Wagh! a little bacca, if its a plew a plug, an' Dupont an' G'lena, a Green River or so," and he leaves for the Bayou Salade. Darn the white diggins, while thar's buffler in the mountains. Whoopee! ... are you for Touse?

This is a gloss on the text:

> I [this horse, i.e., Hatcher] am not a bear, which likes to hibernate all winter. I [this chil', that is, child: Hatcher again refers to himself] hate someone from the settled parts of the United States who hasn't seen Indians scalped and can't tell a Ute moccasin from a Kiowa moccasin [that is, someone who is so much of a greenhorn that he can't tell one Indian tribe from another simply by the footprints of their moccasins]. I say: Wagh! All I need is a little tobacco [bacca], even if it's extremely expensive [a plew a plug: a plew is a beaver pelt and a plug is one pound of tobacco], some gunpowder [made by the DuPont company], lead for bullets [galena is the principal ore of lead], a butcher knife [especially one stamped on the blade with the Green River trademark], and I'm off to a wilderness teaming with game [the Bayou Salade]. Who cares about settled life [the white diggins] while there's buffalo in the mountains. Whoopee! Are you heading for Taos, New Mexico, too?

In the same conversation, another mountain man, Louy (sic) Simonds, reminisces with Hatcher about their fights with Indians. Simonds says "this coon has raised har so often sence, he keers fur nothing now. Mind the time we took Pawnee topknots away to the Platte, Hatch?" In modern English this means: "I [this coon, i.e., Simonds himself] have scalped so many Indians that nothing bothers me any more. Do you remember the time, Hatcher, that we scalped the Pawnee Indians near the Platte River?"

It must be noted here that mountain men were given to telling tall tales. Jim Bridger, for example, held a group of emigrants spellbound with a long, graphically detailed story about the time he was attacked by six Indians. He said that with his only weapon, a six-shot revolver, he had downed five of the Indians who were pursuing him.[85] Forced by the remaining Indian to the brink of a high cliff, Old Gabe, with his last shot, killed the Indian's horse but the Indian fired at the same time, killing Bridger's horse. "We now engaged in a han'-to-han' conflict with butcher knives," Bridger continued earnestly. "He was a powerful Injun — tallest I ever see. It was a long and fierce struggle. One moment I had the best of it, an' the next moment the odds was agin me. Finally...." Here Bridger paused for a few seconds, as if to catch his breath, and one of his listeners asked eagerly, "How did it end?" Bridger then replied with slow deliberation: *"The Injun killed me."*[86]

In his own reply to Louy Simmons, Hatcher is doubtless mixing a little bit of fact with a lot of tall-tale fiction when he says:

> Wagh! ef we didn't ... an' give an owgh-owgh, longside of thar darned screechin', I'm a niggur. This chil' doesn't let an Injun count a coup on his cavyard always. They came nigh rubbing me out, t'other side of Spanish Peaks — woke up in the mornin' jist afore day, the devils yelling like mad. I grabs my knife, keels one, and made for timber, with four of their cussed arrows in my meatbag. The Paches took my beaver — five packs of the prettiest in the mountains — an' two mules, but my traps was hid in the creek. Sez I, hyar's a gone coon ef they keep my gun, so I follers their trail, an' at night, crawls into camp, an' socks my big knife up to the Green River, first dig. I takes t'other Injun by the har, and makes meat of him, too.... I got old bullthrower, made medicine over him, and no darned niggur kin draw bead with him since.

A rough gloss:

> Well, if we didn't hold our own and give the Indians war cry back for war

cry, I'll be damned! I never let an Indian steal my band of horse or mules.[87] The Apaches came close to killing me on the other side of the Spanish Peaks in southern Colorado — I woke up just before dawn and heard the Indians yelling like devils. I grabbed my knife, killed one Indian and ran off to hide in the forest, despite having four arrows in my belly. The Apaches took my beaver pelts — five packs of the best furs in the mountains — and my two mules, but my beaver traps were hidden in the creek. I said to myself: I'm a dead man if they keep my rifle, so I followed their trail, crawled into their camp at night and on the first stroke buried my big knife into one Indian, all the way up to the Green River trademark, and killed him. I grabbed another Indian by his hair and killed him, too.... I got my stolen rifle back again and called on the gods to protect it; now no darned Indian will ever be able use it.[88]

There were no houses and very few log cabins in the mountains, so where did the mountain men live? The English traveler George Frederick Ruxton gives us the answer:

> A hunter's camp in the Rocky mountains is quite a picture. He does not always take the trouble to build any shelter unless it is in the snow-season, when a couple of deerskins stretched over a willow frame shelter him from the storm. At other seasons he is content with a mere breakwind.... Some hunters, who have married Indian squaws, carry about with them the Indian lodge of buffalo skin, which is stretched around a conical frame of poles.... The camp is invariably made in a picturesque locality, for, like the Indian, the white hunter has ever an eye for the beautiful.[89]

A fuller description of winter camps comes from Warren Angus Ferris, an American who traveled in the Rockies

"Captain Walker (Joseph Reddeford Walker)" or "A Bourgeois and His Squaw" (Alfred Jacob Miller, Joslyn Art Museum, Omaha)

from 1830 to 1836 as a member of fur trapping expeditions:

> The season having become far advanced, we pitched quarters in a large grove of aspen trees, at the brink of an excellent spring that supplied us with the purest water.... Our camp presented eight leathern lodges, and two constructed of poles covered with cane grass, which grows in dense patches to the height of eight or ten feet along the river. They were all completely sheltered from the wind by the surrounding trees.... One who has never lived in a lodge, would scarcely think it possible for seven or eight persons to pass a long winter agreeably, in a circular room, ten feet in diameter, having a considerable portion of it occupied by a fire in the centre.... I moved from the lodge into a comfortable log house, but again returned to the lodge, which I found much more pleasant than the other.[90]

Since the mountain men carried no food with them except for a little salt, what did they eat? The answer is that they ate only what they themselves could kill. In good times they had more than enough. In addition to beaver tails and the best cuts of buffalo, they also ate deer. Indeed, blacktail deer were so common in the Rockies that the hunters of Ferris' party frequently killed seven or eight deer apiece in the course of one day; the trees in his camp "were soon

"Trapping Beaver" (Alfred Jacob Miller, Walters Art Gallery, Baltimore). Rheumatism, caused by standing for hours in streams fed by melting snows, was one of the mountain man's occupational ailments.

decorated by several thousand pounds of venison."[91] Still, there was not much variety in this high-protein diet. When Bridger visited St. Louis during the winter of 1839–40 — the first time he had been out of the mountains in 17 years — he said that not once during those years had he tasted bread.[92]

In "starvin' times," however, survival was problematical and death from hunger or thirst was never far away. For example, John Kirk Townsend, a naturalist who went West in 1834, was reduced to drinking the still warm blood directly from the heart of a dead buffalo. As soon as the blood touched his lips, he says, "my burning thirst, aggravated by hunger (for I had eaten nothing that day), got the better of my abhorrence; I plunged my head into the reeking ventricles [the heart was still in the body cavity of the buffalo], and drank until forced to stop for breath."[93]

The Last Big Rendezvous

As the number of beaver declined because of overtrapping and as silk hats began to replace beaver hats, the economic underpinnings of the fur trade crumbled. The 1839 rendezvous, held in the upper valley of the Green River about 150 miles north of Fort Bridger, was the last important one. There are many firsthand descriptions of how the mountain men traded, drank, fought each other and found girlfriends at earlier rendezvous, but F.W. Wislizenus, a German physician who attended the 1839 rendezvous, felt a note of sadness among the mountain men. "The days of their glory seem to be past," he wrote. "Only with reluctance does a trapper abandon this dangerous craft, and a sort of serious home-sickness seizes him when he retires from his mountain life to civilization."

However, Wislizenus goes on to give us some insights into the Indians who came to that last-but-one rendezvous.[94]

Several thousand Shoshoni, Flathead and Nez Percé attended. Wislizenus was impressed by the long rows of their teepees, extending for a full mile along the Green River. An army of wolfish dogs milled around the teepees and from some tents came the sound of music, in the form of drumbeats and monotone chanting. Squaws were playing a popular game called "the hand," in which a small piece of wood or some other object was passed from hand to hand by women seated in a circle. A given player had to guess in whose hand the object was at that moment. Warriors played, too; in fact, both sexes "were so carried away by the game that they often spent a whole day and night at it."

For the Indians, a rendezvous meant barter. They offered to trade tanned skins, moccasins, thongs of buffalo leather or braided buffalo hair, and fresh or dried buffalo meat. In exchange, they wanted gunpowder and lead, knives, tobacco, bright red pigment for painting their faces, kerchiefs, pocket mirrors and ornaments. If an Indian for some reason decided not to part with one of his wares, however, Wislizenus noticed that "he obstinately adheres to his refusal, though ten times the value be offered him."

Having sold their beaver pelts, the mountain men had some money. But, as we have seen, prices were sure to be high: in this case, flour was $1.00 a pint; pints of coffee beans, cocoa beans or sugar were $2.00 each; a pint of diluted alcohol was $4.00; a pint of tobacco went for up to $2.00. In addition, Wislizenus found that, "Guns and ammunition, bear traps, blankets, kerchiefs and gaudy finery for trappers' squaws [this finery was called *foofuraw* by the mountain men, who had to pay a good deal for it], are sold at enormous profit...."

Occupational Hazards: Brawls, Grizzly Bears and Frontier Surgery

Being a mountain man was a dangerous business. In 1826, James Ohio Pattie, who trapped in the southern reaches of the Rockies, claimed that of 116 men who left Santa Fe that year, only 16 survived until the next season. In later years, another trapper, Antoine Robidoux, asserted that of the 300 men he knew who had gone into the mountains, only three were still alive. A conservative estimate today is that at least 20 percent of the trappers died in the wilderness.[95]

Even partying could be dangerous for a mountain man. Writing for a Scottish magazine in 1846, George Frederick Ruxton remembered a fandango (a lively Spanish dance) in Santa Fe attended by half a dozen mountain men. As the night wore on and as alcohol flowed freely, the Mexican men lining the walls of the room where the fandango was held became furious because the trappers were monopolizing all the pretty women. Losing his temper, one Mexican pulled a girl away from her partner, a huge mountain man named La Bonté, who retaliated by lifting the Mexican over his head and throwing him against the wall. What happened next was predictable:

> The war, long threatened, has commenced; twenty Mexicans draw their knives and rush upon La Bonté, who stands his ground and sweeps them down with his ponderous fist, one

after another, as they throng around him. "Howgh-owgh-owgh-owgh-h!" the well-known war-whoop, bursts from his companions, and on they rush to the rescue.... Knives glitter in the light, and quick thrusts are given and parried.... [As Mexican reinforcements arrive the] odds began to tell against the mountaineers, when Kit Carson's quick eye caught sight of a high stool ... with three long heavy legs. In a moment he had cleared his way to this, and in another the three legs were broken off and in the hands of himself, Dick Wooton [another famous trapper] and La Bonté. Sweeping them round their heads, down came the heavy weapons amongst the Mexicans with a wonderful effect ... mowing down a good half-dozen of the assailants. At this the mountaineers gave a hearty whoop, and charged the wavering enemy with such resistless vigor that they gave way and bolted through the door....

No mountain men were injured in this brawl but two Mexicans died that night of the knife wounds they had received. The trappers agreed to pay some compensation to the friends of the deceased and to have Catholic masses said for the repose of their souls. "Thus," says Ruxton, "the affair blew over; but for several days the mountaineers never showed themselves in the streets ... without their rifles on their shoulders."[96]

Grizzly bears posed a real threat, too. Trappers feared them because, as Zenas Leonard found during his own travels in the West, "The grizzly bear is the most ferocious animal that inhabits these prairies, and are very numerous. They no sooner see you than they will make at you with open mouth ... if you turn and run they will most assuredly tear you to pieces."[97] The most famous story about encounters with grizzlies involves the trapper Hugh Glass. Improbable as it may sound, this account comes from two different and reputable sources.[98]

In 1823 Glass was traveling in South Dakota with the Ashley-Henry expedition. One of the members of this party was 19-year-old Jim Bridger. These men were passing through Arikara country and for reasons of safety Major Henry told them to stay close together. But Glass never obeyed orders and went on ahead, alone. Half an hour later, his colleagues heard screams and ran forward to see what had happened. This is what they found:

> ...a huge Grizy Bear, with two Cubs — The monster had seized [Glass], torn the flesh from the lower part of his body, & from the lower limbs — He also had his neck shockingly torn ... & his breath to exude at the side of his neck — Blood flowed freely, but fortunately no bone was broken — & his hands & arms were not disabled.

The bear and her cubs were killed, Glass was strapped to a litter and his party continued on their way. But Glass was so badly wounded that his comrades "every moment waited for his death." After six days of slow travel, Major Henry, knowing that the trapping season was drawing to a close, offered $400 to any two of his men who would stay with Glass until he died and bury him before catching up with the expedition. John S. Fitzgerald and Jim Bridger volunteered.[99] They took care of Glass as well as they could, but after several days, "Quite discouraged & impatient for his death, as there remained no hope of his recovery, the two resolved to leave him there to die alone in the wilderness." They took his rifle, knife and camp kettle. Glass could hear every word they said but could not speak or move any part of his

"Hunting of the Grizzly Bear" (Karl Bodmer, courtesy of Alecto Historical Editions, London). This hunt took place along the Missouri River near Fort Union, Montana.

body except his arms. He was abandoned to his fate.

Fortunately, he was lying near a spring which was overhung by great clusters of "Buffaloberries" and could thus sip water from the hollow of his hand and pluck the berries. After some time had passed, one morning he found a huge rattlesnake by his blankets, killed it with a stone, threw the head away and gnawed on the carcass from time to time. Later on, wolves pulled his blankets out from under him and tore them to pieces. This left him lying on a bed of leaves.

In the meantime, Fitzgerald and Bridger had caught up with Major Henry. They told him that Glass had died, that they had buried him and that they had brought back his personal possessions as proof. Major Henry gave them the promised $400. Glass, however, was far from dead. Gradually his strength returned. At first he could only crawl; later, he could walk. As Maguire et al. relate on page 34 in *A Rendezvous Reader*, sometimes he would find the carcasses of buffalo which had been wounded and left to die:

> From these he gained nourishing food, by pounding out the marrow from the bones, & eating it seasoned with Buffaloberries & moistened with limped water from the brooks & springs — With sharp stones he would dig from the earth nourishing roots, which he had learned to discriminate while sojourning with the Paunees [the Pawnee Indians].

Major Henry's company at Fort Kiowa — a trading post variously described as being either 60 or 200 miles from Glass's encounter with the grizzly bear — "saw a man slowly approaching … as he came nearer their eyes rested on a cadaverous figure with a head so disfigured as to be unknown." It was Hugh Glass. John S. Fitzgerald was no longer at the fort, and when Glass finally caught up with him later on, seeking vengeance, Fitzgerald had joined the U.S. Army and was thus safe from violent retaliation. Bridger was still at Fort Kiowa, however. But Glass charitably forgave him because he was so young and inexperienced.[100] Glass himself recovered from all his wounds and continued to trap in the Rockies until he and two other mountain men were killed by the Arikara Indians in the winter of 1833.

Glass was extraordinarily lucky to have made it to Fort Kiowa but he was also lucky not to have undergone frontier surgery. In 1826, for example, a Westering man named Broadus pulled his rifle out of a wagon muzzle-first. It went off and the bullet hit him in the arm. We learn that,

> the bone being dreadfully shattered, the unfortunate man was advised to submit to an amputation…. [The only instruments available to his companions were] a handsaw, a butcher's knife and a large iron bolt. The teeth of the saw being considered too coarse, they went to work and soon had a set of fine teeth filed on the back. The knife having been whetted keen and the iron bolt laid upon the fire, they commenced the operation, and in less time than it takes to tell it, the arm was opened round to the bone, which was in an instant sawed off; and with the whizzing hot iron the whole stump was so effectively seared as to close the arteries completely. Bandages were now applied and the company proceeded on their journey as though nothing had happened. The arm commenced heal-

ing rapidly and in a few weeks the patient was sound and well….[101]

The ordeal of mountain man Thomas "Pegleg" Smith was similar. In 1828 Smith was part of a group of trappers wintering along the Green River, probably at Brown's Hole in northwestern Colorado. It is unclear precisely how Smith was wounded: contemporary accounts differ considerably. He was shot by an Indian in a fair fight, or perhaps from ambush. The bullet, or perhaps it was an arrow, shattered the bones of his lower leg just below the ankle, or perhaps at the ankle, or perhaps below the knee. Smith reached for his rifle but collapsed before he could get to it, or perhaps he managed to raise the rifle and kill his hidden enemy.

Fortunately, another Westering mountain man, George C. Yount, compiled an accurate account of what happened after Smith was wounded. Yount was born in North Carolina, began trapping in New Mexico in the mid–1820s, and later became a rancher in California. He tells us that Smith's colleagues were certain his leg would "mortify" (i.e., gangrene would set in), so death was certain unless the limb was amputated. Smith asked the leader of the party, Milton Sublette, whether he knew how to cut it off.

"Well," said Sublette, "I seen it done once when I was huntin' with the Crow Injins and I think I can do it their fashion." "Go ahead, then," said Smith, "it's my duty not to lose a chance." So the men sharpened a hunting knife "till it would cut a hair"; made a rudimentary saw by using a hatchet to chop notches along the back of another knife; and poked the barrel of an old rifle into the campfire to heat it. They then tied Smith

"Trappers Starting for the Beaver Hunt" (Alfred Jacob Miller, Walters Art Gallery, Baltimore)

to a tree so he could not move and in lieu of an anesthetic gave him a pint of "Old Baldy" (cheap whiskey) to drink. After tying a strip of deer hide tightly around his leg as a tourniquet, Sublette took the razor-sharp knife and quickly cut down to the bones.

Smith said later that he withstood this pain fairly well because by that time his leg was numb from the tourniquet. Sublette then took the sawknife and sawed off both bones. As soon as the leg dropped to the ground, a trapper handed Sublette the gunbarrel, which was now red-hot, and Sublette *"rubbed it over the stump till it fizzled and smoked worse nor a venison steak!"* Mercifully, during this process Smith fainted.

When he came to, he found that his leg was heavily bandaged, with a poultice of birchbark on the stump itself and a flask of water which was perforated so that it dripped onto the stump. He was taken to a Ute village, where the squaws nursed him by chewing up roots and spitting on the stump. But despite their care, fragments of the severed bones worked loose. Then, assisted by Sublette and using a bullet mold as forceps, Smith pulled the fragments out of his own leg. Later, he whittled a peg leg out of oak, which let him move about more easily. When unstrapped, it was also very useful as a club to swing during a brawl.[102]

Chapter V

Gentiles and Saints: The Great Migrations

On 10 December 1843 at Fort Union, at the junction of the Missouri and Yellowstone Rivers in North Dakota, Jim Bridger dictated a letter to the fur-trading firm of Pierre Chouteau and Company at St. Louis; Bridger reported that his last beaver hunt had been "particularly unsuccessful owing to the lateness of the season" and that he had only three packs of beaver pelts to show for his efforts. This poor showing, however, probably reflected something more fundamental than the onset of winter: beaver populations in the Rockies were being severely reduced by overtrapping.[103]

By the early 1840s this depletion, coupled with the change in men's fashions from beaver hats to silk hats, was bringing the era of the mountain man to an end. But just as the old order was changing, new commercial possibilities were opening up. Some of the mountain men left the mountains and became farmers. The following conversation took place in 1840:

"Come," said Newell to Meek [his colleague and brother-in-law]; "We are done with this life in the mountains — done with wading in beaver-dams and freezing or starving alternatively — done with Indian trading and Indian fighting.... Let us go down to the Wallamet [the Willamette River in western Oregon] and take farms.[104]

A few other mountain men, however — Bridger is the best example here — saw that new sources of income were beginning to arrive virtually at their front door. These were the great overland migrations.

Fort Bridger: The Early Years

Although some beaver trapping continued, Bridger understood the changing conditions and figured out how to adapt to them — he was perhaps the first mountain man to do so. This adaptation is evident from his 10 December 1843 letter, in which he reported that he had entered into a partnership with another trapper, Louis Vasquez. Bridger explained that,

I have established a small store with a Black Smith Shop, and a supply of iron in the road of the Emigrants, on Black's Fort, Green River, which promises fairly. They [the emigrants], in coming out are generally well supplied with money, but by the time they get there, are in want of all kinds of supplies. Horses, Provisions, Smith work, &c, bring ready cash from them; and should I have the goods hereby ordered [from St. Louis], will do a considerable business in that way with them! The same establishment trading with the Indians in the neighborhood, who have mostly a good number of Beaver among them. The fort is a beautiful location on Black's Ford of Green River, receiving fine, fresh water from the snow on the Uintah range. The streams are alive with mountain trout. It passes the fort in several channels, each lined with trees, kept alive by the moisture of the soil.[105]

This was actually the third fort built by Jim Bridger. The first, he and another mountain man, Henry Fraeb, had built in midsummer 1841 on the Green River between the mouths of the Big Sandy and Black's Fork. This was about 50 miles northeast of the present Fort Bridger. After Fraeb was killed by the Sioux later that year, Bridger built another fort near Black's Fork in the early summer of 1842. The third and last post, Fort Bridger itself, was occupied in early August 1843.[106]

Not everyone believed that Bridger and Vasquez would be successful in their venture, however. William Laidlaw, who forwarded Bridger's letter to St. Louis, recorded in his own journal:

> Bridger has come in with a mountain party of thirty or forty men. He is not a man calculated to manage men, and in my opinion will never succeed in making profitable returns. Mr. Vas-

quez, his partner, is represented to be, if possible, even more unable than he, as by drinking and frolicking at the Platte [River], he neglected his business.[107]

Despite these forebodings, though, from small beginnings Bridger managed to make the fort a success. One of the earliest descriptions of Fort Bridger was written by a Westering traveler, Joel Palmer, in July 1845. He was the leader of a train of 41 covered wagons and 150 emigrants out from Independence, Missouri. The party spent 200 days on the Oregon Trail before finally arriving at Oregon City, near Portland, Oregon. Palmer agreed that Bridger had built the post in an excellent location and that it served a useful function, but he was not at all impressed by its outward appearance:

> The fort is owned by Bridger and Basquez [Vasquez]. It is built of poles and dogwood mud. It is a shabby concern. There are about twenty five lodges of Indians or rather white trapper lodges occupied by their Indian wives. They have a good supply of robes, dressed deer, elk, and antelope skins, coats, pants, moccasins, other Indian fixins which they trade low for flour, pork, powder, lead, blankets, butcher knives, spirits, hats, ready made clothes, coffee, sugar, etc. They have a herd of cattle, twenty or thirty goats, and some sheep.[108]

Little had changed one year later. Heading west with his family, John McBride wrote in July of 1846:

> [We] arrived at Fort Bridger so called by courtesy. It is only a camp where some fifty trappers were living in lodges. A single cabin of logs where the roof composed of willow brush covered with earth composed the fort. There was a large village of Indians of

the Snake Tribe encamped here and a brisk traffic in dressed deer skins, buffalo robes, and logs [firewood] went on during our stay with them which was half a day and the following night. The mountaineers and the Indians alike wanted to buy whiskey and brandy, but were not provided with this kind of merchandise. The next most desirable articles were coffee, sugars, soap, and flour.[109]

J. M. Shively, author of the guidebook *Route and Distances to Oregon and California* (1846), had nothing good to say about Fort Bridger. He told his readers that if they took the trail to the fort, rather than taking a shortcut known as Sublette's Cutoff, they would lose at least 100 miles. "I was one of the company that made the road to Bridger's," he added, "and opposed it all I could. There is no use in going that way; they have no provisions, nor anything else that you want."[110]

His view was shared by Edwin Bryant, whose book, *What I Saw in California* (1848), is one of the most informative and readable records left by any overland traveler. Bryant was at Fort Bridger on 17 July 1846, where, as already mentioned, he found 500 Shoshoni Indians. Upon learning that the Sioux planned to invade their territory, most of the Shoshoni immediately left to form a war party to counter this threat. Bryant described Fort Bridger itself as consisting only of "two or three miserable log cabins, rudely constructed, and bearing but a faint resemblance to habitable houses." But he was more favorably impressed by the location. The fertile river bottom produced, he said, "the finest quantities of grass, and in great abundance." This was important to emigrants because by the time they got to Fort Bridger, the oxen pulling their covered wagons were thin from overwork and from grazing on the dry grass of the Great Plains. Bryant went on to note that, "The water of the stream is cold and pure, and abounds in spotted mountain trout."

Bryant was also impressed by the mountain men from Taos, New Mexico, who came to Fort Bridger bringing tanned skins and buckskin shirts, trousers and moccasins to trade with the emigrants:

> The countenances and bearing of these men, who have made the wilderness their home, are generally expressive of a cool, cautious, but determined intrepidity. In a trade, they have no consciences, taking all the "advantages"; but in a manner of hospitality or generosity they are open-handed — ready, many of them, to divide with the needy what they possess.[111]

Trails West

Major starting points for overland travel to the Far Western frontier included Independence and Westport, Missouri; Council Bluffs, Iowa; and Nauvoo, Illinois. There were at least six different and well-defined routes to the new frontier, which were known, respectively, as the Oregon, Santa Fe, Mormon, Gila River, California and Old Spanish Trails. Since two of these trails overlapped (the Oregon and the Mormon Trails) and two had shortcuts known as cutoffs (the Oregon and the California Trails), it may be best to describe them in geographic terms rather than by name alone.

1. From the Missouri River to the eastern edge of the Oregon Territory (i.e., southwestern Wyoming), via the Oregon and the Mormon Trails

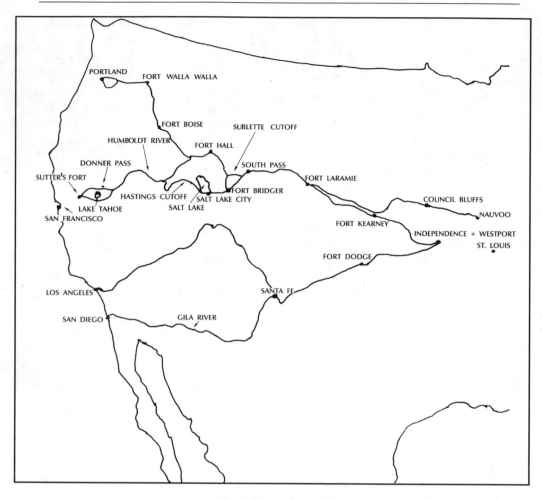

Map 3: Westering Trails

The Oregon Trail began at Independence or Westport. It followed the Little Blue River to Fort Kearney and then continued along the Platte River and the Sweetwater River to South Pass. This was the best wagon route over the Continental Divide — the long ridgeline which emigrants called "Uncle Sam's backbone" — but South Pass itself was not very dramatic. The final ascent to the point where the continent fell away to the Pacific and Atlantic sides was so gradual that John Charles Frémont, the best-known member of the U.S. Army's Corps of Topographical Engineers, said it was only like the gentle rise of Capitol Hill in Washington, D.C. South Pass turned out to be such a good route, though, that wagons continued to use it until as late as 1912.

The first large-scale emigration over the Oregon Trail occurred in 1843 when over 1,000 people made the 2,000-mile, six-month trip. Eventually, nearly 500,000 men, women and children would end up taking this route across the country. The advantages of the Oregon Trail were evident from the very beginning. In 1859 Captain Marcy, who knew all the trails well from his long service on the frontier, recorded that,

"River Eau Sucre" (Sweetwater River) (Alfred Jacob Miller, Walters Art Gallery, Baltimore)

This was the great emigrant route from Missouri to California and Oregon, over which so many thousands have traveled within the past few years. The track is broad, well worn, and can not be mistaken. It has received the major part of the Mormon emigration, and was traversed by the army in its march to Utah in 1857.[112]

For its part, the Mormon Trail began at Nauvoo, went through Council Bluffs and then headed for the Platte River, where it at first paralleled the Oregon Trail and then, at Fort Laramie, overlapped it.

2. From the eastern edge of the Oregon Territory to Oregon, Utah or California, via the Oregon, Mormon, and California Trails

The Oregon Territory initially began at Dry Sandy Creek in southwestern Wyoming, on the Pacific Ocean side of South Pass, but its boundary was later moved westward to coincide with the western border of Wyoming. At Dry Sandy Creek, emigrants had to make a choice.

One possibility was to turn southwest along a longer but well-watered route to Fort Bridger itself. Captain Marcy warmly recommended Fort Bridger because it offered "Good camps above and below the fort. Military post, mail station, and store." The fort prospered because it was located near the Sublette Cutoff (discussed below), a key junction point on the Oregon and Mormon Trails. Fort Bridger soon became the second most important emigrant resupply point between the Missouri River and the Pacific Ocean. (Fort Laramie in southeastern Wyoming was the most important; Fort Hall in eastern Idaho was the third most.)

From Fort Bridger the emigrants could head west to Salt Lake. Then, via the Hastings Cutoff in the Great Basin, they could press on to Sutter's Fort in Sacramento, California, crossing the Sierra Nevada mountains by Donner Pass north of Lake Tahoe or by Carson Pass south of the lake.

Alternatively, from Dry Sandy Creek the emigrants could continue due west along the arid Sublette Cutoff. By 1849 this was already a well-marked trail; the Forty-niner Joseph Goldsborough Bruff chose to follow it rather than turn south to Fort Bridger. This was a shorter route but not an easy one. Bruff recorded some of the hardships in his journal:

> Quite a sandy & dusty trail; first few miles level, latter part rolling, and perfectly arid ... dusty sage bushes scattered over the country, and hosts of dead oxen. About Sun-Set a mule in wagon next to rear failed ... we left him to the tender mercy of the wolves. Ox trains rolling along, enveloped in a cloud of dust. Men & oxen suffering much from dust, heat and sandy trail.... Another mule fell, in harness, and finding that plunging the blade of a penknife into his shoulder, created no sensation, we left him also, as a tribute to the lean lank wolves.[113]

The waterless stretch of the Sublette Cutoff was variously estimated at 35 to 55 miles but once negotiated successfully it put emigrants back onto the Oregon Trail north of Fort Bridger. To get to the Pacific Ocean, all they had to do then was to continue northwest on the trail.

The California Trail had two branches. The first branch began at Fort Bridger itself. From there, overlapping with the Mormon Trail, the emigrants went on to Salt Lake. Continuing westward, the Hastings Cutoff brought them to the Humboldt River. The second branch of the trail came off the Oregon Trail west of Fort Hall and ran southwest to the Humboldt River. By following the Humboldt across Nevada, wagon trains could then cross the Sierras near Lake Tahoe and end their journey at Sutter's Fort.

3. From the Missouri River to New Mexico or California, via the Santa Fe, Old Spanish, and Gila River Trails

Emigrants bound for the Southwest took the Santa Fe Trail, which began in Westport. At Santa Fe itself, the Old Spanish Trail swung northwest into Utah and then turned southwest toward Los Angeles. In contrast, the Gila River Trail went southwest from Santa Fe down to the Mexican border and ran west along the Gila River until it reached San Diego.

Westering and the West

The excitement, danger and romance of the Westering migrations constitute a high point of the American experience and are not likely to be forgotten. Indeed, in the 1940s, during the early days of World War II, the enormous surge of workers from eastern states to the shipyards and aircraft manufacturing plants of California, Oregon and Washington reminded people of the frontier days already a century past. "It wouldn't take any imagination at all," said one wartime migrant to the West Coast, "to think that you were going West in a covered wagon and were a pioneer again." In these war years, California alone grew by two million people, a fact which prompted a journalist to remark that this boom had been "the real gold rush in California's colorful history."[114]

Californians today still remember how their ancestors came to the West. Here is a lightly edited but otherwise verbatim account of what one California lady's research into her family history has revealed:

> Our great-great-grandparents, Charles and Priscilla (Hancock) Lee, traveled by oxen-pulled covered wagon to California in 1852. They had been married in Wisconsin in 1850, and lived in northern Illinois until they decided to leave for the west in 1852. They left with their not-quite-2-year-old daughter, Sarah; Priscilla was pregnant with their second child at the time. Sarah died of cholera in June of 1852, while on the wagon trail, and her brother, John, died the day after he was born, in August of that year, also of cholera. I do not know exactly where they are buried. It took six months and 15 days to arrive in California. They settled in Santa Clara County — and raised seven more children to adulthood there. Charles was an orchardist — he grew apricots, figs, and prunes on his ranch in Berryessa, which is now part of San Jose [today's Silicon Valley].

Another part of this lady's family came by sea from Plymouth, Maine, where their forebears had lived since Mayflower days. She now picks up their story:

> Ahira Holmes, our great-great-grandfather, arrived in San Francisco in the "early days of 1852." He sailed north from Nicaragua, having crossed from the Atlantic to the Pacific through that Central American country, something commonly done at that time as [an] alternative to [crossing at] Panama. His older brother, Ellis H. Holmes, had arrived prior to 1852, but I've not yet found any records to give me a date. They were both educators. Ahira was the first principal of the State Normal School in 1852, which became San Jose State University. It was established to train teachers, first in San Francisco, and later it moved to San Jose. Ahira's son, Arthur, married Charles' daughter, Nancy.[115]

These 19th century migrations across the plains and through the mountain passes of the West constitute one of the great adventure stories of the United States. They are also the most interesting part of American frontier history — not so much because of the physical challenge of making epic journeys but because of the human element involved, as seen in the quotations above. This is what the American novelist John Steinbeck had in mind when he wrote *The Red Pony* (1938). One of Steinbeck's characters — an old man who had been "a leader of the people" (that is, a wagonmaster) reminisced that, "It wasn't getting here [California] that mattered, *it was movement and westering. We carried life out here and set it down.*"[116]

Indeed, one can argue that this Westward movement captures the American spirit better than any other single episode in the entire history of the United States. How remarkable it was for emigrants to leave their farms, towns, homes and friends; to spend six months or more traveling by horseback, covered wagon or on foot for thousands of miles into a new frontier; and to carve out new communities and new lives for themselves. This is in fact so remarkable, so contrary to the normal run of human experience, that we may well ask: just *why* were these people so bold?

There seem to be at least two answers. The first is that this was primarily an economic migration — that is, people wanted to improve their own lot in life. Moving to the frontier usually did not appeal to the minority of men and women in the older regions of the United States who were already highly educated, financially successful and socially well-connected. For the average American, however, as well as for large numbers of upwardly mobile foreigners, the West was seen as the land of opportunity and promise, where there was no rigid social stratification, where new approaches to problems were welcomed and where anything seemed possible. Horace Greeley, the most influential journalist of his time (he founded and edited the New York *Tribune*), struck a responsive chord with his famous advice, "Go West, young man, go West."

A second and perhaps even more compelling reason why people were willing to pull up stakes and move West was that they had a strong streak of independence in them. They wanted to be their own masters. Specifically, they rejected social distinctions based on birth rather than on personal achievement. A frontier anecdote makes this point: an English lord came to Wyoming to visit the ranch of an American friend. When the nobleman rode up to the corral, he saw a cowboy sitting on the topmost rail. "Is your master at home?" asked the Englishman in his upper-class accent. The cowboy looked at him silently and then slowly turned his head to the side and spat into the dust. "The son-of-a-bitch ain't been born yet," he replied.

Fall–l–l–l In!

With a bellow like this from a leather-lunged wagon-master or at some other agreed signal, such as a trumpet blast, the covered wagons began each day's journey. Regardless of which of the major trails they took, the emigrants would face similar experiences. The horses and the mule pack trains of the mountain men had used parts of all these trails for many years. But a major turning point was reached on the Oregon Trail in 1836, when the first wagon (a light Dearborn model) and the first white women (Narcissa Whitman, the wife of Dr. Marcus Whitman, and Eliza Spalding, the wife of Reverend Henry Hart Spalding) crossed over South Pass, bound for Oregon.[117] The trapper Osborne Russell recorded in his journal that these two ladies "were gazed on with wonder and astonishment by the rude savages, they being the first white women ever seen by these Indians and the first that had ever penetrated into these wild and rocky regions."[118] These missionaries were following in the old footsteps of mountain men but they had a new purpose in mind — the permanent settlement of the West.

Within a few years of the Whitmans' crossing, what began as a trickle of emigrants over the Oregon Trail soon became a flood. In 1841, for example, a typical party leaving the Missouri consisted of 70 people, including five women and seven or more children, and 12 covered wagons. In 1850 alone, the peak year of the emigrations, 55,000 people "pulled up stakes" (left their homes) and headed West to start new lives. Most of these families traveled in covered wagons known as Conestoga wagons or "prairie schooners." These are generic terms

"Wagon Boss" (Charles M. Russell, from the collection of Gilcrease Museum, Tulsa, no. 0137.900). As the wagon boss checks to make sure the wagon train is in good order, a bullwhacker snaps his long whip over the heads of the oxen to encourage them up the hill.

which cover a wide variety of vehicles, from light farm wagons to specially modified or custom-made rigs.

Typically, though, the bed of the wagon was a rectangular box made of oak, hickory or maple, about four feet wide and up to 12 feet long, which if necessary could be detached from the undercarriage and hauled up rock faces by ropes or chains. The only metal parts of the wagon were the iron tires, the axles and the connecting bars known as hounds. A framework of curved wooden bows held up the cover, which was made of canvas or cotton and could be rolled up in hot weather. Virtually all the emigrants began with too heavy a load (up to 2,500 pounds) and were forced to jettison their oak chests of drawers and other heavy furniture when the going got tough. Moreover, since the clutter of household goods took up so much space in the wagon bed and since the wagons did not have any springs, many emigrants chose to walk most of the 2,000 miles from the Missouri River to the Pacific Coast.

On the Trail

The best time to leave the Missouri River for points west was in March or April. Although this meant that at first the draft animals would have to be fed on grain because the nutritious new grass had not yet appeared on the prairies, an early start would get the emigrants off before the spring rains turned

Scale model of the covered wagons used on the Oregon Trail from 1841 to 1871 (Oregon Historical Society, negative no. 837)

the roads into quagmires. Prior to starting, however, the first order of business for the 50 to 70 men in a typical wagon train was to elect a commander and to draw up an agreement binding the signatories to obey him and to assist each other. These were elementary precautions because, as Captain Marcy warned his readers,

> On long and arduous expeditions men are apt to become irritable and ill-natured, and oftentimes fancy they have more labor imposed on them than their comrades, and that the person who directs the march is partial toward his favorites, etc.... Unless a systematic organization be adopted, it is impossible for a party of any magnitude to travel in company for any great length of time, and for all the members to agree upon the same arrangements in marching, camping,

etc. I have several times observed, where this has been attempted, that discords and dissentions sooner or later arose which invariably resulted in breaking up and separating the company.[119]

Emigrants also had to be careful that they carried enough food and, equally important, that it was the right kind of food. Supplies of wine, champagne, candied fruit and olives did not provide sufficient nourishment and exhausted the teams which had to pull them. In the end, most of these luxuries simply had to be thrown away, along with the oak tables, heavy chairs, gilt-frame mirrors and other cumbersome household items stuffed into the covered wagons by inexperienced travelers. It was recommended instead that the following minimum provisions be taken for every adult making the long trip from the Missouri to California, which usually took at least 110 days[120]:

- 150 pounds of flour, or the equivalent in hard bread which would keep well.
- 25 pounds of bacon or cured pork (some of the cattle of a wagon train were used for additional meat).
- 15 pounds of coffee.
- 25 pounds of sugar.
- Dried or canned vegetables.
- Yeast for making bread.
- Salt and pepper.
- Citric acid (to prevent scurvy).

Suitable clothing was as important to the prairie traveler as suitable food. An ideal outfit for one man for a three month journey included the following:

- 1 heavy woolen coat.
- 2 pairs of thick, soft pants, lined with buckskin to keep them from excessive wear against the saddle.
- 2 blue or red flannel overshirts, open in front, with buttons.
- 2 woolen undershirts.
- 2 pairs of thick cotton underpants.
- 4 pairs of woolen socks.
- 2 pairs of cotton socks.
- 4 colored silk handkerchiefs.
- 2 pairs of durable shoes (for men who walked).
- 1 pair of high-topped boots and 1 pair of shoes (for horsemen).
- 3 towels.
- 1 waterproof poncho.
- 1 broad-brimmed hat of soft felt.
- 1 comb and brush.
- 2 toothbrushes.

- 1 pound of hand soap.
- 3 pounds of soap for washing clothes.
- 1 broad leather belt with belt-knife and whetstone.
- 1 small buckskin or cloth bag containing a sewing kit consisting of strong linen thread, large needles, a bit of beeswax, some buttons, pins and a thimble.[121]

Emigrants usually slept on the ground because there was little room in their covered wagon, which was filled with all the items needed to begin a new life in the West. These included tables, chairs, a plow, spades, axes, other tools, weapons, a wood-burning stove, a bed, a Bible, and, not infrequently, even a grandfather clock. At night on the overland trails, bedding typically consisted of two thin blankets, one thick comforter, a pillow and a waterproof tarpaulin. This last item protected the sleeper from the dew and from the dampness of the ground, although in a heavy rainstorm everyone was likely to be soaked. During the day the bedding was rolled up in the tarpaulin so it could be stowed easily in the covered wagon.

The success of an overland journey depended to a large extent upon the strength of its draft animals. Men were strongly advised not to work the oxen too hard, especially at the beginning of the trip, and never to whip them unless absolutely necessary. The best teamsters, when they swung their long, powerful bull whips, rarely if ever let the "popper" at the end of the whip actually touch an ox because it would draw blood if it did. A more humane and equally effective method was to crack the whip so close to the head of an ox that the noise alone would scare it into pulling harder.

A Leader of the People: Jesse Applegate

One of the early emigrants was Jesse Applegate. In 1843, he led an unusually large, well-organized and well-equipped party of several hundred west along the Oregon Trail, together with their 5,000 cattle and horses. A typical day for Applegate and his party would have been a typical day for the hundreds of thousands of others who took the trails West. The day begins early.[122]

It is 4:00 AM. The men on guard duty fire their rifles into the air as a wake-up call. Men, women and children clamber sleepily out of their wagons and tents. Campfires are built using buffalo chips (sun-dried buffalo dung) because there are so few trees on the prairies. Cattle and horses are rounded up. Breakfast is eaten. Tents are struck. Wagons are loaded and ox teams yoked up. And ten to fifteen young men are sent off to hunt buffalo.

Sixty wagons, divided into 15 groups of four wagons each, are ready to roll by 7:00 AM. As Applegate himself describes the line of march,

> the leading division of wagons moves out of the encampment and the rest fall into their places with the precision of clockwork.... The wagons form a line three quarters of a mile in length; some of the teamsters ride upon the front of their wagons; scattered along the line companies of women and children are taking exercise on foot; they gather bouquets of rare and beautiful flowers that line the way.

Resting during a midday stop ("nooning," it is called), the ox teams are turned loose to graze. Applegate and his council of elected representatives meet then to discuss the day's problems and to settle disputes. Under the stresses of travel, personality differences and political ambitions could become disruptive — it was not unusual for a wagon train leader to be voted out of office, although this did not happen to Applegate himself.

In the afternoon, Westering continues. Just before it gets dark, at a spot designated by a guide who was sent on ahead, the wagons form a 100-yard circle for the night. "So accurate the measurement and perfect the practice," Applegate writes, "that the hindmost wagon always precisely closes the gateway. Within ten minutes from the time the leading wagon is halted, the barricade is formed."

This defensive tactic worked quite well. Although film and television productions in our own time have delighted in showing Indians attacking a circle of corralled wagons, in point of fact this rarely if ever happened. Captain Marcy tells us why:

> The Comanches, Sioux, and other prairie tribes make their attacks upon the open prairies. Trusting to their wonderful skill in equitation and horsemanship, they ride around their enemies with their bodies thrown on the opposite side of the horse, and discharge their arrows in rapid succession while at full speed; they will not, however, often venture near an enemy who occupies a defensive position. If, therefore, a small party is in danger of an attack from a large force of Indians, they should seek the cover of the timber or a park of wagons, or, in the absence of these, rocks or holes in the prairies which afford good cover.[123]

Thus like their 19th century contemporaries, the pirates of the South China sea, the Indians preferred to attack only "soft" (poorly defended) targets. In this they were very wise: it would have been suicidal for them to face the concentrated firepower of well-armed emigrants, firing from shelter behind their wagons and fighting for their own lives and for those of their families.

The typical day for the Applegate party is not over yet. After the circling of the wagons, tents are pitched, fires are lighted, and dinner is cooked and eaten. Just before 8:00 PM the night watch is set and "near the river a violin makes lively music, and some youths improvise a dance; in another quarter a flute whispers its lament to the deepening night." Soon only the night guard and Applegate are still awake. Later on, the night guard hears that the buffalo hunters have returned, but Applegate is too tired to learn how they fared: "the last care of the day being removed, he [Applegate] too seeks the rest that will enable him to go through the same routine tomorrow." Still, despite his fatigue, he concludes that, "It has been a prosperous day; more than 20 miles have been accomplished."

This was in fact a good day's travel. Sixteen to 18 miles per day was more common, although with careful planning much longer distances were possible. In the deserts of New Mexico, for instance, there was one waterless stretch 78½ miles long, known as the *Jornada del Muerto* ("Journey of the Dead Man"). Even this could be crossed safely by oxen or mule teams, however, during two night-long drives.

The Mormons

"Mormons" is an unofficial but familiar term for members of the Church of Jesus Christ of Latter-Day Saints. It is perhaps impossible adequately to define the beliefs of any religion or sect in a single paragraph, but this is how the Mormons describe their own in the official *Encyclopedia of Mormonism* (1975):

> Mormonism refers to the divinely inspired doctrine taught by Joseph Smith and the succeeding leaders of the Church.... Basic Church doctrines include belief in a personal God vitally concerned with his children, the divinity of the Savior Jesus Christ and his infinite Atonement, the universal need for repentance and baptism by proper authority, continuing revelation through living prophets, the brotherhood and sisterhood of all human beings, the eternal sanctity of marriage and family, and the responsibility to be self-reliant and to help others.[124]

Mormonism was founded in 1830 in western New York State by Joseph Smith. Members called themselves "Saints"; nonbelievers were known as "Gentiles." The Mormons developed a successful and unique way of life but one which infuriated their Gentile neighbors, who frequently took offense at their self-righteousness, religion-based government, system of plural marriage (polygamy) and "sharp" (unethical) business practices. As a result, the Mormons were persecuted so violently — first in Ohio, then in Missouri and finally in Illinois, where Smith was murdered by militiamen in 1844 — that they resolved to find a sanctuary somewhere in the frontier West, far beyond the reach of their enemies. Their solution was to settle in the uninhabited Salt Lake valley of Utah.

The first wave of the Mormon migration crossed over South Pass in 1847, when Brigham Young, Smith's successor, led an advance party of 143 men, two women and three children to Salt Lake. On 28 June 1847, Young met with Jim Bridger on the banks of the Big Sandy, about 75 miles northeast of Fort Bridger. When Young asked Bridger what the land in the Salt Lake valley was like, Old Gabe replied that he "considered it imprudent to bring a large population into the Great Basin until it was ascertained that grain could be raised; he said he would give one thousand dollars for a bushel of corn grown in the basin."[125] Undeterred by this negative opinion, the Mormons listened attentively as Bridger told them about the climate, minerals, timber and the Indians of the valley. He did not mention the Shoshonis, presumably because they were so well-disposed to the emigrants, but he did warn the Mormons about the Utes, whom he described as "bad people around Utah Lake." Although warriors of this tribe would not attack large groups of armed emigrants, they might rob or even kill anyone found alone.[126]

One of the early Mormon pioneers, William Clayton, was at Fort Bridger in 1847 and described it thus:

> Bridger's fort is composed of two double log houses about forty feet long each and joined by a pen for horses about ten feet high constructed by placing poles upright in the ground close together, which is all the appearance of a fort in sight. There are several Indian lodges close by and a full crop of young children playing around the door. These Indians are said to be of the Snake tribe, the Utes inhabiting beyond the Mountains. The latitude of Fort Bridger is 41°19'13" and its height above the level of the sea according to Elder Pratt's observation is 6,665 feet. It is doubtless a very cold region and little calculated for farming purposes.[127]

Another Mormon traveler, George A. Smith, had similar impressions in 1847. "Bridger's Fort," he reported, "consists of two long, low, rough cabins built in the form of an L with a small enclosure for stock built of upright poles. The surrounding countryside was beautiful, but the fort itself was an unpretentious place."[128] Visitors usually found that neither Bridger nor Vasquez was present. They were usually off on hunting or trapping expeditions, rather than spending their days minding the store.

The 1848 Mormon migration was much larger than the first one. (A total of 15,000 made the journey to Salt Lake during these two years, And, all in all, from the late 1840s through the 1860s, more than 70,000 Mormons would pass by Fort Bridger.) In 1848, the Mormons found that only Vasquez, not Bridger, was in residence. Business must have been good then because the fort had grown. John D. Lee wrote that, "The FT [fort] consists of 8 Block Houses and a smaul [sic] Enclosure picketed in. Land exceedingly rich, grass durable winter and summer, all though there is Frost every month of the year."[129]

The Mormons were a very dedicated and, some of their Gentile contemporaries would have added, a very headstrong people. There was considerable friction between Mormons and Gentiles even in Utah itself. Captain Marcy, for example, warned prospective emigrants to carry enough food and supplies with them because, he said,

> It is true that if persons choose to pass through Salt Lake City, and the Mormons *happen* to be in an amiable mood, supplies may sometimes be procured

from them; but those who have visited them well know how little reliance is to be placed upon their hospitality or spirit of accommodation.[130]

Missionary activity was (and still is) an important part of Mormon life. In the 1850s Mormon missionaries made thousands of converts in Europe and encouraged them to come to Utah. Many of them did, including the families of the so-called Handcart Battalion, who walked 1,300 miles from Iowa, pulling all their worldly goods behind them in heavy two-wheeled handcarts because they could not afford to buy covered wagons.

The Mormons who came in covered wagons were tough, too. In 1853, William K. Sloan drove one of the 20 teams of oxen which made up a wagon train from St. Louis. The trip was long and tiring for Sloan and his colleagues. Indians demanded some of their scarce supplies in return for unmolested passage across tribal lands, forcing the emigrants to live on "rusty pork," dried apples, sugar and coffee. When they were five miles east of Fort Bridger, they were met by a wagon sent out from Salt Lake to bring them more food. But the wagon contained only one side of beef, some flour and a few sacks of potatoes (hardly enough for 20 families). The emigrants, however, were so hungry that "a grand rush was made for the potatoes, half of which were devoured raw on the spot."[131]

Sloan went on to describe Fort Bridger in now familiar terms. It consisted of

> a string of log houses built in the shape of a quadrangle, with a gate on one side opening into the square. The doors and windows, or rather openings, were on the inside…. The place was occupied by a number of mountaineers, the majority of whom had lately come

from their trading stations along the mountain road to spend the winter…. From Fort Bridger to Salt Lake the roads were terrible, rain and snow every day, grass very scarce, and cattle perishing from cold and hunger.[132]

The Forty-Niners

On 24 January 1848, James W. Marshall, a 35-year-old carpenter working in central California, discovered gold in the millrace (watercourse) of a sawmill he was building for a German-born Swiss entrepreneur named John Augustus Sutter. The news spread quickly. The *Californian*, a San Francisco newspaper, carried this article on 15 March 1848:

> GOLD MINE FOUND.— In the newly made raceway of the Saw Mill recently erected by Captain Sutter, on the American Fork, gold has been found in considerable quantities. One person brought thirty dollars worth to New Helvetia [Sutter's Fort], gathered there in a short time. California, no doubt, is rich in mineral wealth; great chances here for scientific capitalists. Gold has been found in almost every part of the country.[133]

This was the first report of the California goldfields to appear in print and it was in large measure true. Indeed, these fields are said to have produced a total yield of about half a billion dollars between 1848 and 1858 alone, using a variety of mining techniques which will be discussed in Chapter VII, "Gold, Silver and Diamonds."[134]

Marshall's discovery sparked the great California gold rush of 1849, which has given the name "Forty-niners" to the 100,000 miners who swarmed into California, either overland or by ship, soon

The earliest (1850) photograph of San Francisco, showing the building boom during the gold rush (Bancroft Library, University of California)

thereafter.[135] In 1847, San Francisco had been a sleepy Mexican village of perhaps 450 people. When the gold rush was at its height (1849–52), however, the population swelled to around 40,000 and the town's waterfront became a forest of masts as officers, crews and passengers abandoned their ships to look for gold in the foothills.

In the first year or so of the gold rush, the shipping that set out from Eastern ports for San Francisco was vast. It included 242 full-rigged ships, 218 three-masted barks, 170 brigs, 132 schooners and 15 steamers. The average passage took 182 days. Describing this great odyssey, the California historian J.D.B. Stillman wrote in 1877 that, "Never since the Crusades was such a movement known…."[136]

In the mid–1850s as many as 500 ships lay rotting at anchor, many still laden with cargoes which no one took the trouble to unload. By 1858 San Francisco had a population of about 100,000 people and was the financial and social capital of the West. So much money could be made there by selling luxuries to newly rich miners that one recent arrival wrote:

> I have seen purer liquors, better segars, finer tobacco, truer [more accurate] guns and pistols, larger dirks and bowie knives and prettier courtesans than any other place I have ever visited. California can and does furnish the best bad things that are available in America.[137]

Many of the men who went overland to California during the gold rush passed through Fort Bridger. Joseph Goldsborough Bruff, leading a group calling itself the Washington City and California Mining Association, learned from a colleague that "Capt. Bridger and 2 sons at Ft Bridger, had a fine store there, with necessaries and indian goods, and very good whisky for only $1 per pint.— And that he had horses, ponies & mules for sale."[138] As Bruff's party drew nearer to Fort Bridger, they met three mountain men from the fort who were horse traders. It turned out that Bridger had a good deal of business acumen. Where the Sublette Cutoff left the Oregon Trail, Bruff met some other men "sent here by Old Bridger, to trade with the emigrants, who have mostly come this way; thus trying to cut off the 'cutoff' folks."[139] Bridger also signposted the trail to bring customers to him. Bruff soon met up with

> another detachment of Old Bridger's traders [who] were camped here, and had put up a notice at the branching of the road for the emigrants to take the left one [which led to Fort Bridger], as the best. They had horses, &c. to sell. Their camp was within 200 yds. of mine. The traders told me that during the month of June [1849], 3,200 wagons passed through this valley.[140]

After getting supplies and repairing their wagons at Fort Bridger, to reach California the Forty-niners first had to cross the Great Basin and then get over the high passes of the Sierra Nevada mountains before the winter set in. Elisha Stevens, an old mountain man, aided by a Paiute Indian named Truckee, had pioneered the first wagon trail over the Sierra Nevada in 1844. This route was improved in 1845 by the Dog Valley detour, which avoided the difficult Truckee Canyon, and was further improved in 1846 by the discovery of two higher but broader passes, Coldstream Pass and Roller Pass, over the backbone of the mountains.[141]

Still, getting over the mountains was difficult at best and was sometimes impossible. Thirteen-year-old Virginia Reed was a member of the Donner-Reed party, which became snowbound and had to resort to cannibalism to survive. In a 16 May 1847 letter to her cousin Mary, Virginia recounted how the party's troubles began:

> My dear Cousan I am a going to Write to you about our trubels geting to California; We had good luck til we come to big Sandy [River] thare we lost our best yoak of oxons we come to Brigers Fort & lost another ox....
>
> We had to Walk all the time we was a travling up the truckee river.... we went on that way 3 or 4 days tell we come to the big mountain or the California mountain the snow was about 3 feet deep thare was some wagons thare.... thay said they had attempted to cross and cold not.... the further we went up the deeper the snow got so the wagons could not go.... [After the party sought shelter in a makeshift cabin] there was 15 in the cabon we was in and half of us had to lay a bed all the time
>
> thare was 10 starved to death.... it snowed and would cover the cabin over so we could not git out for 2 or 3 days.... There was 3 [emigrants] died and the rest eat them thay was 10 days without anything to eat but the Dead.... thank the Good god we all got throw and the onely family that did not eat human flesh we have left everything but I dont cair for that we have got through but Dont let this letter dishaten anybody and never take no cutofs and hury along as fast as you can.[142]

Today, the placenames Donner Pass and Donner Lake remind modern travelers of Virginia's terrible experience. But although other emigrants were not snowbound, they still had to overcome enormous obstacles.[143] Joseph E. Ware's *Emigrants' Guide to California* (1849) warned travelers about 7,088-foot "Truckie's Pass" (Donner Pass), where "You will be tried to the utmost. Pack everything over the summit, then haul your wagons up with ropes. You will certainly save time, and perhaps hundreds of dollars."[144]

This was good advice because at the pass the narrow trail was blocked by walls of rock six to eight feet high. To surmount them, the emigrants had to unyoke their ox teams, drive the animals around the rocks until they were above them and then yoke them up again. While some men were doing this, others were cutting long poles strong enough to bear the weight of the wagons and were laying them against the rocks. One end of a long chain was hitched to the tongue of a wagon; the other end was made fast to the ox yoke. With much cracking of whips and much strong language to encourage the oxen, each wagon was slowly pulled up the rock face.

A similar procedure was used at Roller Pass, where a big log was put at the summit of a steep hill to serve as a roller for chains. The chains were passed over the log, fastened to a wagon and 12 yoke of oxen pulled the wagon up the steep incline. Going uphill was hard enough but going downhill was more dangerous because a runaway wagon could be lethal. The emigrant Isaac Wistar left this description of getting down Steephollow Crossing in 1849:

> we chained the wheels [so they would not turn], took out the four lead mules, leaving only the wheelers [the mules nearest the front wheels], cut

and chained to the rear axle as large a tree as we could handle for a drag, put all hands on the back ropes, and lowered away. The descent was two miles long, with some bad turns and jump-offs, but it was at length accomplished.[145]

Because the emigrant trail proved to be the best route over the Sierras, it has been in use ever since. The transcontinental railroad followed it in 1869, as did the first automobile road in 1916. When improved in the 1920s, this road became U.S. Highway 40. After further improvements in the 1960s, it became the Interstate 80 of today.

But some emigrants during the gold rush chose to avoid the Sierras. One way they took was a more southerly route toward San Bernardino (about 60 miles east of Los Angeles), and then north through the Sacramento-San Joaquin Valley to the goldfields in the foothills of the mountains of central California.

Whichever route they took, though, patience was critical — the lack of it was a recipe for disaster, as the following account shows. In September 1849, a sizable wagon train — 200 people, 110 wagons, 500 horses and oxen — left Salt Lake City under the leadership of Captain Jefferson Hunt. To avoid the burning, waterless Great Salt Lake Desert due west of the town, where many oxen had died and emigrants had suffered greatly, Hunt took his party south. Some of his charges, however, began to complain that by this route it would take them too long to get to the goldfields: they were sure it would be faster to head due west. Fierce arguments arose over which trail to take, to the extent that two men who jointly owned a wagon sawed it in half because they could not agree. In the end, though, most of the party followed Hunt. Eventually, after a hard trip, this group reached San Bernardino safely.

Those who did not follow Hunt had no guide, squabbled among themselves and came to grief as they were trying to cross the Mojave Desert on the California-Nevada border. Some of the older men in this group died on the trail due to hunger, thirst and exhaustion. It was easy to make fatal mistakes. One emigrant, for example, deserted the group and went off on his own but changed his mind at some point and tried to make it back to camp. He was later found dead not far away, on his back, with his arms outstretched, without any food or water.

Those who did not die suffered tremendously from bitter water and lack of food. Since it was clear that everyone would die if nothing was done, a last-ditch effort was made to find help. Two men — Lewis Manly, who had been a hunter for the emigrants and who later told the story of their disaster, and John Rogers, another member of the party — set out on foot, each carrying a knapsack packed with the dried flesh of an emaciated ox.

They crossed 200 miles of desert mountains before reaching a Spanish ranch 30 miles from Los Angeles. Twenty-five days after they had left the other emigrants, they returned, still on foot because their horses had given out. They were leading a small black mule laden with supplies.

Some days later, as the emigrants were crossing the Panamint Mountains and knew they were safe, some of the men climbed a peak to look back at the valley which had nearly killed them. "Good-bye, Death Valley," muttered one of them, thereby giving it the name by which it is still known.[146]

Captain Stansbury's Adventures

So many Forty-niners began to come overland that the U.S. Army decided to build more forts and to conduct surveys of the West. Captain Howard Stansbury, en route to find a suitable location for Fort Hall and to survey the Great Salt Lake valley, arrived at Fort Bridger on 11 August 1849. He described it as a trading post for the Indians, with buildings located around a hollow square and protected from attack by a strong wooden gate. "We were received with great kindness and lavish hospitality," Stansbury continued,

> by the proprietor, Major James Bridger, one of the oldest mountain-men in this entire region, who has been engaged in the Indian trade, here, and upon the banks of the Missouri and Columbia, for the last thirty years. Several of my wagons needing repair, the [wagon]train was detained five days for the purpose, Major Bridger courteously placing his blacksmith-shop at my service.[147]

After Stansbury finished his survey of the Great Salt Lake valley and was heading east in September 1850, Bridger agreed to help him find a short-cut through the Great Divide Basin in south-central Wyoming. They found what came to be called Bridger's Pass (elevation 7,550 feet), near Rawlins, Wyoming. This new trail cut 61 miles off the previous route over South Pass. Old Gabe was such a superb pathfinder that Bridger's Pass was later used by the stage-coaches of the Overland Mail, by the Union Pacific Railroad and is now followed by Interstate 80.[148]

Stansbury and his party made their way to the Laramie Plain, which was thick with buffalo. One of the mountain men killed four buffalo, even though their mules could only carry the meat of one, and Stansbury recorded his distaste for what he called this "wanton butchery."[149] In the process, he left us such a graphic account of how to extract the best and most nourishing cuts of meat from a buffalo that it is worth reading (see Appendix III).

Chapter VI

Crossroads of the West

By the middle years of the 19th century Fort Bridger was firmly on the map, playing a key role in maintaining the new military, transportation and communication links across the frontier. It served as a U.S. Army base before, during and after the Mormon War (a conflict in which no one was killed) and as a supply point for stagecoaches, the Pony Express, the transcontinental telegraph line and the Union Pacific Railroad. The frontier was a crossroads for European hunters, too, and as a renowned guide and a hunter himself, Jim Bridger was in his element.

The Odyssey of Sir George Gore

With his usual literary facility, Captain Marcy captures the unique relationship which sprang up between Bridger and Sir George Gore:

> Bridger had been the guide, interpreter, and companion of that distinguished Irish sportsman, Sir George Gore, whose peculiar tastes led him in 1855 to abandon the luxurious life of Europe and bury himself for two long years [1855–1857] among the savages in the wildest and most unfrequented glens of the Rocky Mountains.
>
> The outfit and adventures of this titled Nimrod, conducted as they were upon a most gigantic scale, probably exceeded any thing of the kind ever attempted before on this continent.... Some conception may be formed of the magnitude of his equipment when it is stated that his party consisted of about fifty persons, comprising secretaries, steward, cooks, fly-makers [for fishing lines], dog-tenders, hunters, servants, etc., etc. He was provided with a train of thirty wagons, besides numerous saddle-horses and dogs.[150]

Marcy met Gore at St. Louis at the end of this epic trip and estimated that "during his protracted hunt [Gore] had slaughtered the enormous aggregate of forty grizzly bears, twenty-five hundred buffaloes, besides numerous elk, deer, antelope, and other *small* game." Gore himself had more precise figures. He said he had spent $500,000 on the hunt; had traveled 6,000 miles; and had killed 2,000 buffalo, 1,600 deer and elk, and 105 bears.[151]

Of greater human interest, perhaps, is the fact that during the hunt Gore usually invited Bridger to join him for dinner.

After dinner, Gore would read aloud from one of the books he had brought along and would ask Bridger (who, as we know, was illiterate) what he thought about it. Marcy reports that Gore's favorite author was Shakespeare. Bridger, however, confessed that Shakespeare's work "was a leetle too highfalutin for him" and "rayther calculated that that big Dutchman, Mr. *Full-stuff* [Falstaff], was a leetle bit too fond of lager beer."

When Gore read to Bridger some of Baron Munchausen's writings (Munchausen was an 18th century German soldier, adventurer and raconteur famous for his tall-tales), Bridger at first said that "he be dogond ef he swallered every thing that thar *Baren* Mountchawson said, and he thout he was a durn'd liar." But after turning the matter over in his mind for a time, he added that some of his own experiences among the Blackfeet would be equally marvelous, "ef writ down in a book."

Fort Bridger and the Mormon War

Fort Bridger was first used by the U.S. Army in 1849 because it was a convenient base for protecting the growing flood of emigrants bound for Oregon and California. It was only a modest example of the 150 forts eventually strung out along the major rivers and trails of the West. But it got caught up in the 1857 clash between the Mormons and the U.S. Government which became known as the Mormon War.

One tangential dispute in this conflict involved the murky question of who owned Fort Bridger itself. Mexico had lost the war of 1848 and was forced to concede huge chunks of land to the United States, e.g., California, Utah, Nevada and parts of Arizona, New Mexico, Colorado and Wyoming. In 1853, the Mormons asserted that Jim Bridger had sold his fort to their representative, Louis Robinson, for $8,000, half of this sum to have been paid in cash. Bridger denied that such a transaction had taken place and claimed he still owned the land around the fort (as well as the fort itself, which he and Vasquez had built) through a Mexican grant of 30 square miles. However, when the Mormon leader Brigham Young tried to confirm Bridger's grant claim in Washington, D.C., he was unsuccessful. Although some former Mexican lands in New Mexico and California had in fact been transferred to private owners through grants from Mexico, for some reason the U.S. Government did not recognize Bridger's particular claim as being valid.

There are three explanations for this imbroglio. One theory is that Bridger simply made up the land grant story in order to sell to the Mormons property which he did not legally own. Another thesis is that he honestly thought he did have title to the land but was mistaken. A third possibility is that the Mormons forced Bridger to sell out against his will. This is at least what Bridger himself wanted his friends to believe. Captain Marcy first met Bridger in 1857 at Fort Laramie and later (in 1866) wrote that Bridger's life, "pregnant as it is with scenes of startling personal incident, interested me supremely." According to Marcy, Bridger told him that Fort Bridger's commercial success in trading with Indians and emigrants alike

had excited the cupidity of the Mormons, and they intimated to [Bridger] that his presence in such close proximity to their settlements was not agreeable, and advised him to pull up stakes and leave forthwith; and upon his questioning the legality or justice of this arbitrary summons, they came to his place with a force of "avenging angels" [Mormon zealots], and forced him to make his escape to the woods in order to save his life. He remained secreted there for several days and, through the assistance of his Indian wife, was enabled … to make his way to Fort Laramie, leaving all his cattle and other property in possession of the Mormons.[152]

At a later meeting with Marcy in 1873, Bridger stuck to this story: "I was robbed and threatened with death," he said.[153]

Whatever the reasons, the Mormons took over Fort Bridger in 1853 and that year they also built another trading post, known as Fort Supply, 12 miles to the southwest. This new fort, designed to help the Mormon emigrants heading for Salt Lake City, consisted of log buildings protected by a high palisade and was surrounded by irrigated fields. Both forts also traded with Gentile emigrants and were a good defense against any possible Indian attacks, which the Mormons claimed Jim Bridger, now their bitter enemy, was trying to encourage. The Mormons invested $60,000 in these two forts before hostilities with the U.S. Army began.

The Mormon War had its origins in 1849 when the Mormons organized their own territory called "Deseret," which encompassed all of Utah, most of Arizona and Nevada, parts of Idaho, Oregon, California, New Mexico and Colorado, and the southwestern quarter of Wyoming. Brigham Young was elected governor of this huge new territory. Deseret immediately applied to join the

United States as the 31st state of the union, but Congress refused. Instead, in September 1850, it created the Utah Territory, which comprised the whole of Utah, the northern four-fifths of Nevada, the western third of Colorado, and the southwestern corner of Wyoming. Because of his position as leader of the Mormons and head of the proposed state of Deseret, Young was appointed governor of Utah in 1850. But in 1857, the newly elected president, James Buchanan, decided to replace him with a non–Mormon governor.

Young was not popular among the Gentiles in Utah or elsewhere. His many critics claimed that he defied Federal authority at every opportunity and that he was ruling Utah as a Mormon kingdom. Moreover, he had grossly offended almost all other Americans, particularly those living in the cities of the East, by having between 19 and 55 wives (the exact number seems to be unclear) by whom he had a total of 47 children.[154] Buchanan named Alfred Cumming, a former Indian agent, to be the new governor of Utah but it was clear that the Mormons would never let Cumming take up his position. Faced with this defiance of Federal authority, in July 1857 Buchanan took the drastic step of ordering the U.S. Army to intervene.

Under the command of General Albert Sidney Johnston of the 2nd U.S. Cavalry, a force of 2,500 soldiers marched out from Fort Leavenworth, Kansas, to bring the Mormons into line. Johnston hired Jim Bridger as his chief guide and gave Old Gabe the rank of major. It was 1,200 miles from Fort Leavenworth to Salt Lake City, and winter overtook the troops in the mountains. They suffered terribly, and many of their horses and mules died. To defend Mormon Utah,

The route from Fort Bridger to Salt Lake City was first used by the Mormons' covered wagons and then by the Union Pacific Railroad. (Photograph by the author)

Brigham Young called up the Nauvoo Legion (the territorial militia) and sent out a 75-man "Corps of Observation" to report on Johnston's progress. The Corps and other groups of Mormon raiders sallied forth with the following orders from Young:

> On ascertaining the locality or route of the troops, proceed at once to annoy them in every possible way. Use every exertion to stampede their animals, and set fire to their trains.... Keep them from sleeping by night surprises. Blockade the road by felling trees, or destroying the fords when you can.... Take no life, but destroy the trains, and stampede or drive away their animals.[155]

The Saints promised they would burn Salt Lake City itself to prevent it from falling into Federal hands. They did not have to carry out this threat but they did burn both Fort Bridger and Fort Supply. Johnston immediately occupied the remains of Fort Bridger and turned it into a temporary U.S. military reservation. Fort Supply was left in ruins and was never rebuilt. The Nauvoo Legion's guerrilla warfare tactics proved to be so effective that by the time Johnston finally got to Salt Lake City in November, his men were exhausted and had to wait for additional supplies, horses and mules to reach them in the spring.

Before any actual fighting could occur, though, a face-saving compromise was worked out under which Cumming would be permitted to take up his duties in Salt Lake City. The Army made a show of force by marching into and then immediately out of the town. The soldiers never occupied Salt Lake City itself but they did remain in the Salt Lake valley for the next three years. Buchanan pardoned the Mormon militia. Young and the other Mormon men were permitted to keep their unique institution of "plural marriages" and all their wives: polygamy continued to be tolerated by the Federal government until it was finally outlawed in 1882. The Mormon Church officially abandoned the doctrine of polygamy in 1890 but some Mormon men continued to have more than one wife, a custom which survives today in a few remote corners of the West.

In the meantime, however, Mormon intransigence paid off. The Saints made money selling food and supplies to the soldiers stationed in the Salt Lake valley. After Abraham Lincoln became President in 1861, he was preoccupied with the Civil War. When T.B.H. Stenhouse, the Mormon representative in Washington, D.C., asked him what his intentions were toward the Mormons, Lincoln replied,

> Stenhouse, when I was a boy on the farm in Illinois there was a great deal of timber we had to clear away. Occasionally we would come to a log which had fallen down. It was too hard to split, too wet to burn, and too heavy to move, so we plowed around it. That's what I intend to do with the Mormons.[156]

Lincoln's policy, in short, was that the Saints would be left to their own devices — which was precisely what they wanted.

In 1858, after the Mormon War, Fort Bridger was officially made a U.S. military reservation and a building program was started.[157] The fort was used as a camp for troops en route to Utah and to help keep the growing number of trails open at a time when Indian depredations were making travel hazardous. Had it not been for Washakie, the great Shoshoni chief, bloodshed would have been likely because the waves of emigrants were scaring away the game on which the Indians depended. Captain Lander, a newly appointed Superintendent of Indian Affairs, met Washakie near South Pass in July 1858 and sent a revealing report to the Commissioner of Indian Affairs in Washington, D.C.[158]:

> After leaving the South pass ... I met the whole of the great tribe of the Eastern Shoshones, under the direction of the celebrated Wash-i-kie. They were on their annual hunt near the headwaters of the Green river, surrounding antelope.... [I] talked with him upon the subject which brought me to the country.... He remarked that it was never the intention of the Shoshonee tribe, at least his portion of it, to fight the whites; that he himself had been fired upon by emigrants but had always taught his young men that a war with the "Great Father" [the President of the U.S.] would be disastrous to them.

Washakie went on to tell Lander that before the emigrants began to pass through his country, all manner of game — buffalo, elk and antelope — could be seen in the mountains. But now, when he looked for game,

> he saw only wagons with white tops and men riding upon their horses ... his people were very poor and had fallen back into the valleys of the mountains to dig roots and get meat for their little ones.... He said he did not even propose to fight, notwithstanding the building of [a new emigrant road which] would destroy many of their root grounds and drive off all their game.

Fort Bridger in 1858: the U.S. Army's headquarters during the Mormon War (Wyoming Division of Cultural Resources)

Lander therefore advised the Commissioner that, "Although Wash-i-kie declares his intentions to be friendly, the Snakes will be much injured by the passage of this new road by emigrants." To reward Washakie for his cooperation and to pay for any damage to their root and herding grounds which the emigrants' horses and oxen might cause, the Shoshonis were given some payments, in the form of goods rather than money, beginning in July 1859.

Transportation and Communications Links at Fort Bridger

Because of its strategic location, Fort Bridger was a natural convergence point for the stagecoach, the Pony Express, the telegraph and the Union Pacific Railroad. It was also a military strongpoint which could offer some protection to the other activities going on around it. At first, U.S. Army troops were stationed there, but after the Civil War began in 1861, Fort Bridger was left without an armed garrison for a whole year. William A. Carter, the post sutler (a merchant who sold provisions to the Army) later organized a group of mountain men to defend the fort. These were replaced by volunteer soldiers from Nevada and California, who in turn were replaced in 1866 by two companies of regular infantrymen under the command of Brevet Major A.S. Burt.[159]

Moving Freight and People

By the end of the 1850s, military supplies and other goods, passengers, mail, gold dust and bullion were being carried across the West by a far-flung network of freight and stagecoach lines. A few of them are mentioned below.

WELLS FARGO

In the 1840s, Henry Wells and William G. Fargo decided to expand their express business (the shipment of parcels, money and other items) westward to St. Louis. In 1850 they founded the American Express Company and two years later set up Wells, Fargo & Company in San Francisco. This new firm provided banking, express and mail delivery services to miners and merchants in the California goldfields. It transported strongboxes full of California gold and was so reliable that the miners swore "by God and by Wells Fargo." The company's honesty was legendary. A Wells Fargo superintendent instructed one of the company's agents in the gold diggings: "Pay no more for gold dust than it is worth, nor pay any less. This is the only true motto to do any kind of business on." Wells Fargo is probably the only company to have a Colt revolver named after it. This was the five-shot .31 caliber Wells Fargo model, which is virtually identical to the .31 caliber Baby Dragoon except that it has a rounded rather than a square-backed trigger guard. (See Chapter IX for details on these pistols.)

Wells Fargo's success can hardly be overstated. In the 1860s, this firm became the West's most important express service, its richest bank, one of its biggest freighting companies and its most extensive stagecoach line. Long-distance passengers on its coaches were promised "good meals at reasonable prices" at stage stations such as Fort Bridger. Still, this mode of travel was not without its difficulties. Demas Barnes, a cross-country traveler in 1866, reported that,

> It is not a *pleasant*, but an *interesting* trip. A through-ticket and fifteen inches of seat, with a fat man on one side, a poor widow on the other, a baby in your lap, a bandbox [a lightweight cylindrical box used to transport hats] over your head, and three or four more persons immediately in front, leaning against your knees makes the picture, as well as your sleeping place, for the trip.[160]

It is not too much to say that in its heyday Wells Fargo was the most powerful single institution in all of the West — even more powerful than the Federal government, whose on-the-ground presence across the Mississippi was usually limited to a scattering of post offices, military forts and Indian agencies.[161] For this reason the Wells Fargo History Museum in San Francisco is well worth visiting today. It has an excellent library which was the source of some of the information used here. The biggest and most noteworthy item in the museum, however, is a century-old stagecoach. Other exhibits include gold and gold mining equipment, money, treasure boxes, postal envelopes, art, tools, photographs, original papers and equipment from 19th century Wells Fargo offices.

RUSSELL, MAJORS & WADDELL

This firm signed an exclusive and lucrative contract with the War Department in 1855 to carry military freight westward from the Missouri. In its heyday Russell, Majors & Waddell deployed 500 wagons, 7,500 oxen and 1,700 men to move freight across the West.

Wells Fargo strongbox used to transport gold dust and other high-value items (Photograph by the author)

THE OVERLAND MAIL

In 1859, the westbound schedule of John Butterfield's Overland Mail line called for two departures a week (Monday and Thursday) from St. Louis, Missouri, or Memphis, Tennessee. Butterfield's wagons followed a long southerly route which first cut southwest across Texas to El Paso and then followed the Gila River westward toward California, finally arriving at San Francisco 2,800 miles and 25 days later.

OVERLAND STAGE AND MAIL LINE

Ben Holladay's Overland Stage and Mail Line operated 3,145 miles of stagecoach and freight lines in Kansas, Nebraska, Colorado, Nevada, Utah, Oregon, Idaho and Montana. One of its two routes from Denver to Salt Lake City ran directly through Fort Bridger. Holla-

day's company employed 15,000 people, owned 150,000 draft animals (horses, mules and oxen), and carried passengers and goods in 20,000 vehicles, 110 of which were the world-famous "Concord" stagecoaches built by the Abbot-Downing Company in Concord, New Hampshire.[162]

The Ultimate Stagecoach

A Concord coach was at the same time a triumph of engineering and a work of art. Drawn by either four or six horses, its woodwork consisted of carefully chosen, well-seasoned basswood, elm, oak and hickory. The carriage itself was not suspended on springs but was supported instead by two long, thick pieces of leather known as thorough-braces. These imparted such a gentle,

Concord stagecoach on display at Wells Fargo headquarters in San Francisco (**Photograph by the author**)

rocking motion to the coach that Mark Twain described it as being in "a cradle on wheels."

The exterior of each Concord coach was painted with an original landscape or the name of its new owner (for example, "Wells Fargo & Overland Stage," picked out in gold-colored paint against a russet background) and each wagon was personally inspected by either Abbot or Downing before it left their factory. The result of all this care and attention was a nearly indestructible coach which weighed more than 2,000 pounds, stood eight feet high and cost between $1,200 and $1,500.

A Concord coach could carry as many as 23 people, although admittedly under exceptionally cramped conditions. A driver and a shotgun-wielding guard sat out in front in the driver's box, next to the driver. (This is the origin of the phrase "to ride shotgun," which passed into American folklore to mean riding in a vehicle as a passenger rather than as the driver.) Nine passengers could be crammed inside the coach itself, sitting cheek by jowl on three upholstered benches, knees and other body parts pressed tightly against each other for long days on the trail. For short journeys, as many as 12 more people could perch on the flat roof, held precariously in place there by a thin iron railing.[163]

Close-up of the heavy leather thoroughbraces which cradled the carriage of the Concord stage-coach (Photograph by the author)

Keep Your Seat, Horace!

Understandably, traveling long distances in a stagecoach was not always pleasant. As mentioned in Chapter I, the editor Horace Greeley made his way from New York to San Francisco in the summer of 1859. In *An Overland Journey*, he tells us that Fort Bridger marked the end of the Great American Desert, a region inhabited only by "rude [uncultured], nomadic, lawless, but hardy, bold, and energetic pioneers."[164] From Fort Bridger itself, he reported, the trail to Salt Lake City went over a high, broad ridge, descended a steep, rocky, difficult hill down to a creek known as the Big Muddy, and then crossed another broad ridge. After Greeley's coach narrowly escaped an upset in a gully gouged in the trail by a sudden rainstorm, his driver kept on going well after dark. The stage

finally stopped shortly after 11:00 PM, at which point Greeley and the other passengers rolled up in blankets and slept, under a light drizzle, on the wet ground near the coach.

At dawn they rose again and pressed on to the stage company's little outpost on the Bear River, where two men who had been sleeping in wet blankets on the grass arose and sold them canned sardines, canned lobster and vile coffee. Some of Greeley's companions wanted to top off this meager breakfast with a stiff shot of "rot" (rotgut, i.e., hard liquor of the lowest quality). This beverage was duly provided but Greeley refused to touch the stuff. "Its look alone," he said, "would condemn it — soapy, ropy, turbid, it is within bounds to say that every pint of it contains as much deadly poison as a gallon of pure whisky." Greeley agreed wholeheartedly with a

Mule-drawn wagons deliver supplies to Union Pacific Railroad workers building the line westward through Utah in 1869. The coming of the railroad marked the beginning of the end for long-distance travel by covered wagon. (Andrew J. Russell Collection, Oakland Museum of California)

"log-tavern-keeper" on the Weber River, his next stop, who said about the "rot" being sold there, "There a'an't nothing bad about this whisky; the only fault is, it isn't good."

Greeley wrote articles in the *Tribune* supporting the transcontinental railroad. (The Central Pacific Railroad was to be built from California eastward and join up with the Union Pacific Railroad coming westward across the Great Plains.) The 19th century humorist Artemus Ward joked that these articles had so greatly "endeared Greeley to the citizens of the Golden State ... [that at] one town, the enthusiastic populace tore his celebrated white coat from his back to pieces, and carried the pieces home to

remember him by."[165] Ward himself passed through Fort Bridger in 1864 and was not overly impressed. "Here are a group of buildings," he reported, "built around a plaza, across the middle of which runs a creek. There are a few hundred troops under the command of Major Gallagher."

In any case, the Californians flocked to Greeley's lectures. On one occasion, he was scheduled to speak in the mining camp of Placerville, formerly known as Hangtown because two Frenchmen and one Chilean, none of whom could speak English, had been hanged there after a 30-minute trial conducted entirely in English. Greeley was at the town of Folsom and had to be in Placerville, 40

miles away, at 7:00 PM. But his stagecoach was delayed and did not leave Folsom until late in the afternoon. The local
agent for the stagecoach company therefore told the driver, Henry Monk, "Henry,
this great man must be there by 7 to-
night." Monk answered, "The great man
shall be there."

The roads were in such bad shape,
however, that at first the coach could
make only slow progress. Greeley repeatedly urged Monk to go faster, but with
no effect. Finally, however, the horses
broke into a wild gallop, encouraged by
yells from Monk: "Git up! Hi yi! G'long!
Yip-yip!" Greeley was bounced around
in the coach so much that he ordered
Monk to slow down. But Monk replied,
"I've got my orders!" and tore along at a
breakneck pace. The coach finally hit
such a big bump in the road that Greeley's bald head broke through the lath-
and-canvas roof. "Stop, you _____ ma-
niac!" Greeley roared. Monk's answer
has gone down in Western history: "I've
got my orders! *Keep your seat, Horace!*"

The citizens of Placerville had sent a
delegation, complete with a brass band
and a wagonload of pretty young women
in white dresses, to Mud Springs, a nearby
village, to welcome their distinguished
guest and to escort him into Placerville.
They saw the stage coming and tried to
get Monk to stop, but he only shouted at
them, "*I've got my orders!* My orders don't
say nothing about brass bands and young
women. My orders says, 'git him there by
seving!' Clear the away there! Whoo-up!
KEEP YOUR SEAT, HORACE!" Monk
did get Greeley to Placerville by 7:00 PM.
At first Greeley, who was bleeding from
the nose because of his encounter with
the roof of the stagecoach, was furious
with Monk but then he laughed and later
presented him with a new set of clothes.

Other Stagecoach Travelers: Richard Burton and Raphael Pumpelly

The greatest of the Victorian lin-
guists, Sir Richard F. Burton, left St.
Louis in 1860 in a Concord coach, en
route to Salt Lake City and San Francisco.[166] He had a less harrowing ride than
Greeley and admired the construction
and decoration of the stagecoach, especially the fact that the carriage rested on
strong leather thoroughbraces, which
"are found to break the jolt better than
the best steel springs, which moreover,
when injured cannot readily be repaired."
He warned, though, that, "The comfort
of travel depends on packing the wagon;
if heavy in front or rear, or if the thoroughbraces be not properly 'fixed' the
bumping will likely cause nasal haemor-
rhage."

When he got to Fort Bridger, Burton, like many other visitors, remarked
on its good location:

> Fort Bridger lies 124 miles from Gt.
> S. L. [Great Salt Lake] City; according
> to the drivers, however, the road might
> be considerably shortened. The posi-
> tion is a fertile basin cut into a num-
> ber of bits by Black's Fork, which dis-
> perses itself into four channels about
> 1.5 miles above the station, and forms
> again into a single bed about two miles
> below.... The material of the houses is
> pine and cedar brought from the Uinta
> Hills, whose black flanks supporting
> snowy cones rise at the distance of
> about thirty-five miles ... they are said
> to shelter grizzly bears and an abun-
> dance of smaller game.

But the fort itself, Burton said, was
"a mere cantonment without any attempt at fortification ... garrisoned by
two companies of foot [infantrymen],

under the command of Captain F. Gardner of the 10th Regiment." The captain introduced Burton to the officers under his command. In the manner of soldiers the world over after a round of drinks, these men were quick to complain to a sympathetic listener about the rigors of their life. Fort Bridger was too isolated, they said, and their own duties were not very challenging, consisting only of "keeping the roads open for, and the Indians from cutting off, parties of unmanageable emigrants, who look upon the Federal army as their humblest servants." The officers also raised a subject which was "still sore to military ears" — the fact that during the Mormon War, Colonel Johnston's troops had to spend part of the severe winter of 1857–58 camping outdoors in the snow at Fort Scott, not far from Fort Bridger.

Bridger himself was not at the fort because he was off on an exploratory expedition with Captain Reynolds but Burton heard fine things about him: "He [Bridger] divides with Christopher Carson, the Kit Carson of the Wind River and the Sierra Nevada explorations, the honour of being the best guide and interpreter in the Indian country; the palm for prudence is generally given to the former; for dash and hard fighting, to the latter." Burton found that during Bridger's absence William A. Carter was in charge of the fort, simultaneously discharging to everyone's satisfaction the triple duties of postmaster, post sutler and probate judge.

While Burton was learning all about life at Fort Bridger, his traveling companions had a less scholarly objective — refilling their whiskey jug. Burton joked that its emptiness must have been due to "the rapid evaporation at such an elevated region imperfectly protected

by timber." His stagecoach driver commented facetiously that although the quantity of whisky remaining in the keg did not diminish too rapidly, the quality lost strength every day. Someone, of course (probably the driver himself), was drinking the whiskey surreptitiously and replacing it with water.

Another first-rate account of a stagecoach journey in 1860 comes from Raphael Pumpelly's *Across America and Asia* (1870). Pumpelly was a mining engineer en route to the silver mines of Arizona and was traveling along the southerly trail used by Butterfield's Overland Mail. He did not have an easy time of it.

> The coach was fitted with three seats, and these were occupied by nine passengers. As the occupants of the front and middle seats faced each other, it was necessary for these six people to interlock their knees.... An unusually heavy mail in the boot, by weighing down the rear, kept those of us who were on the front seat constantly bent forward, thus, by taking away all support from our backs, rendering rest at all times out of the question.... At several stations, six wild horses were hitched blind-folded into their places. When everything was ready, the blinds were removed ... the driver had no further control over his animals than the ability to guide them; to stop, or even check them, was entirely beyond his power....[167]

By the time the stage got to El Paso, Texas, Pumpelly was half-delirious from exhaustion and lack of sleep. His only memory of the stretch between the Rio Grande River and Tucson, Arizona, was the sight of Indian campfires at Apache Pass. The next recollection, he tells us, was being woken up by a pistol shot. He was amazed to find himself lying on the floor of a crowded room where a heated argument was going on at a gaming table. He then remembered that upon reaching Tucson he had thrown himself into the first room he could enter: he had slept soundly on the floor of a saloon until the pistol shot woke him up 12 hours later.

The Pony Express

The need to get high-priority business mail across the country quickly, regardless of the cost, led to the brief but dramatic career of the Pony Express. The Pony, as it was called, was initially operated by Russell, Majors & Waddell's Central Overland California & Pikes Peak Express (COC & PPE) to prove that a direct 1,966-mile route across the middle of the United States through Fort Bridger was quicker and more profitable than the long southern route used by the Overland Mail.[168]

The Pony began operations in April 1860 but without government subsidies or lucrative mail contracts the COC & PPE soon became known as the "Clean Out of Cash & Poor Pay Express." In April 1861 Wells Fargo took charge of the western end of the route, carrying mail between San Francisco and Salt Lake City, while the COC & PPE continued to handle the eastern route.

A letter carried by the Pony was usually written on tissue paper to save weight and cost $5.00 in gold for each half-ounce. The mail left San Francisco on Wednesdays and Saturdays, securely locked in the four pockets of a light saddle covering known as a *mochila,* which carried about 10 pounds of mail. The Pony took only ten days to make its east-

west runs, either from St. Louis to San Francisco or from San Francisco to St. Louis. Sometimes even better time was made. President Buchanan's last message to Congress in December 1860 was carried from St. Louis to Sacramento, California, in eight days plus a few hours. President Lincoln's inaugural address in March 1861 reached Sacramento in only seven days and 17 hours.

These speedy deliveries were possible only because the Pony's riders were exceptionally able horsemen. Each man rode about 75 miles, changing horses five times and going at a full gallop day and night, regardless of the weather. Riders were selected with the utmost care. The ideal candidate for this dangerous job was a 20-year-old man who was brave, unmarried, did not weigh more than 125 pounds and who was, of course, an expert rider. A Pony Express rider had to rely on his speed rather than on his weapons for defense because he was permitted to carry only one light Colt revolver, perhaps with an extra cylinder so that he could reload the pistol quickly, and one knife. But he was well paid at $125 dollars per month and was greatly admired by men and women alike for his daring.

One of the greatest Pony Express riders was Robert H. "Pony Bob" Haslam, who once covered 380 miles in about 36 hours of riding.[169] He had been assigned to a desert section of the trail which linked an outpost known as Friday's Station (located at Lake Tahoe on the California-Nevada border) with Fort Churchill on the Carson River in Nevada, 75 miles to the east. Haslam began his eastward mail run on 11 May 1860 but soon encountered difficulties. He could not get a fresh horse at Carson City because the townsmen had commandeered them all to chase the Paiute Indians. They had attacked some settlements between Carson City and Fort Churchill, killing the residents and stealing or driving off their horses. At Fort Churchill, the next rider refused to take over, so Haslam mounted a fresh horse and kept on going. He changed horses again at Sand Springs and Cold Spring, finally reaching Smith's Creek early on 12 May riding 190 miles in about 18 hours.

After sleeping for eight or nine hours, Haslam then picked up the westbound mail from another rider who had just arrived and headed back toward Friday's Station. But the Paiutes had burned the station at Cold Spring, killed the stationkeeper and stolen the horses, so he had to go on to Sand Springs to get a new mount. He changed horses again at Carson Sink, pressed on to Fort Churchill, where he rested one hour, and headed toward Carson City, finally returning safely to Friday's Station on 13 May. Summing up his ride, Haslam later said, with justifiable pride, "I had traveled 380 miles within a few hours of schedule time, and surrounded by perils on every hand."[170]

Not many writers saw a Pony Express rider in action, but Mark Twain, who was traveling through Nevada by stagecoach in 1861, was one of them. Riders had often passed Twain's stagecoach at night but at last the Pony turned up in broad daylight. The driver of the coach shouted, "HERE HE COMES!" As Twain remembered the scene years later:

> Every neck is stretched further, and every eye strained wider. Away across the endless dead level of the prairie a black speck appears against the sky, and it is plain that it moves. Well, I should think so! In a second or two it becomes a horse and rider, rising and falling, rising and falling — sweeping toward us nearer and nearer — growing more and more distinct, more and more sharply defined — nearer and still nearer, and the flutter of the hoofs comes faintly to the ear — another instant a whoop and a hurrah from our upper deck [the roof of the stagecoach], a wave of the rider's hand, but no reply, and man and horse burst past our excited faces, and go winging away like a belated fragment of a storm![171]

Before this long-distance mail service came to an end in October 1861 (due to the linking of transcontinental telegraph wires), Pony Express riders successfully carried 34,753 pieces of mail, much of it through regions where outlaw and Indian attacks were an ever-present danger. Only one rider was captured and killed by the Indians but his horse escaped and made its way, alone, to the next relay station — probably still carrying the mail locked in the *mochila*.

Over its 18 months of operations, however, the Pony Express managed to lose a good deal of money — between $300,000 and $500,000, according to one estimate. Some of its financial problems arose because mail deliveries were interrupted for weeks at a time by Indian hostilities, but even in peaceful times the Pony was a money-losing proposition. It charged an average of $3.00 to deliver a letter but had to spend about $16.00 to get that letter into the hands of the reader. If the Pony did not make any money, its intrepid riders did prove one important point: that the central route through Fort Bridger, rather than the longer southerly route through Texas and along the Gila River, was the best way to cross the continent. As a result, this was the route that the Union Pacific Railroad and the interstate highways followed later on.

Spanning the Continent with Wire and Rails

THE TELEGRAPH

The telegraph lines linking the Atlantic and Pacific Coasts were finally joined at a Western Union office in Salt Lake City on 24 October 1861.[172] The first coast-to-coast message was sent from California Chief Justice Stephen Field to President Lincoln, congratulating the President on the successful completion of the line and pledging California's loyalty to the Union cause. Although telegraph rates were quite high (up to 75 cents per word), they spelled the end of the Pony Express and the beginning in the United States of the communications revolution which in later years would have such a major impact on American life. Fort Bridger itself soon profited from this revolution: Wyoming's first newspaper appeared here, featuring daily bulletins on Civil War battles and other newsworthy developments. These were supplied by H. Brundage, the post's telegrapher, probably beginning in June 1863.[173]

THE RAILROADS

Under the leadership of a group of financiers known as the Big Four (Charles Crocker, Leland Stanford, Mark Hopkins and Collis P. Huntington) and with the help of 15,000 nameless Chinese coolies, many of whom risked their lives every day laying explosive charges to blast a path through the granite faces of the Sierra Nevada mountains, the Central Pacific Railroad gradually made its way eastward from California.

The role of the Chinese on the frontier has not received the attention it deserves. During the winter of 1866-67, for example, the Chinese drove a tunnel 20 feet in diameter through 1,559 feet of solid granite, just below the crest of Donner Pass. Snowdrifts 60 feet deep forced them to cut passageways in the snow between their barracks and the entrance to the tunnel. Even when using nitroglycerin, a dangerous new invention which was eight times more powerful than blasting powder, progress was very slow — only about 16 inches in every 24 hours. Track was finally laid through the completed Summit Tunnel in November 1867.[174]

In an era when Chinese laborers in California were very much discriminated against on a social basis, the Americans who actually worked with them were favorably impressed. In his 1872 travel book, the writer Charles Nordhof reported that when a spur of the railroad was being built to bring tourists into Yosemite National Park, the American engineer who was in charge of 700 Chinese and 100 white laborers said that "the Chinese make, on the whole, the best road builders in the world." His colleague, an American contractor, added that "they learn all parts of the work very quickly." Both men agreed that the Chinese were cleaner than the white men, ate a wider and better variety of food and were much more frugal, managing to save about $13 of the $28 they earned each month. They did not drink, fight or strike. Their only vice was gambling.[175]

Racing across the desolation of the Bonneville salt flats on the Nevada-Utah border, the 10,000 men in Crocker's crew once managed to lay a record-breaking 10 miles of track in a single day.[176] For their part, the Irish laborers laying rails westward for the Union Pacific were prodigious workers, too. One mile of railroad track required 400 steel rails, each weighing 500 pounds, 12,000 spikes, each of

Wells Fargo — i.e., Concord — stagecoach at Fort Bridger in 1869 (Courtesy of Wells Fargo)

which had to be driven in with three blows from a sledgehammer, and 10 pairs of strong arms. Watching the Irish at work, one newspaper reporter, reminded of Verdi's opera *Il Trovatore*, described this cacophony of sound as nothing less than "a grand Anvil Chorus."

The Indians of the northern Rockies and the Great Plains soon realized, however, that for them the Union Pacific only meant more settlers and less game, especially buffalo. Some Indians tried to resist the inroads of what they called the Iron Horse. On the night of 6 August 1867, for instance, a Cheyenne war party near Plum Creek, Nebraska, cut the telegraph line and used the wire to lash together a barricade of railroad ties. When six railroad workers went down the tracks in a hand-pump car (a platform moved by muscle power) to repair the telegraph line, they were derailed by the barricade. Five of the six men were killed by the Indians. On another occasion, an Indian war party tried to capture a locomotive

by tying their lariats (ropes) across the tracks. Since the ends of these lariats were lashed to the Indians' saddlehorns, when a train came through at 25 miles per hour, several of the Indians, along with their ponies, were jerked into its drive wheels and dismembered.[177]

By 1868 the railroad reached the vicinity of Fort Bridger, running along Muddy Creek, about 15 miles north of the fort. It is said that the reason the Union Pacific did not go directly through Fort Bridger, as had originally been planned, is that one of the men who was surveying the right of way became furious when he could not buy a quart of whiskey at the fort on a Sunday.[178] Nevertheless, Fort Bridger immediately became an important supply center for the railroad. In addition, the U.S. Army troops there offered emigrants and railroad crews protection against possible Indian attacks. In 1868 the Shoshonis bowed to the inevitable and Chief Washakie signed a peace treaty at Fort

Bridger with Governor Doty of Utah. Under its terms, the Shoshonis agreed not to molest the stagecoach routes or the telegraph lines and to give the Union Pacific a right of way across their ancestral lands.[179] In 1869 the Union Pacific and Central Pacific Railroads were finally joined at Promontory, 56 miles west of Ogden, Utah. The last spike, driven home by a silver hammer, was made of solid gold. It bore this patriotic slogan, engraved in the fine, elegant style known as copperplate hand:

> May God continue the unity of our Country as this Railroad unites the two great Oceans of the world.

The era of the prairie schooner as the best means of family transportation across the West was not over yet but the writing was on the wall. Prairie schooners, freight wagons and stagecoaches continued to be used long after the transcontinental railroad was finished in 1869. It was not until after other rail lines had been completed — the Southern Pacific and the Northern Pacific (both 1883), the Atchison, Topeka and Santa Fe (1885), and the Great Northern (1893) — that a newspaper could confidently report: "The prairie schooner has passed away and is replaced by the railway coach with all its modern comforts."[180]

Chapter VII

Gold, Silver and Diamonds

Most of California's gold was located on the western slope of the Sierra Nevada mountains. This is rugged country and it is still one of the most attractive parts of the West, known today primarily for its superb hiking and skiing. It is characterized by blue skies, dry sunny summers, snowy winters, narrow ridges, deep canyons, dense coniferous forests, exposed granite faces and small lakes nestled deep in rock basins. From the more pragmatic point of view of the Forty-niners, however, the only attraction of the Sierras was the boulder-filled rivers and streams which thread their way through the mountains. Today the names of these small rivers — some euphonious (the Mokelumne, Stanislaus, Toulumne, San Joaquin, and Yuba) and others more prosaic (the Feather, Bear, American, and Merced) — still evoke memories of the gold rush days. These and their tributary streams were critically important to the Forty-niners for two reasons.

The first was that at low water during the dry summer months the rocky banks and beds of these waterways provided access routes through the long chain of the Sierras, which would oth-

erwise have been quite impassable for wagons. Following the course of a riverbed in a wagon, though, was never easy. Writing in his diary on 18 September 1850, the emigrant John Steele recorded that, "We followed the brook [the Yuba River] upon a bed of large granite boulders, difficult for teams and dangerous to the wagons, until we reached the brink of a deep abyss down which the stream, by a succession of cascades, fell in a spray."[181]

The second and more important reason why the rivers and streams were important was that they contained gold. Thanks to the heavy snowfall in the Sierras, these watercourses become virtual torrents in the spring. When in spate, over the millennia they carried down from the gold-rich outcroppings of the highest peaks not only boulders, rocks, pebbles, dirt and sand, but also nuggets and flakes of gold and gold dust. As these rivers reached gentler gradients lower down in the foothills of the mountains, their currents slowed. Gold, being a heavy element, was deposited there in sand-and-gravel bars and in pockets of the stream beds; it was not washed all the way down into the Sacramento-San

Gold mining equipment used by the Forty-niners. Shown here are two wooden rockers (also called cradles); a tin or iron wash pan; and, visible near the stairs, a small brass nozzle used in hydraulic mining. (Photograph by the author)

Joaquin Valley. Using a Spanish word meaning an underwater plateau, the Forty-niners referred to the gold which had been deposited in this way as "placer" gold.

Being on or reasonably close to the surface of the ground, placer gold could be mined with only rudimentary pick-and-shovel technology. "Panning" for gold was the most popular way, but it was also the slowest and least comfortable method of trying to strike it rich because it meant standing or squatting for hours in a cold stream. A miner would fill a shallow, slanted-edged metal pan with dirt and gravel, gently swirl it around under the water to wash off the lightest residues, then bring it above the water and continue the swirling motion, occasionally tilting the pan slightly

to allow some of the water and sand to escape. If the panning was done by an expert, any gold the original panfull had contained would be left in the bottom.[182]

But panning for gold was such a cold and slow process that enterprising miners soon built wooden devices to help them process dirt and gravel more efficiently. These were known by different names — rockers, cradles, long toms, sluices — but they all worked on the same basic principle as the pan: that is, they used running water to separate the heavier gold from the lighter debris surrounding it. Such devices worked so well that by the mid–1850s most of the easy gold, that is, the placer gold which could be retrieved by one man or by a small group of men using primitive equipment, had already been found. Miners therefore found it necessary to move on to a more advanced technology.

When they did this, entire rivers were diverted to lay bare their stream beds, long tunnels were dug into the mountains, and great "hoisting wheels," which looked like Ferris wheels without seats, were built to lift dirt and gravel from deep pits to the surface. The most dramatic and certainly the most destructive method, though, was hydraulic mining. This involved forcing millions of gallons of water a day (collected and canalized from mountain rivers by long narrow wooden sluices) through metal nozzles which were up to eight inches in diameter and were known as monitors. The most powerful of these jets of water could cut a man in half at very close range; at longer range, they washed away whole hillsides and created man-made canyons.

The long-term damage caused by hydraulic mining has to be seen to be believed. For example, it is only now, over 115 years after such mining was finally outlawed in 1884 (not for environmental reasons but because it was impeding navigation of the Sacramento River by silting it up), that a few trees are struggling to grow on the desolate, rust-colored hillsides near Dutch Flat on the Overland Emigrant Trail in the Sierras about 70 miles northeast of Sacramento. Such denuded mining areas, their topsoil and vegetation blasted away by the torrents of water extracted from the Bear River and forced through monitors, were known as "diggings." And the names that the diggings at Dutch Flat bore during the gold rush days — Placer, Little York, Blue Devil, Buckeye and Liberty Hill — are still used on modern topographic maps.

Other Western Goldfields

As placer mining gave way to hard rock mining, advanced technology was needed. But this was so expensive that only big companies could afford it. Not many Forty-niners had struck it rich. Even so, not many of the majority who hadn't wanted to stay on in California as day-laborers for these companies. So, rather than returning home in disgrace, many of them fanned out over the West to look for new Golcondas. ("Golconda" refers to a ruined city in southern India. This term was used in the 19th century to describe a rich mine or some other source of great wealth.) They met with varying degrees of success — only the Comstock Lode, discovered in Nevada in 1859, was truly a great bonanza. But in the process of looking for buried treasure in the West, enough gold and silver was in fact found to whet miners' and investors' appetites and, ultimately, to set the stage for the Great Diamond Hoax of 1872.

Pike's Peak, Cripple Creek and the Comstock Lode

In 1858 a little gold was discovered west of Colorado Springs near Pike's Peak, Colorado. The next spring 100,000 eager prospectors sallied forth in wagons painted with the confident slogan "Pikes Peak or Bust." So few of them found gold, though, that most returned home disillusioned, their wagons now bearing a much different slogan: "Busted, by God!"

Still, there were some major finds. In 1859, for instance, George Jackson discovered gold flakes in a gravel bar near Clear Creek, 30 miles west of Denver — one decade later, Colorado was producing more gold than California. In 1878

Bob Womack found faint traces of gold at Cripple Creek, 100 miles south of Denver, and spent the next 12 years looking for what was called the mother lode, i.e., the original source of all the gold washed downstream. Womack finally located this treasure-trove in 1890 and named it the El Paso Mine. It eventually produced $3,000,000 worth of gold. But Womack saw none of it — he had sold the mine for $300 when he was drunk.

By far the greatest find occurred in 1859 when Henry Comstock, a former mountain man, discovered a fabulously rich gold-and-silver deposit on Mount Davidson, near Virginia City in western Nevada. It came to be called the Comstock Lode. The two small towns immediately south of Virginia City are still known, respectively, as Gold Hill and Silver City, reflecting the fact that gold and silver often occurred together in the West. (The silver, however, was not as easy to detect as the gold and was more difficult to refine.)

The Comstock Lode itself was only four miles long but it contained a vein which was chock-full of gold and silver. Indeed, for the two decades after its discovery the Comstock Lode was the primary source of all the gold mined in the United States. This vein was so rich that towns grew explosively around it. In 1860 Gold Hill and Virginia City consisted only of "frame shanties, pitched together as if by accident; tents of canvas, of brush, of blankets, of potato sacks, and old shirts." By 1864 a woman from Massachusetts who came out to the Comstock Lode to join her new husband reported that, "The houses are furnished well and there is much more dress displayed here than on Beacon Street [Boston] when the ladies make calls."[183]

Over the next 30 years, huge amounts of capital were poured into the Comstock Lode to sink vertical shafts 3,000 feet deep and to honeycomb Mount Davidson with horizontal tunnels. To prevent collapse, both shafts and tunnels had to be shored up by an intricate network of heavy timbers. Special rooms containing big blocks of ice had to be built underground so that the miners could cool off after working for hours in temperatures of up to 130 degrees Fahrenheit. But these investments paid off handsomely. The Comstock Lode produced about $400,000,000 worth — 55 percent of it silver and 45 percent gold. But Henry Comstock himself never profited from his great discovery: he sold his share for $11,000. He eventually went mad, and shot himself in 1870.

The Comstock Lode not only enriched its investors but also had a major impact on journalism. The mine gave a failed California placer miner named George Hearst a new start in life. He bought part of Comstock's share in the mine and later parlayed it into ownership of the Homestake Mine in the Black Hills of South Dakota. After huge investments in rock-crushing machinery and chemical processing plants, Homestake produced about $1,000,000,000 worth of gold. (Tailings — the residue of mining after pulverization and milling — still contained some gold and silver. Much of this could be recovered by a chemical refining process involving sodium cyanide and zinc.) Backed by the Comstock Lode fortune, Hearst's son, William Randolph Hearst (1863–1951), would go on to become one of the world's most famous publishers and editors.

GOLD NEAR FORT BRIDGER

New discoveries continued to hearten the optimists who believed that the West was an inexhaustible store-house of treasure. Gold was first reported in the South Pass area in 1842. It was discovered by a fur trader from Georgia who had come west for his health. Ironically, he was killed near South Pass by the Indians. No mining seems to have occurred there until 1855. It subsequently continued at low levels until 1862, when the U.S. Army troops stationed at Camp Stambaugh (18 miles northeast) were withdrawn to serve in the Civil War. The Indians' hunting trails crossed over South Pass and, once the troops were gone, renewed Indian attacks drove the miners out of the region.[184] They also forced the Overland Stage Company to move the Oregon Trail farther south.

Gold had been found in Idaho in 1860 and in Montana two years later. Encouraged by this and by seeing the rotten remains of mining equipment near South Pass, in 1865 Major Noyes Baldwin of Fort Bridger and his colleague John F. Skelton, "grubstaked" (that is, they provided food and mining tools for) two prospectors, John A. James and D.C. Moreland, for a six-month exploration of the region.

James and Moreland did find some good mining sites, but only after a great deal of hard, tedious work. During the winter of 1865, for example, they had to shovel their way through 10 feet of snow to get to the bottom of a promising gulch — a deep, narrow, possibly gold-bearing ravine marking the bed of a mountain stream. With the approach of spring, James wrote a long letter to Major Baldwin on 18 March 1866, chiefly to bring him up to date on the mining prospects (which were good) but also giving him some insights into local conditions. "We have had such good luck this winter killing buffalo," he reported,

"that we will have becan [bacon, but in this context, dried buffalo meat] enough to last us all summer, consequently our outfit will not be so expensive as it was last fall." Even excluding the danger of Indian attacks, however, life in the mountains was not without its dangers. James added in a postscript:

> I forgot to mention above that Mountain Jack was killed a few days ago by a man named Johnson, who used to stay about grangers [farmers]. Jack was a desperet character, had on several occasions thretend Johnson's life. in fact all the crowd with him were afraid of him. I have talked with several who were known to the circumstance, and they all agree, the Johnson was justifiable, it happened about two miles below where we camped....

Rumors of gold near South Pass spread quickly in 1867, after reports that soldiers were using their knives to dig gold out of gopher holes. When the Carissa mine was discovered that same year, greatly exaggerated accounts of the amounts of gold to be found around South Pass acted like a magnet to attract even greater numbers of miners and adventurers. Another sizable find in 1867 led to the opening of a mine known as the Miner's Delight. At the high point of the South Pass gold rush there were about 2,000 residents there, dozens of mines and hundreds of placer claims. A few of these mines and claims turned out to be valuable but most were disappointments, even though they were graced with colorful and optimistic names: the Young American, the King Solomon, the Mary Ellen, the Caribou, and the Buckeye.

But South Pass was not destined to become another Comstock. By 1872 the rich paydirt of the placer claims was

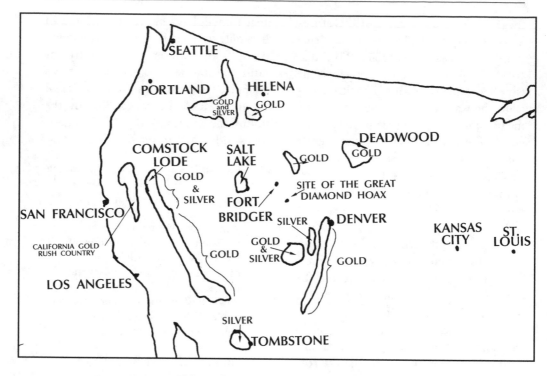

Map 4: Treasure Troves of the Frontier

gone, leaving only lower grade ores hidden deep in the ground. These could not be exploited without capital, heavy machinery and better transportation, so the pick-and-shovel miners moved on. Usually they were lured away by reports of richer goldfields elsewhere but sometimes they were also worried about the danger of Indian attacks. Not infrequently, finding that they could not make a living as miners, they abandoned mining altogether and took up safer, more secure and better paying jobs on the Union Pacific construction crews.

The population of South Pass fell to about 300 people in 1872 and to 100 people in 1875, when the nearby military post of Camp Stambaugh closed. Although some mining continued thereafter — a man named Lewis discovered the Bullion Lode in 1876, made a small fortune and even had a town (now long vanished)

named after him — the area around South Pass gradually sank back into the obscurity from which it had emerged. The best guess is that its goldfields produced a total of nearly $6,000,000. In the latter years of the 20th century, only a few diehard prospectors continued to pan for gold near South Pass and only one or two optimistic miners still dug there for ore. South Pass City, however, is now one of Wyoming's State Historic Sites. It has 30 log, frame and stone buildings set on 39 acres of land, as well as 30,000 artifacts related to mining and associated activities.

The Great Diamond Hoax

So much gold and silver had been found in the West that by the 1870s even hard-headed businessmen were prepared to believe that unlimited riches still awaited them. Thus it was that on the morning of 29 October 1872, a small group of geologists packed mules, swaddled themselves in big woolen mufflers, mounted their horses and set out from Fort Bridger to look for something entirely new in the annals of the West — a diamond field.[185]

GEOLOGISTS IN ACTION: EMMONS AND KING

One of these geologist horsemen was Samuel Franklin Emmons, who had just spent six years conducting geological surveys in Nevada, Utah and Wyoming. He would later remember how on that ride from Fort Bridger he had worn four flannel shirts and two pairs of socks to save space on the pack mules. Even so, it was "a bitterly cold journey on tired and worn-out animals, whose legs from crossing the frequent thinly frozen mountain streams became encased in balls of ice, which rattled … like crude castanets."

Emmons was the man who had launched his fellow geologists on this intensive search for the diamond field which had been the subject of rumors in the West since early in 1872. (Clarence King, the chief of the U.S. Government's Fortieth Parallel Survey, is the best known of these geologists because he was such a good writer.)

TWO CON MEN: ARNOLD AND SLACK

These rumors arose because two filthy, bearded prospectors — Philip Arnold and John Slack — had appeared early one morning at the Bank of California in San Francisco with a small leather pouch which they wanted to put into one of the vaults. Swearing a bank clerk to secrecy, they poured the contents of the sack onto a table: rough diamonds glittered in the light. The clerk was only too happy to take charge of these gems — and to show them to the officers of the bank as soon as the prospectors left. Arnold and Slack themselves quietly disappeared into the San Francisco fog.

With great fortunes in the offing, the Bank of California organized the "New York and San Francisco Mining and Commercial Company," which was led by prestigious businessmen. It paid Arnold and Slack about $600,000 for information about the diamond field. The diamonds themselves were sent to New York, where Charles Lewis Tiffany, the head of the prominent jewelry firm Tiffany and Company, personally assessed them as bona fide gems worth about $150,000. As an additional check, however, the cautious men in charge of the New York and San Francisco Mining and Commercial Company decided to send Henry Janin to the diamond field to produce a report.

JANIN TAKES THE BAIT

Henry Janin was at that time one of the best-known mining engineers in California. (See Appendix IV for a biographic sketch.) Like Bridger, he is a good example of Westering but, unlike Bridger, he was also a member of the 19th century's educational and social elite. According to Emmons, Janin was an extraordinarily conservative specialist who had made his reputation by "condemning almost every new scheme he had been called to report on." Another contemporary source (Asbury Harpending) said that Janin had examined something over 600 mines without once making a mistake and never caused his clients to lose a dollar.

Janin went to the diamond field in June 1872, found that there were indeed diamonds there and formally claimed on behalf of the company the most promising 3,000 acres of land. While Janin focused on securing water rights for this claim, Arnold and Slack, working by themselves, washed out from 1½ tons of gravel something like 1,000 diamonds, four pounds of rubies and a dozen sapphires. On 1 August 1872 Janin was quoted in a California newspaper as saying the diamond field was so rich that 25 men could wash out gems worth $1 million a month.

DIAMOND HUNTERS

Emmons was on a train headed west through Nevada in early October 1872 when he and his colleague James T. Garner noticed that their fellow passengers included "a rather suspicious looking set of men whose rough clothes, top boots, and bronzed faces seemed somewhat at variance with a certain citified air." Emmons and Garner decided, correctly as it turned out, that these men were diamond hunters returning to San Francisco. Among them was Henry Janin, whom they knew.

Janin told Emmons and Garner that he had tried to go back to the diamond field again (this would have been his second trip) but he had been followed so closely that to prevent the field from being found by others, he had asked a surveyor to take his place. The surveyor, accompanied by nine other men, had found the diamond field and in one hour these ten, using only their pocket knives,

had collected 280 diamonds, as well as rubies "too common to count." These gems ranged in size from "a grain of wheat to a small pea."

Janin also told Emmons that on his first trip his party had camped at the foot of a pine-covered mountain which still had snow on its slopes in June. In a conversation with the surveyor, who was also on the train, Garner got another bit of useful information: no high peaks could be seen from the camp, which was located on the northwest side of a mountain. This was not much to go on but the geologists knew that part of the West so well that when Clarence King returned to San Francisco and heard the story (he had been conducting geological surveys in the southern Sierra Nevada mountains) he agreed that the diamond field was probably located about 80 miles southeast of Fort Bridger, near a 9,658 feet mountain (later known as Diamond Peak) about nine miles southeast of the point were the borders of Wyoming, Utah and Colorado meet.

THE HOAX IS EXPOSED

King immediately saw that his own professional reputation was on the line. If diamonds did indeed exist within the regions explored by his Fortieth Parallel Survey and if he had not mentioned them in his reports, the rest of his geological work might well be discredited. He saw that the matter merited urgent investigation and, together with his colleagues, he went to Fort Bridger by train. As already mentioned, on 29 October these men set out from Fort Bridger on horseback to find the diamond field.

After a cold four-day trip, they reached the most likely area and found, nailed to a tree, a notice which had been

Henry Janin after graduation from the School of Mines in Paris, c. 1861 (Photograph courtesy of the author)

signed by Henry Janin in June 1872 claiming the water rights of a nearby stream. Then, Emmons says,

> Throwing down our bridle reins we began examining the rock on our hands and knees, and in another instant I had found a small ruby. This was indeed the spot. The diamond fever had now attacked us with vigor, and while daylight lasted we continued in this position picking up precious stones.... That night we were full-believers in the verity of Janin's reports, and dreamed of the untold wealth that might be gathered.[186]

Their suspicions were aroused, however, when they found that the number of diamonds and rubies declined drastically away from a centrally located flat area. And King worked out that for every 12 rubies they were sure to find one diamond. The men then began a meticulous search which even included the ant hills — and there they found conclusive proof that the field had been "salted," that is, the gems were there not as a result of geological processes but because Arnold and Slack had put them there. King and his colleagues soon found that any ant hill which had a human footprint beside it and a tiny hole in its crust would yield a small ruby or two, but that no gems were ever found in an ant hill without a footprint or a hole. "Our explanation," says Emmons, "was that some one must have pushed a ruby or two on the end of a stick. We dug in the gulch again, and found the rubies decreased as we left the rock, until at a certain distance, sift the sand as we would we got none at all."[187] Further tests confirmed that the diamond field was an out-and-out fraud.

Returning to San Francisco on 10 November, King immediately sought out Janin and spent nearly the whole night telling him what had been found. At last Janin was convinced that King was right. The next day, when the board of directors of the New York and San Francisco Mining and Commercial Company was given the bad news, these businessmen were also convinced. Nevertheless, they decided to send King, Janin and some others back to the diamond field for a final check. The results of this last trip were grim. No diamond or ruby was found naturally and one man even found some rubies lying exposed on a bare rock. "In my opinion," he later said, "it would have been as impossible for nature to have deposited them there as for a person in San Francisco to toss a marble into the air and have it fall on Bunker Hill Monument [in Massachusetts]."[188]

When all this was reported to the board of directors in San Francisco, they publicly denounced the fraud and immediately took steps to try to recover the money given to Arnold and Slack. Investigations revealed that these rogues had planned the hoax very carefully and had made trips to Amsterdam and London, where they had bought somewhere between $20,000 and $50,000 worth of South African "niggerheads," flawed diamonds in the rough. Thus the diamonds found by Janin and the others were in fact real diamonds but of little value.

Tiffany, for his part, sidestepped any responsibility by claiming that his company's expertise was only in cut and polished gems, not in rough diamonds. Janin himself, who upon learning about the hoax had immediately put into escrow all the fees paid to him, was exonerated by his fellow mining engineers. But he was deeply humiliated by his mistakes, especially by the error of letting Arnold and Slack wash out gravel without his direct supervision. This oversight gave the two men the opportunity they needed to sprinkle gems into the gravel.

Janin wrote a "Brief Statement" describing his own role in the hoax. He gave a copy of this document to the Huntington Library in California, writing on it a wry comment in French: "On peut être plus fin qu'un autre, mais pas plus fin que tous les autres." (Perhaps one can be shrewder than the next man, but not shrewder than all other men.)

ON THE TRAIL OF THE CON MEN

The public did not lose any money in the Great Diamond Hoax because no stock was ever sold. However, $12,000,000 worth of stock would have gone on sale within 30 days had it not been for the remarkable investigative work of King and his colleagues. The major losers in the hoax were William Ralston, the head of the Bank of California, who lost $250,000, and the San Francisco financier William Lent, who lost $100,000.

What happened to the "prospec-tors" Arnold and Slack? Arnold, for one, came to a violent end. He escaped to Elizabethtown, Kentucky, with an estimated $300,000–$600,000 and was never brought to justice, although he may have paid one creditor $150,000 to settle his claim. He lived very well in Kentucky, announcing that he had discovered a silver deposit there worth $9,000,000. He bought 500 acres of rich farm land, and put up the first store in Elizabethtown, which had plate-glass windows.

Success went to his head, however, and he overreached himself by going into the banking business. This brought him into conflict with another bank run by two partners. Although Kentucky was no longer purely a frontier state, some disputes were still settled with weapons. In a gunfight with the two rival bankers, Arnold wounded one of them in the arm, but the other came up behind him with a shotgun and put a fatal charge of buckshot into his back.[189]

As for Slack, there is no further record of him after the Great Diamond Hoax. He simply disappeared without a trace.

Chapter VIII

Frontier Ways of Life:
Soldier, Cowboy, Outlaw,
Sheepman, Buffalo Hunter

In the last quarter of the 19th century, an adventuresome young man could hold down different jobs on the frontier at different times. Let us conjure up one such young man and call him "Jed Simpson," a name which must have been common enough on the frontier.

Let us first imagine that Jed is much like the protagonist in *The Red Badge of Courage* (1885), Stephen Crane's classic novel about the Civil War:

> He had, of course, dreamed of battles all his life — of vague and bloody conflicts that had thrilled him with their sweep and fire. In visions he had seen himself in many struggles. He had imagined peoples secure in the shadow of his eagle-eyed prowess.... His busy mind had drawn for him large pictures extravagant in color, lurid with breathless deeds.[190]

Inspired by dreams of glory, Jed enlists in the U.S. Army and is assigned as an infantryman to a remote post in the West — at Fort Bridger, perhaps. After six months of garrison duty, Jed finds that barracks life is far from exciting: indeed, it is unbearably monotonous. So he deserts and makes his way to Cheyenne, Wyoming, where he gets a job as a cowboy, driving cattle north toward Fort Laramie.[191]

Once the cattle are delivered to the buyers at Fort Laramie, Jed and his fellow cowboys are paid off and go out on a night-long spree in the local bars and whorehouses. The next day, however, he is hung over, broke and without a job. He lets one of the other cowboys talk him into what sounds like a promising line of work — rustling cattle, stealing horses and holding up stagecoaches or trains.

But after a few months as an outlaw, Jed sees that the risks are too great for the evanescent profits involved. (If they stayed in their trade, most outlaws ended up getting killed in gunfights, dangling from the end of a rope or languishing in jail.) So Jed goes back to the world of legitimate work. Because some

"In Without Knocking" (Charles M. Russell, oil on canvas, 1909, Amon Carter Museum, Fort Worth, accession no. 1961.201). This shows the cowboy's famous "spree at the end of the trail."

ranchers in Wyoming and elsewhere on the frontier raise sheep in addition to cattle, alternating between sheep and cattle in response to changing market conditions, Jed is able to find a job as a sheepman.

Always restless, it is not long before he gets bored taking care of these "wooly locusts," which is what the 19th century naturalist John Muir called sheep because of the damage they did to the open range. So, with the last of his meager savings, Jed invests in a second-hand rifle, some tools to reload ammunition, two skinning knives and a horse. These are all he needs to become a professional buffalo hunter on the plains of eastern Wyoming.

The most important item is the rifle. Jed chooses a "Big Fifty." It's a powerful, accurate .50 caliber Sharps rifle which

fires a cartridge 2½ inches long, loaded with 100 grains of black powder and a 473-grain lead bullet. With a Big Fifty, a hunter can kill buffalo at up to 600 yards. The dead beasts are skinned and their dried hides shipped east by the trainload to be turned into winter coats for city dwellers and into leather drive-belts to power factory machines. The carcasses of the buffalo are left to rot. Later on, the sun-dried bones are collected, shipped east and ground into fertilizer.

With this mythical example of Jed Simpson in mind, we can now look at five quintessentially western occupations which for one reason or another might have attracted an energetic, carefree young man on the frontier. Listed in the order discussed below, these jobs are: soldier, cowboy, outlaw, sheepman and buffalo hunter.

Soldier

At 2.5 million square miles, the trans–Mississippi West was so huge that it could be garrisoned only lightly. In 1874, the U.S. Army's Military Division of the Missouri, which included most of the Great Plains and the Rockies, embraced more than one million square miles of land and contained 99 different Indian tribes totaling about 192,000 people. According to General Philip Sheridan, the military resources available to the U.S. Army to protect the emigrants from the Indians (and sometimes to protect the Indians from the emigrants) were stretched very thin. In all the Military Division of the Missouri, there were only 76 posts or camps, many of them, like Fort Bridger, quite small, and a total of only 17,819 officers and men.[192]

THE FOOT SOLDIER ON THE FRONTIER

Thanks to films and television, the cavalry has become in the public eye the sole important military force in the West. This is rather unfair because although the infantryman lacked the glamour of the cavalryman, he, too, played a vital role in opening up the West. Marching from 15 to up to 40 miles per day, infantrymen could outlast the cavalry's horses on long campaigns. One proof of their effectiveness was that the Indians considered a foot soldier to be a more dangerous adversary than a cavalryman. The reason was that Indians on horseback often were, man for man, more than a match for the cavalry. So the Indians preferred to fight the cavalry rather than charge against the disciplined volleys of the "steady foot" fighting from an entrenched position.

An enlisted man on the frontier was usually badly paid, badly fed, badly housed, badly dressed and sometimes badly led. Only his weapons were first rate. In the last quarter of the 19th century these included the six-shot .45 caliber Colt Single Action Army revolver (see Chapter IX) and a heavy, nearly indestructible single-shot rifle — the .45–70 caliber "trapdoor" Springfield, so named because of the way its action (firing mechanism) opened.[193] The U.S. Army was aware of the much greater firepower offered by the repeating rifles which became available after 1866 (a lever action Winchester rifle held up to 15 shots). But it decided that in comparison with its time-proven Springfields, the new lever action rifles were not suitable for military use because they were weaker, less powerful, more prone to jam under muddy conditions, slower to reload and inaccurate beyond 200 yards.[194]

THE ARMY AT FORT BRIDGER

Infantrymen made up the bulk of the forces at Fort Bridger but occasionally a cavalry unit was stationed there, too. In 1873, for example, the garrison at Fort Bridger was commanded by Lt. Col. Albert G. Brackett of the Second Cavalry and consisted of part of the Second Cavalry and part of the Thirteenth Infantry.[195] Cavalrymen were assigned to escort and scouting duties where rapid mobility was necessary.

Whatever their branch of service, soldiers at isolated posts such as Fort Bridger did not have an easy time of it. Virtually all the newly arrived people on the frontier — the miners, ranchers, farmers, town dwellers, stagecoach drivers and railroad workers — expected the Army to protect them from the wrath of the

Plains Indians, whose way of life was being destroyed by the white invasion.

This was a thankless task. With the coming of the railroads, soldiers might be able to take trains to get part of the way to a theater of operations, but most of their journeys still had to be made in all weathers just as they always had: for the infantryman, on foot, carrying a heavy rifle and a heavier pack; for the cavalryman, mounted on a horse which required food, care and attention. When pursued by the Army, whether infantry or cavalry, the Indians usually scattered rather than standing and fighting. This meant that military expeditions sometimes went on for weeks altogether and ranged over hundreds of miles. When the soldiers finally returned to their forts, often without having accomplished a great deal in the field, they were exhausted and had long hair, shaggy beards and ripped clothing.

Once back at camp, the deadening monotony of garrison duty (standing guard, close-order drill, inspections, training, cleaning the barracks and latrines, washing clothes, cooking and cleaning up, being bellowed at by the sergeants and ignored by the officers) was broken only rarely. Near Fort Bridger, the infantry sometimes built wagon roads and telegraph lines, escorted wagon trains bringing in supplies, accompanied geological explorations and helped keep order in Wyoming towns. We may assume they welcomed such diversions. Otherwise, their life was uneventful.

The one exciting event for foot soldiers at Fort Bridger seems to have been the Bear River Riot. This occurred in November 1868, when fighting broke out in Evanston, Wyoming, about 30 miles east of Fort Bridger, between two groups with conflicting interests.

The first group consisted of Union Pacific railway workers, who wanted to have a good time after the day's work was done and who did not want to be robbed or cheated in the process. The second group included the criminals, gamblers and, we may guess, the "soiled doves" (prostitutes) who preyed upon the railwaymen. It is unclear what specific event caused the riot but the disturbances threatened to become so serious that soldiers from Fort Bridger had to be called in to restore order. Alas for their dreams of glory: by the time the infantrymen had marched the 30 miles to Evanston, the Union Pacific workers had won the battle and the town was quiet once more.

Cowboy

CATTLE ON THE NORTHERN RANGE

Accounts of cowboy life traditionally focus on the men who drove Longhorns from Texas to the railheads of the Great Plains for onward shipment to the slaughterhouses and meat-packing plants of Chicago. However, there was also a thriving cattle business in the vast sweep of the frontier far to the north of Texas. This region was known as the northern range and included northern Colorado, Wyoming, Montana and the Dakotas.

In addition to his other achievements, Jim Bridger was also the founder of the northern range cattle industry in southwestern Wyoming and northwestern Colorado.[196] In the 1840s he pioneered what came to be called "road ranching." This was a small-scale but profitable calling. By the time Westering emigrants finally reached Fort Bridger, their oxen were worn out, gaunt and sore-footed from the long trek across the dry, flinty plains. Bridger saw a good business opportunity here: he would trade one of his fresh oxen for two or even three of the exhausted animals pulling the covered wagons. These tired beasts he turned out to graze on the luxuriant grass of the river bottoms near the fort. In two or three weeks' time, they had regained their strength and Bridger traded them off to other emigrants at the same favorable exchange rate. Perhaps taking his cue from Bridger, further west along the Oregon Trail another former mountain man, Richard Grant, also ran a road ranching business out of Fort Hall, Idaho.

The first man to build up a large herd of cattle in the Fort Bridger area, though, was William A. Carter, the post sutler. In 1868 the Union Pacific railroad tracks were being laid not far from Fort Bridger and the Irish laborers craved beef. To cater to this market, Carter stocked the range with Texas Longhorns. These were the descendants of the cattle brought from Spain to Mexico in the early 16th century. They multiplied rapidly and spread throughout the Southwest. Longhorns had a number of bad points. They were half-wild, evil-tempered, dangerous, with sharp horns five feet long, tip to tip, and not very good to eat because their flesh was dry and muscular. They had only one saving grace: they were so hardy that they could survive on the dry grass of the Great Plains, even during the winter.

Carter and other northern ranchers soon saw the need for better cattle. During the 1870s they imported Shorthorns from Canada and Britain, as well as Aberdeen Angus from Scotland. The great success story, however, was the Here-

ford. Brought from England in the early 1880s, they were manageable and excelled at turning grass into prime-quality beef. They eventually replaced the Longhorns in Wyoming and Montana.

Moreover, thanks to Carter, Fort Bridger itself became, albeit in a very modest way, an island of culture in the Rocky Mountain wilderness. A neighboring rancher, Jesse S. Hoy, whose life is described below, recorded in the mid–1870s that

> We spent the night at Fort Bridger as guests of W.A. Carter, a tall, white-bearded old gentleman. The house he occupied was built of hewn pine logs, plain on the outside but well furnished within. His principal room contained a library of a considerable number of books — must have contained a couple of hundred volumes — the first of the kind I have ever seen. The floor was carpeted and adorned with rugs of the skins of wild animals native to the mountains. Mr. Carter's general appearance denoted the scholar and the thinker, a rare specimen of his kind seen on the frontier.[197]

More and more cattlemen came to the northern range. Elijah Driscoll, who in 1863 had been posted to Fort Bridger as a member of the California Volunteers during the Civil War, set up two trading posts for road ranching, first on Ham's Fork (30 miles northeast of Fort Bridger) and later at Henry's Fork (25 miles southwest of the fort). Driscoll prospered to such an extent that by the mid–1880s he was shipping trainloads of cattle to eastern markets. After the modest beginnings made by Jim Bridger, the Sweetwater region, which takes its name from the Sweetwater River rising near South Pass and flowing east, soon became a major grazing ground and supported more than 500,000 head of cattle.

BROWN'S HOLE

Cattlemen were also attracted to Brown's Hole (also known as Brown's Park), a narrow valley straddling the Utah-Colorado border, located about 80 miles southeast of Fort Bridger. This valley had been a minor rendezvous point for mountain men and for the Indians (Shoshonis, Utes and even a few Navaho from the southwest) who went there to sell their beaver pelts or barter them for other items. William Thomas Hamilton, a mountain man who knew the Indian sign language so well that he was called "Master of the Signs," was charmed by the colorful scenes at the rendezvous:

> Take it all in all, it was just such a crowd as would delight the student were he studying the characteristics of the mountaineer and the Indian. The days were given to horse-racing, foot-racing, shooting-matches; and in the evening were heard the music of voice and drum and the sound of dancing.[198]

In 1849, a band of Cherokee Indians, who were en route to the California goldfields, pioneered a track known as the Cherokee Trail. This began in northeastern Oklahoma and crossed Kansas, Colorado and southern Wyoming before finally joining up with the Oregon Trail at Fort Bridger. In the process of blazing this new trail, the Indians discovered that their cattle could survive the winter in Brown's Hole because it had plenty of dry grass and not much snow. They wintered their stock there and then moved on to California. Brown's Hole subsequently remained unused until 1871, when George Baggs, a rancher from southern New Mexico, was trailing (driving) a herd of 900 steers to the northern range when he was stopped by exceptionally bitter weather. Baggs wintered his cattle in Brown's Hole and, despite a high mortality rate that season among herds in other parts of the West, he did not lose a single animal.

JESSE HOY

Baggs sold his herd to two men, Crawford and Thompson, who had set up a ranch near Evanston, Wyoming. But the winters there were so severe that Crawford and Thompson hired Jesse S. Hoy and some other cowboys to drive their cattle the 100 miles back to Brown's Hole every year. It thus became a permanent winter range.

Hoy's own experiences are of interest here because they are well-documented and show him to have had a "Jed Simpson" approach to frontier life. Like many another young man, Hoy had come to the West in search of adventure. He had been born into a wealthy family at Hoy's Gap, Pennsylvania, in 1847 and could have led a comfortable, sedate, middle class life in the East had he chosen to. At the age of 17, though, he took a job as a bullwhacker on an ox train going from the Missouri River to the Rockies. Then, in 1865, he drove horses pulling freight to Denver and later became a bullwhacker again.

His next job was working a sawmill but he soon tired of this and at the age of 20 he became a professional hunter, supplying the Denver market with antelope he killed on the plains east of the city. By the fall of 1867 Hoy was working in Cheyenne, Wyoming, where he became friendly with Jack Watkins, a hunter for the Overland Stage line. Watkins was also a gunfighter and Hoy has left us a vivid account of this man:

> Uneasy lies the head that wears a crown.... Jack was a fighting man

without being a bully. Owing to his superiority ... he attracted the attention of men generally, and was an object of jealousy, fear, admiration, or hate.... He slept with his right arm above his head with a six-shooter in his hand. So lightly did he sleep, that a rat running across the room brought him to a sitting position with the gun automatically leveled in the direction of the noise. When in a saloon ... he usually stood with his back to the wall, ready for [police] officers or town toughs, who all envied his attainments....

Hoy later bought three span of oxen and a wagon and began to haul railroad ties in southern Wyoming for the Union Pacific. His parents back at Hoy's Gap seem to have been very generous because at some point between 1869 and 1872 he was able to make the Grand Tour of Europe, which was mandatory for young men from prosperous eastern families. By the summer of 1872, however, Hoy was back in Wyoming, where he was hired by Crawford and Thompson to drive their herd of cattle from Evanston back to Brown's Hole. Despite his family connections in the east and his European travels, he was to stay in the Brown's Hole area for the next 50 years, first as a cowboy and then as a ranch owner.

THE COWBOY WAY OF LIFE

As Brown's Hole was coming into prominence, a Massachusetts man named Clay bought the Swan Land and Cattle Company's extensive holdings in southwestern Wyoming and set up several ranches near Fort Bridger itself. Clay's brand became well known because of the thousands of cattle he branded with it and then turned loose on the open range.

Cowboys used a jargon all of their own to describe cattle brands. Clay's brand looked very much like this: VD. But probably to make it more difficult for rustlers to alter it, these two letters were joined at the top. Thus Clay's brand was known as the Vee Dee Connected or the Flying Vee Dee. If a brand contained a numeral or a letter which was lying on its side, this number or letter was referred to as being "lazy." Thus the numeral 2, lying on its side, was read as "lazy 2." One famous brand was 2 lazy 2 P.

Thanks to Clay and to the many other ranchers on the northern range, between 1870 and 1880 there was a huge increase in the number of cattle in Wyoming (from 11,130 to 521,213 animals) and a sizable increase in Colorado (from 70,736 to 791,459).[199] This required a corresponding increase in the number of cowboys on the range.

Despite his glorification in books, films and television, the average cowboy was only a poorly educated young man doing a dead-end job which was inherently seasonal, difficult, monotonous, often dangerous and always badly paid. He was usually improvident as well, sometimes losing hundreds of dollars in a single night by trying, while half-drunk, to beat the marked cards, stacked decks and loaded dice of a professional gambler. Condemned to perpetual bachelorhood because he was dirt-poor, he lived in bunkhouses, changed jobs frequently and had few prospects in life. The only feminine companionship he could look forward to was an occasional fling with a soiled dove.

Any money the cowboy did not drink or gamble away was likely to go on luxuries — a saddle for $85, a Stetson hat costing a lot, or fancy cowboy boots with decorative stitching the same. A few of the more intelligent, ambitious and self-disciplined cowboys dreamed about having a ranch of their own, but it was almost impossible for them to amass enough capital to achieve this goal. The pay per month for a cowboy included food and bunkhouse lodging and ranged from a low of $20 in Texas in 1872 to a high of $75 in Wyoming in 1880–83, Pay for a foreman ranged on average from $50 to $90 per month in the 1880s, and rose to $150 per month in Texas in 1890.[200]

Moreover, since the most labor-intensive activities involving cattle began with the spring roundup and ended with the fall roundup, cowboys were usually out of work during the long winter months and had great trouble making ends meet. In 1885 the magazine *Kansas Cowboy* estimated that on the northern range, cowboys found work for only three or four months a year. To survive when unemployed, they split wood, "rode the grub line" (got free handouts at different ranches), hunted wild game, or dined on "slow elk" (range cattle). Saving any money in these circumstances was out of the question.

As described by Joseph G. McCoy in 1874, who was a cattleman himself and a first-hand observer of the men working for him, the average cowboy was a simple, uncomplicated soul with no upward aspirations:

> He lives hard, works hard, has but few comforts and fewer necessities. He has but little, if any taste for reading. He enjoys a coarse practical joke or a smutty story; loves danger but abhors labor of the common kind; never tires of riding, never wants to walk, no matter how short the distance he desires to go. He would rather fight with pistols than pray; loves tobacco, liquor and women better than any other trinity. His life nearly borders upon that of an Indian. If he reads anything, it is in

A famous cattle brand: 2 lazy 2 P

> most cases a blood and thunder story of a sensational style. He enjoys his pipe [when in the saddle, cowboys usually smoked hand-rolled cigarettes], and relishes a practical joke on his comrades, or a corrupt tale, wherein abounds much vulgarity and animal propensity.[201]

The career prospects for a cowboy were not very bright. Some men rose to become foremen; a handful of others managed to fight, work or steal their way into becoming the owners of big spreads. Perhaps the best example of the cowboy-turned-cattle baron was Charles Goodnight, who by 1873 was one of the richest cattlemen in the West, earning about $500,000 a year by selling 30,000 animals from his herd of more than 100,000 cattle.[202] But the fate of the average cowboy who stayed on indefinitely in this line of work was to be "stove up" — that, is, to be incapacitated by an accident or by illness. If this happened, he would either have to take a more sedentary job, such as camp cook, or would have to fall back on the charity of ranch owners because he had no wife or children to take care of him.

Ironically, despite the media blitz which surrounded them even during their heyday in the 19th century, there were never very many cowboys. One estimate is that no more than 35,000 men drove cattle north or rode the open range.[203] The basic reason for this low figure was that the cattle boom on the Great Plains had a very short life-span. It only lasted about 20 years. The cattle kingdom only began after 1866, when cattle trails to Missouri were closed because of Texas cattle fever. This forced Texas herders to find other markets for their beef by driving the cows north to the railheads. The cattle boom finished about 1886–87, when the long drives came to an end. The invention of barbed wire sounded their death knell, as did the terrible, cattle-killing winter of 1886–87, the appearance of railheads in Texas itself, and the overstocking of the northern range, which depressed beef prices.

CATTLE DRIVES AND ROUNDUPS

Americans may think that they invented the cowboy but in point of fact the earliest cowboys were probably the Scottish cattle drovers — "great stalwart hirsute men, shaggy, uncultured and wild," according to a contemporary observer — who were driving Highland cattle to lowland markets in Scotland as early as the year 1359.[204] For their part, however, the 19th century cowboys of the United States drove wilder cattle over longer distances over a larger lacework of trails.

After the Civil War, in 1866, Texas cattlemen reopened the Shawnee Trail running north from Brownsville to railheads at Kansas City, Sedalia and St. Louis. As the cattle business boomed, other trails began to snake north. The most important of these was the Chisholm Trail, which gathered cattle from Texas ranches and delivered them to Kansas cow-towns such as Dodge City, Ellsworth and Abilene. The Western Trail went from Texas through Dodge City and thence to Ogallala, Nebraska, where it forked into two routes. The western route ran through Cheyenne

and Fort Laramie in Wyoming, terminating at Miles City, Montana. The northern route ended at Fort Buford, near the junction of the Yellowstone and Missouri Rivers in North Dakota.

The Goodnight-Loving Trail also made its way north from central Texas, first by running along the Pecos River and then by skirting the eastern flank of the Rocky Mountains. This trail, laid out in 1866 to supply the mining camps and military bases of Colorado, was later used to stock the northern range. It went through Pueblo and Denver in Colorado before ending at Cheyenne. Cattle from the northern range were used to feed the Union Pacific's tracklaying crews.

One rancher, John Wesley Iliff, followed these crews into Wyoming, setting up a string of small ranches along the way. The demand for beef was so great that some years Iliff bought as many as 15,000 Longhorns which had plodded north along the Goodnight-Loving Trail. Remarkably, thanks to the size and fecundity of Texas cattle spreads, there was never a shortage of Longhorns there. In 1880, for example, despite the fact that 5,000,000 animals had been exported from Texas in the previous 15 years, there were still 6,000,000 left in the Lone Star State.

The spring and autumn roundups were the most active and most dramatic part of cowboy life. A roundup held in Wyoming in May 1880 involved 150 cowboys and 1,200 work horses from 18 different ranches. Organized with an almost military precision to sweep together not only the cattle which were scattered in plain sight across the open prairies, but also to ferret out all those hidden in ravines and thickets, this complex operation gathered 5,000 to 6,000 cattle on the first day alone.[205]

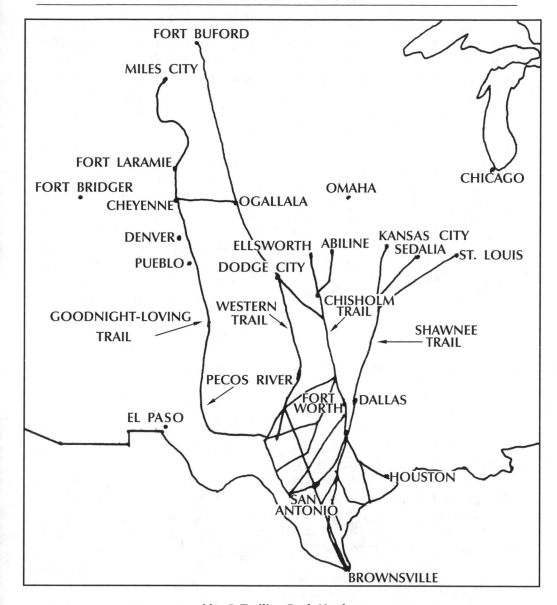

Map 5: Trailing Cattle North

Once assembled on the northern range, the milling herds of cattle had to be kept under control by cowboys riding around them, day and night. There was a great deal of work to be done. The stock belonging to different ranches had to be "cut out" (separated). The new crop of calves had to be branded and, if males, castrated. Some animals needed dehorning or medical treatment. On big ranches, the spring roundup could take as much as three months. A smaller-scale roundup usually took place in the fall, when late calves were collected, spring calves were separated from their mothers for weaning and full-grown steers were taken off the range for shipment to slaughterhouses.

Despite the labor and dangers involved in them, however, cowboys genuinely enjoyed the roundups, probably because it gave them a chance to use the full range of their riding and roping skills. The wife of one rancher described the hurly-burly of a roundup on the northern range:

> The cowboy's life was a strenuous one while on the round-up; nothing but eat, sleep and ride, ride, ride from start to finish; but through it all he was the most happy-go-lucky individual living, always joking or "swapping yarns" or "kidding" someone who had a "bad actor" [a difficult horse] to "wrangle" with [to saddle] in the chilly morning.[206]

THE SPREE AT THE END OF THE TRAIL

The cowboy's desire for a good time after a roundup or a cattle drive sometimes had tragic consequences. One Friday in June 1880, for instance, four Texas cowboys heading for a ranch in the San Juan Mountains of Colorado stopped for the night near the town of Cimarron in northeastern New Mexico.[207] After setting up camp, they rode into town. A contemporary newspaper reported that,

> After a few glasses of Taos lightning [a potent liquor] were had the inevitable pistol was pulled from belt and a firing at lamps, mirror, etc. begun. When fully satisfied with firing at bar-room ornaments the gang betook themselves to a disreputable house, where the desperadoes continued their orgies until a late hour, when they mounted their ponies and rode off to their camp.

The next morning some of the law-abiding citizens of Cimarron complained to Sheriff Burleson, who organized a posse (a group of armed men) to arrest the cowboys at their camp. Hoping to capture the Texans without a fight, the Sheriff ordered his men to sneak up on the camp. But as they approached it Deputy Sheriff Bowman saw one of the cowboys lying down and aiming a Winchester carbine at them. Before Bowman could give any warning to his colleagues, the cowboy opened fire and killed one of the members of the posse, a man named Bragg. Bowman then leveled his own shotgun and killed the cowboy who had shot Bragg. The rest of the posse opened fire, and "so effectual was their aim that all the men were slain. Sheriff Burleson received a serious but not dangerous wound in the arm." The newspaper article ended with the laconic comment, "The names of the Texans killed are not known."

Open Range Ranching Comes to an End

The early pioneers found that the Great Plains were a dry land without wood or rock, the two natural resources which were essential for building the split-rail fences or stone walls which protected farms in the well-watered, settled parts of the United States. Indeed, it was this very lack of fencing which made possible the long drives, the great cattle kingdoms of the 1870s and 1880s and, in short, the whole cowboy way of life. Romantic as these enterprises may have been, what the new wave of homesteaders (farmers) wanted was something very different — a cheap but effective way to keep all those free-ranging cattle from destroying their crops.

The answer to their prayer was

barbed wire, invented in 1874 by Joseph E. Glidden and marketed the next year. Coupled with the spread of railroads across the West, barbed wire ended open range ranching for good. In a conversation in 1941 between two old-time ranchers in Alberta, Canada, one of them blamed "those pesky sheep" for the closure of the range. But his colleague demurred:

> Oh, I wouldn't say sheep were so bad. I'd say barbed wire was what ruined the country. At first we could keep it cut pretty well, and use the posts for firewood, but it got so, after a while, they were putting up the d_____ stuff faster than a guy could cut it down. Every homesteader had his little bit fenced off.... The Cochrane ranch had three strands running for 25 miles, and fence riders ["pliers men" who repaired any breaks in the barbed wire] straddling it all day. When I saw that I said to myself, I says, "This country's done for" — and you see now I was right.[208]

Trying to protect their cattle kingdoms, which were based not on acreage which they owned themselves but on the unrestricted and free use of public land, big ranchers used miles of barbed wire to enclose "their" land illegally. One cattle company in Colorado was instrumental in throwing barbed wire around more than one million acres of the public domain. Abuses were so flagrant that one Western newspaper, the *Wyoming Sentinel*, complained that, "Some morning we will wake up to find that a corporation has run a wire fence about the boundary lines of Wyoming, and all within the same have been notified to move." Finally, the Federal Government had to step in to end this seizure of the public land.

Even the weather seemed to ally itself with the opponents of the open range. In a snowstorm, cattle tend to drift with the wind until they run up against a natural barrier — or a barbed wire fence. There they stand until they freeze to death. The winter of 1885–86 killed many cattle and the following winter was even more deadly on the northern range, with 250,000 cattle perishing in Wyoming alone and about 190,000 more in Montana.[209]

The result of wire and weather was that cowboys had to learn new skills, which were not only tedious and tiring — such as raising, cutting and stacking hay — but which had to be done on foot rather than on horseback. Thus, more and more, the free-spirited cowboy of the open range came to resemble, in his daily work if not in his attitudes, the less colorful farmers, ranch workers, sheepmen and homesteaders who poured into the West during the 1880s and 1890s. Many contemporary observers bemoaned these changing times. Remembering his own happy years as a rancher in the Dakota Territory, President Theodore Roosevelt wrote that the closure of the open range had brought to an end what was "perhaps the pleasantest, healthiest, and most exciting phase of American existence."[210]

Outlaw

It was not uncommon for cowboys to become outlaws, because the lure of illicit gains from rustling cattle, stealing horses, or holding up stagecoaches and trains was difficult to resist. To illustrate this, it is instructive to look at the short but archetypal life of the Texas outlaw

Sam Bass. Even though he was not a particularly successful criminal and is quite forgotten today, he was one of the few outlaws to have had a ballad written about him (see Appendix V).[211]

SAM BASS

There is no known relationship between Bass and Fort Bridger itself. But his story is relevant here because in the northern Rockies there must have been many like him who turned to crime but whose exploits are not recorded.

Sam Bass was born in Indiana in 1851. At the age of 17 he headed west to Denton, Texas, about 60 miles northwest of Dallas. Functionally illiterate (he could only sign his name and decipher a few numerals), he eked out a modest existence there as a sawmill worker, teamster and cowboy. He may also have worked in some minor capacity for the sheriff of Denton County, "Dad" Egan. In his spare time, Bass also "rolled" drunk Mexicans, rustled cattle and raced a fast quarter horse known as the Denton Mare. (A quarter horse, named for the sport of quarter-mile racing, was the ideal mount for a cowboy because of its speed, endurance and agility.)

According to a Fugitive List, there was nothing prepossessing about Bass's appearance: "five feet seven inches high; black hair; dark-brown eyes; brown mustache; large white teeth; shows them when talking; has very little to say." Bass soon teamed up with Joel Collins, who had been at various times a trail driver, a cattle dealer and a petty crook. Collins hired Bass and a couple of other cowboys to help him drive a herd of Texas cattle north to Kansas.

As soon as the cattle were sold there, Collins pocketed the money he should have given to the owners and blew most of it in a spree in Deadwood, South Dakota. He was broke again. In September 1877, near Ogallala, Nebraska, Collins, together with Bass and four other men, held up the Union Pacific train running from San Francisco to Omaha. The outlaws soon discovered that the train was carrying $200,000 but that the money was locked in a "through-safe" which could not be opened en route. They also found a box of silver bricks but these were too heavy to handle.

Finally, however, the men hit the jackpot — six small wooden boxes each containing $10,000 in gold coins. After stealing an additional $400 and assorted jewelry from the passengers, Collins, Bass and the others rode off with their loot. They buried the gold coins in the sandy banks of the South Platte River, and spent the next few days in the flesh-pots of Ogallala. They then went back to the South Platte, retrieved the coins and decided to split up so that the police would have a harder time pursuing them.

Four of the men (Collins, Heffridge, Bass and Davis) went back to Texas; the two others (Berry and Nixon) went to Missouri, where Berry was later shot and killed by the authorities. In the meantime, a former employee of the express company (possibly Wells Fargo) which had sent the gold by train had seen the outlaws dig up the coins and had alerted law enforcement officers. Thanks to the telegraph, the sheriffs and soldiers of Nebraska and Kansas were soon on the alert. Collins and Heffridge were cornered at Buffalo Station, Kansas, on 26 September 1877. They shot it out with a sheriff and a group of soldiers and were killed.

The Sam Bass gang (Western History Collections, University of Oklahoma Library). *Standing left to right:* Sam Bass and J.E. Gardner. *Seated left to right:* Joe and Joel Collins. Joel is holding a Colt Single Action Army revolver, which is probably a studio prop.

Bass and Davis, for their part, slowly drove back to Texas in a buggy. At one point they ran into a squad of soldiers who were hunting for them but the outlaws kept their nerve and pretended to be two flat-broke farmers leaving Kansas to look for jobs elsewhere. The soldiers, satisfied with this story, let Bass and Davis camp near them that night and even loaned them a frying pan and coffee pot.

The two men reached Texas in November 1877 without further incident. Davis fled to Latin America and Bass organized his own gang in Texas. Financially, though, the Sam Bass gang was not a great success. Between 20 December 1877 and 15 April 1878 Bass and his accomplices held up a total of two stagecoaches and four trains in Texas. Their total take was $1,961. Since Bass shared the proceeds equally with his men, his own share for four months of dangerous work came to only $514.

Soon his troubles were not merely financial. Texas Rangers, sheriffs, U.S. Marshals, express company detectives and posses of irate citizens were all looking for him. The Rangers captured one of the gang, a man named Murphy, and persuaded him to rejoin Bass and betray him. Bass and the other outlaws had decided to escape to Mexico but en route they stopped off at Round Rock, Texas, to hold up a bank there. Murphy had previously managed to alert the Rangers to this plan. When Bass and his men went into a store in Round Rock to buy tobacco, the local sheriff noticed that one of them was carrying a pistol in town, which was against the law. The sheriff, for some reason not realizing he was face to face with the Sam Bass gang, tried to disarm them. They drew their pistols, opened fire and killed him.

Bass and his partners in crime ran out of the store and into the street. Texas Ranger Dick Ware was in Round Rock's barbershop and heard the shots. He, too, ran out into the street. Bass saw Ware and fired at him. The shot missed, but not by very much: the bullet hit a doorpost one inch from the Ranger's head. Ware opened fire himself. He killed one of the other outlaws outright, and shot Bass through the body, wounding him

mortally. An autopsy showed that Ware's .45 caliber bullet had cut through two of the cartridges on Bass' gunbelt and lodged in his right kidney. Although dying, Bass managed to escape on horseback. He was still alive when the authorities captured him, but died the following day 21 July 1878. It was his 27th birthday.

THE JOHNSON COUNTY WAR

Cattle rustling became such a problem in northern Wyoming's Johnson County that in 1892 some of the big ranchers, who were prominent members of the Wyoming Stock Growers Association, organized an expedition to surprise and kill more than 20 known or suspected rustlers. This incident is known as the Johnson County War.

The cattlemen mustered a group of 55 mounted men referred to as the Invaders. This force included 22 hired gunmen from Texas, each of whom was armed with a rifle and a revolver. The Invaders set out on horseback from Casper, Wyoming, to hunt down the alleged rustlers but succeeded in killing only two of them before they themselves were surrounded by a posse organized by the sheriff of Johnson County. To prevent any more killings, President Benjamin Harrison, who had been awakened by a telegram in the middle of the night asking him to send troops to quell an "insurrection," ordered the U.S. Army to intervene. The Army took such quick action that within hours the Invaders were forced to surrender to Colonel J.J. Van Horn's cavalry detachment.[212]

The most succinct comment on this sordid affair was made by a Wyoming editor, who wrote that, "Of all the fool things the stock association ever did, this takes the cake." The cattle barons of the Wyoming Stock Growers Association, however, proved to be so well connected politically that in the end the Johnson County authorities had to drop all charges against them and their Texas mercenaries.[213] These hired guns drifted either back to Paris, Texas, where they had been recruited or moved on to other frontier towns in the West. At least one of them came to a bad end directly as a result of the Johnson County War. This was the Texas Kid, who had fired the opening shot in the war. When he got back to Texas, he quarreled with his girlfriend, who hated what he had done in Wyoming. She refused to marry him, so he shot her to death. Just before he was hanged, the Kid said sadly, "I wish I had never gone to Wyoming at all."[214]

TOM HORN

The most famous outlaw on the northern range was Tom Horn. He had been a cowboy, a U.S. Army scout in the campaigns against the Apache Indians, a deputy sheriff in Colorado and a gunman for the Pinkerton Detective Agency. Then he came to Wyoming in 1894 as a stock detective. In this latter capacity he hunted down rustlers and shot them, usually earning $500 per kill from the local ranchers. He once boasted: "Killing men is my specialty. I look at it as a business proposition, and think I have cornered the market." He was an excellent shot, capable of killing a man at 300 yards when using a .30-30 Winchester carbine, which is not very accurate at this range.

Horn made two fundamental mistakes in 1901. First, he allegedly shot and killed from ambush the 14-year-old son of a sheepman, probably mistaking the boy for his father in the dim light of dawn. Second, a deputy U.S. Marshal got Horn drunk and encouraged him to boast about this deed — while a hidden stenographer took down an account of what he said.

Arrested on the basis of his own "confession," Horn claimed that he had only been bragging and that the stenographer's account was inaccurate. Nevertheless, he was convicted of murder and hanged in Cheyenne in 1903. An interesting footnote to this story is that in 1990 a mock retrial was held in Cheyenne, during which evidence — which had not been allowed at the first trial — was admitted. According to the latter-day verdict, Horn was not guilty.[215]

Sheepman

SHEEP NEAR FORT BRIDGER

The Laramie Plains of southeastern Wyoming were considered to be the best region in the state for sheep, but some raising was done in the southwestern corner, too. Jim Bridger was the first to try this line of work, bringing a few sheep and goats from New Mexico to Fort Bridger in 1846–47. In 1848, small bands of sheep were being driven through Wyoming to Utah and Oregon; in the early 1850s the big drives to gold rush California began. William A. Carter, the sutler at Fort Bridger, had a flock of his own in 1859. And by 1872, John "Sheep" Smith and his Indian wife had settled about 60 miles north of Fort Bridger with a band of 500 sheep.

Sheep turned out to be so well suited to southwestern Wyoming that by 1884 there were more sheep there than cattle. This trend picked up speed after so many cows died during the terrible winter of 1886–87. In Wyoming as a whole, in the decade after 1886 the number of cattle fell from 900,000 to 300,000, while the number of sheep rose from 875,000 to 3.3 million.[216] In the late 1890s the Wyoming town of Cokeville, located near the Idaho border on vast grazable prairies, was billing itself as the "Sheep Capital of the World." Given its wealth from sheep and the fact there were not many people living there, Cokeville actually had more millionaires per capita than any other town in the United States.

Disputes between cattlemen and sheepmen were inevitable, both for legal reasons and because of the different ways in which cattle and sheep used the range. Toward the end of the 19th century and in the early years of the 20th, these disputes sometimes erupted into violence.

CATTLEMEN VS. SHEEPMEN: MIGHT VS. RIGHT

The grounds of the legal conflict between cattlemen and sheepmen, between ranchers and "sodbusters" (farmers), can be summed up in one sentence: first in might is first in right. After the Civil War, as the Plains Indians were slowly brought under control and as the great herds of buffalo were gradually killed off, the nutritious grass and clear water of the high plains west of the Missouri River went increasingly unused. These valuable assets were free for the taking by the man — usually the cattleman — who got his livestock there first.

It was not a criminal act for an emigrant to drive a herd of cattle into some unoccupied valley in Wyoming or elsewhere on the frontier and to claim "range rights" to all the land for miles around, even if under the Homestead Act he could hold legal title only to a tiny part of this domain. (The Homestead Act of 1862 had given each man the right to 160 acres of public land. While this was enough for a farm in the well-watered East, much bigger holdings were necessary in the West because it took at least ten acres of scrubland there to support one cow.)

As a practical matter, if a cattleman got to an ungrazed valley first, and was ready to use force to defend "his" property, he could claim what were euphemistically called "possessory rights." But since these had no basis in law, violent quarrels between ranchers and sodbusters, usually over access to water, were likely to break out if a farmer strung barbed wire around his land to keep out the rancher's thirsty, free-roaming cattle.

Bad feelings were likely, too, over the different ways in which cattle and sheep ate the grass. Because they crop the grass more closely than cattle, sheep, it was said, "took over the grass." This meant that when flocks of sheep were introduced into ranges well supplied with grass, they left very little for the cattle or horses which might come after them. When sheep were trailed from one range to another, they left only desolation in their wake: "nothing remained to be garnered by another grazier during the same season."[217] Finally, ranchers claimed that the hooves of sheep left such a strong odor on the range that cattle did not like to feed there after them.

The damage done by these "wooly locusts" was on one occasion put to use by local ranchers in northwestern Colorado. They wanted to keep Wyoming cattle out of Brown's Park, where they had their own stock, so they "fenced in" this lush region by surrounding it with herds of sheep. The Wyoming cattle refused to cross this living fence, because there was nothing to eat there and possibly because of the odor as well. The Wyoming cattle did not get into Brown's Park. Indeed, they ultimately died outside it when they ran out of grass to eat.[218]

THE CATTLE-SHEEP "WARS"

By the 1880s the northern range was getting crowded. There were more and more sheep but no more ungrazed valleys where a cattleman could assert possessory rights. From the Union Pacific railroad line running through southern Wyoming, flocks of sheep were trailed north into the central and northern parts of the state. Cowboys all over the West feared that a flood of sheep would destroy the open range and thus their own way of life. For their part, sheepmen insisted on maintaining their access to grass and water to which they were legally entitled, since these resources were essential for the survival of their flocks.

The first rumblings of violence were heard in the 1870s as cattlemen, sheepmen, homesteaders and rustlers all struggled to maintain their conflicting interests in the public lands. The cattle-sheep "wars" were most bitter in and around Wyoming. But in two separate incidents in Arizona in 1884, cowboys ran wild horses into flocks of sheep to scatter them, and they drove 4,000 sheep into quicksand where they soon perished.

In 1887, 2,600 sheep were burned to death in Wyoming. A gunman named "Diamondfield Jack" was accused of killing two young sheepmen in Idaho in 1896.[219] Wyoming ranchers were feeling so hemmed in that a Stockman's Protective Association was set up in the upper Shoshone Valley in central Wyoming in 1901 to defend cattlemen's interests. Three years later, Wyoming cowboys "rim-rocked" 500 sheep (i.e., drove them over a high cliff) near the Montana border. Later, in 1905, Wyoming cowboys killed 4,000 sheep in the Big Horn Valley in north-central Wyoming. Passions ran so high that the cattle-sheep wars in Wyoming did not finally come to an end until 1912.[220]

Buffalo Hunter

The Indians hunted buffalo simply in order to survive. The whites did not. The Sioux Chief White Cloud understood this very well. "Wherever the whites are established," he complained, "the buffalo is gone, and the red hunters must die of hunger."[221] The mountain men and the emigrants had hunted buffalo intermittently, partly for food and partly for sport. It was not until the 1870s, however, that another group of men turned buffalo hunting into a full-time, profitable business. Using .44 to .50 caliber rifles, they killed up to 150 buffalo per hunter per day.

One of these professional buffalo hunters, John R. Cook, has left us an account of his own experiences in 1874–78 in a remarkable book, *The Border and the Buffalo* (1907). As a young man, Cook teamed up with an experienced buffalo hunter named Buck Wood, who taught him how to skin the animals. Working as a skinner on the southern plains (in Texas and New Mexico), Cook earned 30 cents for skinning each buffalo and pegging out its hide on the ground to dry in the sun. Once dry, the hide was piled onto a wagon. The carcass itself was left to rot, except for the hump and tongue. The hunters fried the humps in tallow and proclaimed them to be "a feast fit for the gods"; the tongues, when boiled, were delicious, too.

On their first day out on the prairies, Cook and Wood saw a vast herd of buffalo which they estimated contained at least 5,000 and perhaps as many as 10,000 animals. Wood was carrying a Big Fifty with 32 cartridges in his belt and a dozen loose in his coat pocket. Cook had an old British Enfield rifle, two skinning knives and a sharpening steel. Another hunter, George Simpson, was with them. Wood rode forward toward the herd. And, as Cook remembered his first day as a buffalo hunter,

> I had not waited long before I heard that loud and boom-like report of the big fifty, that I was to hear more of less of for the next three years. Again I heard it; then about two miles west of where this report came from, pealed out the same deep roar and it came from George Simpson's gun.... Coming up to where Buck was, he informed me that he had killed sixteen buffaloes. I was thrilled with delight; whereas, in less than four months I looked upon such things as a matter of course.[222]

Because of their size, numbers and lack of natural predators, buffalo did not take alarm very easily; indeed, many hunters considered them downright stupid. The next day a herd of about 30 bulls passed within 100 feet of Cook's camp. He got out his Enfield, aimed at the best place to hit a buffalo with a side shot ("anywhere inside of a circle as large as a cowboy's hat, just back of the shoulderblade") and fired at one of the bulls. His aim was good: "in much less time than it takes to tell it, the pale, frothy blood blubbered out of his nostrils, he

made a few lurches and fell over — dead."[223]

Later on, Cook joined another group of hunters who killed 2,003 buffalo. Cook skinned 902 of them in 41 days, an average of 22 buffalo per day. At 25 cents per hide, he earned $225.50 for his work. Not long thereafter, he himself killed four buffalo out of a group of 12. One was at a range of 200 yards while facing away from him, which presented a smaller target than broadside. This was a challenging shot and Cook was proud of himself:

> Sitting down and placing my [.44 caliber] gun in the rest-sticks [an X-shaped arrangement of light poles used by hunters to steady their aim], I drew a fine bead on him, holding the muzzle of the gun just at the top of the rump. When I fired it seemed to me that the whole hind part of his body rose clear of the ground. He made a few lumbering, awkward jumps forward, turned sideways, crouched down on his hunkers, and just as I was getting ready to shoot again he fell over on his left side, kicked his feet violently for a few seconds and gave up to fate.[224]

The carnage continued unchecked. At another site, Cook and the other hunters killed 906 buffalo; by skinning 407 of them, he earned $101.75. He and the other hunters fired so often that they ran low on primers. By good luck, however, Cook and his colleagues met up with another band of hunters, who themselves had killed 3,700 buffalo but still had plenty of primers. A deal was quickly struck: Cook's party gave the other men 50 pounds of flour in exchange for 1,000 primers.

By this time Cook himself was a skilled hunter as well as an excellent skinner. The high point of his career as a professional hunter came when he managed to kill 88 buffalo at one stand. Buffalo usually ran away when hunters opened fire but occasionally, as in this case, the animals would simply stand their ground or slowly mill around in a circle. Captain Marcy tells us that,

> Should there be several animals together ... the hunter can often get several other shots before they become frightened. A Delaware Indian and myself once killed five buffaloes out of a small herd before the remainder were so much disturbed as to move away; although we were within the short distance of twenty yards, yet the reports of our rifles did not frighten them in the least, and they continued grazing during all the time we were loading and firing.[225]

But Cook and his fellow hunters soon shot themselves out of a job. Not long after this stand, what Cook said was "the last great slaughter of the buffaloes" took place on the southern plains. Between December 1877 and January 1878, more than 100,000 hides were taken by an army of professional hunters. These men were followed in the spring of 1878 by a wave of homesteaders, who killed buffalo for their meat as well as for their hides. Soon there were too few buffalo left to support hunting on a commercial basis: by May 1878 the professional hunters were hanging up their Big Fifties and leaving the range. Some became miners in Colorado. Some went to look for other jobs on the frontier. Some abandoned the West altogether and went "back to the States," i.e., east to the settled parts of the United States.[226] They were wise to look for other work because by 1889 there remained on the whole of the Great Plains only about 835 buffalo — 835 out of the 30 to 50 million animals which had roamed there before the white man came.

Chapter IX

Frontier Weapons

Weapons were an integral part of frontier life; on both the old frontier of Kentucky and the new frontier of the trans–Mississippi West, they were usually within easy reach. Wherever some semblance of law and order prevailed, men did not always have go about armed to the teeth. Nonetheless, virtually all of them (and not a few women, too) could lay their hands on a shotgun, a rifle, a pistol or a sizable knife to use for self-defense, to scare off would-be aggressors or simply for hunting.

No understanding of the frontier is complete without some knowledge of these weapons. But a great deal of misinformation about them has found its way into print. Errors have been widely propagated by films and television, too. This chapter tries to set the record straight by describing in general terms a few of the most common weapons of the trans–Mississippi West, and their strengths and weaknesses.

Shotguns

At close range, a sawed-off (shortened) 10- or 12-gauge double-barreled shotgun was the most formidable weapon on the frontier. Shotguns were often loaded with buckshot (heavy pellets), which sprayed out in a dense pattern and increased the probability of hitting a moving target and of registering multiple hits on a stationary target. With buckshot, a shotgun could nearly cut a man in half at 10 yards. This is the reason why stagecoach guards and Wells Fargo agents were armed with shotguns, and why Virgil Earp, the chief of police in Tombstone, Arizona, was carrying one in 1881 when he and his brothers, Wyatt and Morgan, walked into the most famous of all Western gunfights — at the O.K. Corral. At the last minute, Virgil loaned his shotgun to Wyatt's friend, John "Doc" Holliday, who wanted to join the fight. Holliday used it to kill Tom McLaury, one of the Earps' opponents.

Gunmen on both sides of the law had a great respect for the shotgun. One town marshal in Texas, who by his own admission was not a good pistol shot or fast on the draw, compensated for these shortcomings by using a shotgun. He recounted how he had dealt with an outlaw who styled himself the "Terror of the Prairies." The marshal said:

When the Terror come lopin' his big bay hawse into our one main street an' let out a yell, I dropped down behind a rain water bar'l on the street, about as sudden as my knees'd bend. For this Terror, he had a gun in each hand an' like I said, I was no gunman. He come ridin' on, lookin' one way an' another like a mad bull crossin' a pasture.... When he come up even with me, I riz up from behind that bar'l with a sawed-off ten-gauge shotgun lookin' him mean in both eyes. Quick as lightnin', he flipped them six-shooters around to cover me.

Well, sir! The' we was! He could kill me easy. But not quick enough to keep me from blowin' him in two pocket-high. We looked at one another. Then I says to him: "Y' drop them plow-handles [Colt revolvers], Mister, or I'll *about* cut y' in two!"

He never wanted to do it. I could see his thumbs a-quiverin' on the pistol hammers. But the trouble was, he was just wantin' to kill me. He never wanted to kill me so bad he was willin' to sure git killed, hisself, a-doin' it. So he let the Colts drop an' he rode on, right out o' our town, leavin' them fancy six-shooters lie in the dust.[227]

Rifles

Unlike a shotgun, which is smooth bored and is used at ranges of less than 50 yards, a rifle has spiral lands and grooves (rifling) cut inside its barrel and fires a single bullet rather than a number of pellets. The rifling imparts a spin to the bullet, which stabilizes it in flight and makes the rifle a very accurate long-range weapon. In the 1830s, a good shot could hit a 10-inch bulls-eye at 200 yards. Rifles improved so rapidly after the Civil War that by the 1870s a man could kill a buffalo at up to 700 yards. At Adobe

Wells, Texas, in June 1874, a party of 27 buffalo hunters was surrounded by more than 500 Kiowa and Comanche Indians, who had been convinced by their medicine man that they were invulnerable to the bullets of the whites. To show that this was not the case, a young U.S. Army scout named Billy Dixon used his Model 1874 Sharps Sporting Rifle to knock an Indian off a horse at a distance accurately measured at 1,538 yards. This was an extraordinarily lucky shot, however, and one which was probably never duplicated.

THE HAWKEN RIFLE

Westering men soon found that the flintlock squirrel and deer rifles of Kentucky and the 18th century eastern woodlands were not reliable or powerful enough for service on the trans–Mississippi frontier, where big, dangerous, hard-to-kill animals — grizzly bears and buffalo — were common. The light, long-barreled Kentucky rifle was too delicate and too cumbersome for hard use. Frontier gunsmiths overcame these defects by producing a new rifle known, after its makers, as the Plains Hawken. The Hawken brothers (Jacob and Samuel) were in business in St. Louis from 1822 to 1849, when Samuel died. Jacob continued alone until 1861, when he sold out to one of the Hawken workmen, who ran the business until as late as 1915.[228] The heavy (10½ pounds), extremely accurate, shorter-barreled .50 to .54 caliber caplock (percussion) Hawken quickly became the favorite rifle of the mountain men.

Because a bull buffalo had great endurance and could run for miles even when badly wounded, hunters usually tried to get as close to their target as

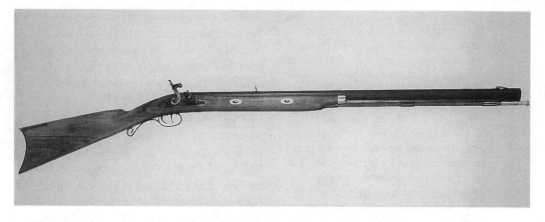

Hawken rifle (Courtesy of Uberti Aldo & Co., Brescia, Italy). In this photo, the ramrod has not been fully seated: it would normally fit flush with the end of the muzzle. Jim Bridger's own Hawken rifle has survived and can now be seen at the Montana Historic Society.

possible. In his classic work, *The Oregon Trail* (1847), Francis Parkman gives a good description of how this was done. He explains that the easiest way to hunt buffalo was to waylay them when they came down to a river to drink. But even then, it took a good marksman to make a quick, clean kill.

> Noiselessly the hunter cocks his rifle [almost certainly a Hawken]. As he sits upon the sand [on the banks of a river], his knee is raised, and his elbow rests upon it, that he may level his heavy weapon with a steadier aim. The stock is to his shoulder; his eye ranges along the barrel. Still he is in no haste to fire. The bull, with slow deliberation, begins his march over the sands to the other side. He advances his foreleg, and exposes a small spot, denuded of hair, just behind the point of his shoulder; upon this the hunter brings the sight of his rifle to bear; lightly and delicately his finger presses the hairtrigger. The spiteful crack of the rifle responds to his touch and instantly in the middle of the bare spot appears a small red dot. The buffalo shivers; death has overtaken him ... still he does not fall but walks heavily forward.... Yet before he has gone far out

on the sand, you see him stop; he totters; his knees bend under him, and his head sinks forward to the ground. Then his whole vast bulk sways to one side; he rolls over on the sand, and dies with a scarcely perceptible struggle.[229]

At one point Parkman watched his guide, Henry Chatillon, worm his way through high grass and prickly pear cactus toward a distant herd of buffalo. Chatillon was carrying two rifles, his own and Parkman's. Soon Parkman heard two shots in quick succession and saw Chatillon rise to his feet as the herd ran off. "You have missed them," said Parkman. "Yes," grunted Chatillon. "Let us go." They reloaded the rifles, mounted their horses and rode off after the buffalo.

The herd itself was out of sight but on the ground where it had been there were two buffalo, one dead, the other dying. "You see I miss him!" joked Chatillon. Parkman was greatly impressed by Chatillon's feat: "He had fired from a distance of more than a hundred and fifty yards, and both balls had passed through the lungs, the true mark in shooting buffalo."[230]

THE WINCHESTER CARBINE

For all its merits, the Hawken was still only a single-shot rifle. Carrying such a weapon, the only way a mountain man could hold off a group of Indians who were pursuing him was to dismount and take careful aim at the nearest, but not to fire. This would make all the Indians veer off; and, if repeated several times, it might even force them to abandon the chase altogether. However, if the mountain man actually fired his rifle, he would probably kill one Indian but the others would certainly kill him.

Inventors had tried for many years to develop a reliable, inexpensive repeating rifle but it was not until the cartridge itself was perfected that this goal was fully achieved, in the 1866 lever action Winchester. Known as the "Yellow Boy" because of its brass frame, this .44 caliber carbine (a carbine is a rifle with a short barrel) held 11 shots. It and its successors became the archetypal rifle of the West during the second half of the 19th century. The Winchester carbine will be familiar to anyone who has ever watched Western films or television.

Cowboys, sheriffs and outlaws liked the carbine because it was well-balanced and fast-handling. Since it was flat-sided it could conveniently be carried on a horse in a leather sheath, known as a scabbard. A further advantage was that some models fired the same cartridges used in revolvers, so only one type of ammunition had to be carried for rifle and pistol alike. Indians appreciated the Winchester, too, because it held a large number of cartridges and was easy to use on horseback. They sometimes decorated it with brass tacks.

Within the inherent limitations of its design (a lever action carbine has a relatively weak action, is slow to reload and is not very accurate at distances exceeding 200 yards), the Winchester was an outstanding weapon. Indeed, it and other carbines like it, usually chambered for the .30-30 cartridge, are still widely used in the United States today for hunting deer and other medium-sized game.

PISTOLS

Because multishot pistols were important in the real West and play an even

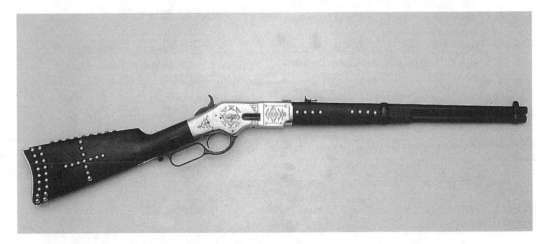

Winchester 1866 Yellow Boy carbine, decorated with brass tacks in the Indian manner (Courtesy of Uberti Also & Co., Brescia, Italy)

more prominent role in the West of our imagination, it is worth spending some time on them here.

THE ALLEN & THURBER PEPPERBOX

Some of the Forty-niners armed themselves with a multibarrel handgun made by Allen & Thurber. Known as a "pepperbox," it consisted of six separate barrels, either welded together around a central axis or bored from a solid block of metal. The result was an awkward, heavy weapon best used as a club. Mark Twain tells us that one of his fellow passengers in a stagecoach carried a pepperbox but that it was woefully inaccurate.

> To aim along the turning barrel and hit the thing aimed at was a feat which was probably never done with an "Allen" in the world. But [it] was a reliable weapon, nevertheless, because, as one of the stage-drivers afterward said, "If she didn't get what she went after, she would fetch something else." And so she did. She went after a deuce of spades nailed against a tree, once, and fetched a mule standing about thirty yards to the left of it.... Sometimes all six barrels would go off at once, and then there was no safe place in all the region round about, but behind it.[231]

THE COLT REVOLVER

In 1830 a 16-year-old American named Samuel Colt went to sea on the brig *Corvo*. During this voyage he carved a wooden model of what was to become the first practical revolving firearm — the Colt revolver — which soon became an essential tool of frontier life and of frontier fiction.

If the truth were known, the average cowboy carried a pistol more for show than out of necessity. Anyone today who has carried a loaded .45 caliber single action revolver in a leather holster on a cartridge-laden gunbelt knows that such a rig is heavy and prone to snag on things. Indeed, this was the reason why cowboys often rolled up their pistols in their blankets during a roundup and left them in the chuck wagon.

There were some practical reasons for carrying a pistol, though. These were best summed up by one veteran of the frontier who said, figuratively tapping the butt of his own revolver, "I don't want this thing often, but when I do want it, I want it damn bad."[232] In the same vein, Captain Marcy offered this stern advice to the emigrants:

> Every man who goes into the Indian country should be armed with a rifle and revolver, and he should never, either in camp or out of it, lose sight of them.... [When] moving about outside the camp, the revolver should invariably be worn in the belt, as the person does not know at what moment he may have use for it....[233]

In addition to self-defense, revolvers had other uses. For example, when a herd of cattle stampeded, the cowboys would race to the head of the stampede and fire their pistols into the air or at the ground, trying to force the lead cows to begin to turn in a circle. If successful, this maneuver would result in a milling herd, which would eventually quiet down and stay put. A revolver could also be used to put out of its misery a cow stuck so deep in a bog that it could not be rescued or a horse with a broken leg. However, blazing away at rattlesnakes, jackrabbits or tin cans was probably the most common use for a pistol.

The earliest Colt revolver to make its mark on the frontier was the single action, .36 caliber, five-shot Patterson model. (With a single action revolver, the hammer must be cocked manually before each shot.) Captain Samuel H. Walker of the Texas Rangers described the Patterson in action in an incident known in firearms history as Hays' Big Fight.

> In the summer of 1844 Col. J.C. Hays with 15 men [armed with Colt Pattersons] fought about 80 Camanche [sic] Indians, boldly attacking them upon their own ground, killing & wounding about half their number. Up to this time these daring Indians had always supposed themselves superior to us, man to man, on horse.... The result of this engagement was such as to intimidate them and enable us to treat with them.[234]

With Walker's help, in 1847 Colt developed a massive .44 caliber, six-shot, 4-pound 9-ounce revolver known as the Walker Model, which was an immediate success and which became the basis for most of the other Colt designs up to 1873. By shortening and lightening the Walker and by making other improvements, Colt went on to produce a famous series of single action cap-and-ball (percussion) revolvers during the middle decades of the 19th century.[235] Captain Marcy, one of the many advocates of Colt revolvers, stated that, "Colt's revolving pistol is very generally admitted both in Europe and America to be the most efficient arm of its kind known at the present time."

One of Colt's best cap-and-ball models was the heavy .44 caliber Dragoon. There were three versions, made from 1848 to 1860, of this exceptionally powerful pistol. Captain Marcy recounts the following episode regarding it:

> In passing near the "Medicine Bow Butte" [in southeastern Wyoming] during the spring of 1858, I most unexpectedly encountered a full-grown grizzly bear ... several mountain men, armed with [the lighter .36 caliber Colt] navy revolvers, set off in pursuit. They approached within a few paces and discharged ten or twelve shots, most of which entered the animal, but he still kept on, and his progress did not seem materially impeded by the wounds. After three men had exhausted their charges, another man rode up with the army revolver [a .44 Colt Dragoon] and fired two shots, which brought the stalwart beast to the ground. Upon skinning him and making an examination of the wounds, it was discovered that none of the balls from the small pistols had, after passing through his thick and tough hide, penetrated deeper than about an inch into the flesh, but that the two balls from the large pistol had gone into the vitals and killed him.[236]

Some other of Colt's best cap-and-ball models were:

- The little .31 caliber Baby Dragoon, which was introduced in 1848 and was so small and light that it could be carried concealed as a back-up gun (the same was true for its .31 caliber sisters, the Pocket Model and the Wells Fargo Model).
- Their mid-size successors, the 1851 Navy (a favorite of James Butler "Wild Bill" Hickok) and the sleek 1861 Navy, both .36 caliber.
- The hard-hitting .44 Army of 1860, which was used by Union and Confederate soldiers alike during the Civil War.[237]

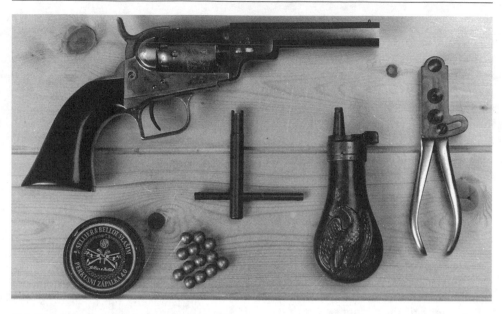

Colt .31 caliber Baby Dragoon revolver with a full set of accessories (Photograph by the author). These are, reading from left to right: a box of percussion caps, lead balls (bullets), a nipple wrench, a powder flask and a bullet mold.

Colt's greatest triumph, however, came in 1873 with the introduction of a solid frame and therefore much stronger revolver using .45 caliber cartridges rather than cap and ball. This new pistol was variously known as the Single Action Army, the Frontier, the Peacemaker, the Plowhandle (so named from the shape of its grip) and the Equalizer. The last name is said to come from one of two frontier sayings. The first was:

God created men;
Colonel Colt made them equal.

The second was:

Be not afraid of any man,
   no matter what his size.
When danger threatens, call on
   me [the Colt revolver] and
   I will equalize.

The Single Action Army revolver was hugely popular on the frontier and was available in a wide range of different calibers, barrel lengths and finishes. This was the pistol typically carried by the cowboy, law officer and outlaw. It was so well designed that with only minor changes it was able to make the transition from black powder to the more powerful smokeless powder and could even be chambered for the modern high velocity .357 Magnum cartridge.

Like the Winchester carbine, the Colt Single Action Army revolver will be familiar to anyone who has watched Western films or television programs. These have implied that the Single Action Army was the perfect pistol. The truth, though, is that it had two shortcomings. The first was that despite the pistol's reputation for reliability, the trigger spring was weak and tended to break. The second defect was that the weapon itself was not very accurate: that is, it could not attain the level of accuracy needed for competitive target shooting.

Colt Single Action Army revolver (Courtesy of Uberti Aldo & Co., Brescia, Italy). This was "the gun that won the West" and is the most famous revolver of all time. Invented in 1873, the Single Action Army is still made today with only minor changes from the original verson.

Fortunately, the Colt mechanism was so simple that the trigger spring or any other broken part could be replaced easily. Fine accuracy was not important to most customers because in practice virtually all combat shooting took place at close range, at five to 15 feet. The minority of shooters who wanted a target-quality Colt revolver had to wait until 1888, when the Single Action Army was modified very slightly and offered for sale as the Flattop Target Model. But this variant was not very accurate, either, and was later superseded by the Bisley Flattop Target Model, named after the firing range in England where the British held their annual shooting matches. The Bisley appeared in 1894 and shot with consistent superiority.

Several common misunderstandings about the use of single action revolvers can be clarified here.

Colt Bisley Target revolver (Courtesy of Uberti Aldo & Co., Brescia, Italy). Although less handsome than the Colt Single Action Army revolver, the Bisley Target was more accurate.

HOW MANY SHOTS ARE THERE
IN A SIX-SHOOTER?

The typical single action revolver held six shots but for reasons of safety it was considered good practice to load the pistol with only five cartridges. The reason was that when the hammer of the revolver was down (uncocked), the firing pin projected into the chamber and rested on the primer of a cartridge. If the pistol was dropped and if it landed on the hammer, it would probably go off. One chamber, therefore, was often left empty but it could still be put to good use: some cowboys rolled up a $10 bill and put it into the empty chamber to pay for their funeral in case they died "with their boots on," e.g., in a gunfight.

With the earlier cap-and-ball revolver, the solution was not to put a percussion cap on the nipple directly under the hammer — or perhaps on any of the nipples. In *Roughing It*, Mark Twain tells us that the leader of his party "had a small-sized Colt's revolver [possibly a five-shot .31 caliber Baby Dragoon] strapped around him for protection against the Indians, and to guard against accidents he carried it uncapped." It would not have taken this man very long to put caps on the nipples and be ready to fire.

Thus, properly loaded, a six-shot revolver contained only five shots, and a five-shot revolver only four shots. The penalties for not taking this simple step could be so severe that prudent shooters willingly accepted the reduction in firepower; those who did not often came to grief. In 1865 or 1866, for instance, the carpenter George Herr and his wife turned their adobe (mud brick) home on the southwestern frontier into a temporary fort because they feared an Indian attack. The first night, Herr slept with a large revolver (probably a .44 caliber cap-and-ball Colt) under his pillow. In the morning, as he was getting out of bed, the revolver fell on the floor, landed on its hammer and went off. The bullet struck Herr in the head, killing him instantly.[238]

In another incident which occurred not far from Fort Bridger, on 18 August 1882, a sheep drover named Lon Murphy was leading his horse along the side of a steep hill, the horse being above him. Suddenly, the horse stopped and shook itself. Murphy's revolver (almost certainly a Colt Single Action Army), which had been in a holster attached to the saddle, fell to the ground, landed on the hammer and went off. The bullet went through Murphy's thigh but did not kill him.[239]

HOLSTERS AND
THE QUICK DRAW

A pistol can be carried in a number of ways. Right-handed shooters today usually carry it in a holster, butt to the rear, on the right side of their belt. But in the 19th century, U.S. cavalrymen carried their Colt Single Action .45 caliber revolvers on the right side with the butt facing forward. The War Department believed this permitted them to draw the pistol more safely and more easily while in the saddle. Some experts, notably Wild Bill Hickok, probably the most famous of all Western gunfighters, dispensed with holsters entirely. Hickok simply tucked two Colts and a Bowie knife into a sash around his waist. His lack of holsters was certainly no handicap. An eyewitness reported that,

> Mr. Hickok ... showed us his weapons [1851 .36 caliber Navy Colts], and

James Butler "Wild Bill" Hickok (Kansas State Historical Society, Topeka, Kansas). Armed with a pair of ivory-handled .36 caliber Navy Colts and an unsheathed Bowie knife, Hickok was not a man to trifle with.

offered to do a little shooting for us ... outside the city limits.... His last feat was the most remarkable of all: A quart can was thrown by Mr. Hickok himself, which dropped about 10 or 12 yards distant. Quickly whipping out his revolvers, he fired alternately, with right and left. Advancing a step with each shot his bullets striking the earth just under the can he kept it in continuous motion until his pistols were empty.[240]

The quick draw involves pulling a pistol out of its holster and firing a shot as rapidly as possible. But there are two problems here. The first is that with a single action revolver the quick draw almost invariably involves cocking the hammer with the thumb while the pistol is coming up out of the holster. If during this process the trigger is inadvertently touched or the weapon is dropped, the pistol will probably go off, possibly putting a bullet through the shooter or a bystander.

The second problem is that a quick draw invariably results in shooting too quickly: often a fatal mistake in the West. Western gunfighters understood that being able to draw a pistol fast was much less important than a willingness to kill and the ability to stay calm when someone was shooting at them. Wild Bill Hickok killed an estimated total of ten men before he was shot in the back of the head while playing poker at a saloon in Deadwood, South Dakota, in 1876. He was famous for his own coolness under fire, and Hickok is reported to have told Colonel George Ward Nicols in 1865, "Whenever you get into a row be sure not to shoot too quick. I've known many a feller to slip up for shootin' in a hurry."

Hickok's role in one gunfight shows that he practiced what he preached. After he and an Arkansas man named Dave Tutt got into an argument during a card game, they met on opposite sides of the town square on 21 July 1865 to iron out their differences. Tutt drew and fired first — and missed. Hickok, still walking toward him with his own pistol drawn but unfired, paused, steadied his gun hand on his left arm and shot Tutt through the heart at a range of about 75 yards.[241]

A similar point about calmness and taking one's time was made by a later firearms expert, Herbert W. McBride. He who was a cowboy and a coalminer in Colorado and New Mexico in the early 1890s, and subsequently saw a great deal of combat as a sniper during World War I. He said that the old gunfighters in the West always told him the most important thing in a gunfight was *never to get excited*. They said that pistols were seldom used at distances greater than 20 or 30 feet — in other words, inside a barroom — and that "outside shooting" was almost never effective. As McBride puts it,

> They have told me innumerable tales of how this one and that one had emptied their guns, reloaded and emptied them again at adversaries who were doing the same thing, within less than one hundred feet and with scant damage on either side.[242]

PISTOL ACCURACY

Under good conditions, an experienced shooter who is sitting or lying down, who is using a sandbag or some other rest to steady his aim, and who is holding a long-barreled .44 or .45 caliber single action revolver with both hands, can hit a man-sized target several hundred yards away. If the same marksman is standing up, however, and is holding the pistol with one hand at arm's length, accuracy suffers greatly. Under these conditions it is surprisingly difficult, even when using a modern, exceptionally accurate .177 caliber air pistol, to put ten consecutive shots into a small bulls-eye only 10 yards away.

In light of this fact, it can be seen that much of what has been written about pistol accuracy on the frontier falls into the category of tall tales. George W. Romspert, who crossed the West in a covered wagon in the mid–19th century, obviously recognized this when he joked about how cowboys treated a tenderfoot (a newcomer to the West).

> They will make him stand still and hold out his hand, and then try to shoot between his fingers, or shoot a hole through his ears, or see how closely they can shoot to the top of his head by shooting through his hat.... There is not much danger until they get pretty full and want to make *too fine* a shot, such as shooting between the flesh and skin, and then the thing is too fine to be pleasant.[243]

Romspert was giving free rein to his imagination to make his point. The average cowboy did not take good care of his guns and, even when sober, was not a good shot. The only gunplay a cowboy was ever likely to try on a tenderfoot was to make him "dance" by repeatedly firing into the ground close to his feet. This initiation rite, of course, did not require a high level of accuracy.

Indeed, cowboys were usually much better at *missing* rather than *hitting* what they aimed at. Court records in New Mexico reveal that in 1884 a group of about 80 cowboys, over a period of 36 hours, fired more than 4,000 shots into a *jacal* (a small house) in which Elfego

Baca, a young Hispanic cowboy, was hiding. Baca, who went on to become a sheriff, a lawyer and a prominent politician, later wrote that, "At the *jacal* the only big object was *Nuestra Señora Santa Anna*, a statue supposed to be over six hundred years old. And neither the statue nor I was hit."[244]

"FANNING"

The quickest way to empty a single action revolver is to grasp the weapon firmly in one hand at waist level, squeeze the trigger and hold it there, then use the heel of the other hand to sweep the hammer back to the fully cocked position. Once the hand releases the hammer it will fly forward and fire the revolver. Repeating this process with the sweeping hand as fast as possible, until all five or six cartridges have been fired, is known as "fanning."

Films and television programs about the West have depicted fanning so often that it may seem the best and, indeed, the only way to have fired a single action revolver rapidly. But there were two problems here. The first was that it was nearly impossible to hit anything by fanning. The second was that reloading a single action took a long time, so emptying a revolver in the general direction of an enemy without hitting him would have left the shooter quite defenseless. This was one of the reasons why Hickok and other gunmen on both sides of the law often carried two revolvers. When the great linguist and world traveler Sir Richard Burton went to San Francisco by stagecoach in 1860, he wrote: "For weapons I carried two revolvers: from the moment of leaving St. Jo. [St. Joseph, Missouri] to the time of reaching Placerville or Sacramento, the pistol should never be absent from a man's right side — remember it is handier there than on the other — or the bowie knife from his left."[245]

There were two additional reasons for carrying a pair of revolvers. The first was that black powder was hydroscopic — that is, it absorbed moisture easily — and after it had been in the cylinder of a cap-and-ball revolver for some time it could become too damp to fire. The second reason was that the percussion cap on a cap-and-ball revolver could split into several small pieces when it exploded. If one of them fell into the pistol's mechanism and prevented the cylinder from turning, another shot could not be fired until the jam was cleared — which might have involved taking the revolver apart. For all those reasons, it was a good insurance policy for a gunfighter to have a second pistol immediately at hand.

SHOOTING TO KILL

Another film and television myth is that a gunman was able to shoot a pistol out of his opponent's hand or could shoot him in the arm or leg simply to wound him. The truth is that in a gunfight it was kill or be killed. The professional gunfighter therefore took his time and aimed for the biggest target — his opponent's torso. This is what Hickok told his friend Charles Gross in 1871:

> Charlie I hope you never have to shoot any man, but if you do shoot him in the guts near the navel, *you* may not make a fatal shot, but *he* will get a shock that will paralyze his brain and arm so much that the fight is all over.[246]

Knives

Of the large variety of knives used on the frontier, the Bowie and the Green River deserve special mention.

THE BOWIE KNIFE

When the British historian Thomas Carlyle heard about the exploits of the great knife fighter Jim Bowie (whose surname is pronounced "Boowie"), he was moved to exclaim: "By Hercules! The man was greater than Caesar — nay, nearly equal to Odin or Thor! The Texans ought to build him an altar." Carlyle must have been thinking about two of Bowie's fights.[247]

Most of the single-shot pistols of the early 1800s were inaccurate, unreliable and slow to reload. As a result, men preferred to rely on their knives instead. Bowie's first battle took place in 1827 on a Mississippi River sandbar near Natchez, Tennessee. Armed with a butcher knife, Bowie disemboweled one opponent and cut another one to ribbons, even though he himself had been shot in the hip and shoulder, stabbed in the chest and beaten on the head. After this fight he decided to have a frontier blacksmith make a knife to his own specifications — a heavy weapon which would be equally good at cutting, chopping and stabbing.

The result was the famous Bowie knife, which is now a generic term for any heavy-duty knife, with or without a handguard, which has a long blade and, usually, an upturned point. A typical Bowie knife of the mid–19th century was strictly a fighting knife and had a 12-inch blade, although scaled-down Bowies were widely used as hunting knives. The top (non-cutting) edge of the blade of a

Bowie knife made in Sheffield, England, with a six-inch blade marked I*XL ("I excel") (Photograph by the author). This is a replica of a knife found in the Alamo (a fort in Texas) after the battle of 1836, in which all 183 defenders of the fort, including Jim Bowie himself, were killed by Mexican soldiers.

big Bowie sometimes contained a strip of soft metal, such as brass. The theory was that in a knife fight this might have momentarily caught and held an opponent's blade. If so, this would have given the owner of the Bowie knife a split-second advantage, which could have proven decisive.

In the second battle, which occurred in Texas in 1830, Bowie was carrying his new knife when he was attacked by three knife-wielding enemies. He practically beheaded the first man and then, although slightly wounded in the leg, he ripped open the second man's belly. The last man tried to run away but Bowie "split his skull to the shoulders" with one blow. Despite his prowess as a fighter, Bowie himself came to a violent end. He was one of the defenders of the Texas bastion known as the Alamo. Lying on his cot there, delirious with fever, he was bayonetted to death by Mexican soldiers when they overran the Alamo in 1836.

Two other men who put their Bowies to bloody use were the veteran mountain man "Long" Hatcher and his young protégé, John Johnson (a variant spelling is Johnston), who became known as "Liver-eating Johnson." This man killed Crow Indians and ate their livers in order to get revenge: the Crows had murdered his pregnant wife.[248] In one incident in the Rockies, Hatcher and Johnson were attacked by a dozen Arapaho Indians. The mountain men drove them off with their rifles, downing three of them, but Johnson was wounded in his right shoulder by an arrow. Before moving forward to scalp the fallen Indians, Hatcher cut out the arrow with his Bowie, removing a quantity of flesh in the process. Johnson did not even flinch during this surgery. Once the operation was finished, Hatcher sheathed his Bowie. But one Indian was still alive and tried to draw his scalping knife. Hatcher redrew his Bowie first and buried it to the hilt in the Indian's chest.

Hatcher then taught Johnson the best way to take a scalp. First he cleaned his Bowie by thrusting it into the soft earth. Then he put his foot on the dead Indian's face, twisted the hair together with one hand, cut a quick circle around the base of the hair, using the point of his blade, and finally yanked sharply upward. The scalp came off with a popping sound. Hatcher swung it around several times to get rid of some of the blood, then slipped it through a ring in his belt, bloody side outward so that it would dry more quickly. Johnson, for his part, proved to be a quick learner. On his first try he scalped one of the two remaining Indians. Hatcher scalped the other, remarking that, "Fust time I skinned a red coon [an Indian] I wuz cold and shuk all over." Johnson, however, was unmoved. "Slicin' a man don't bother me none," he said grimly.

THE GREEN RIVER KNIFE

The Bowie was an excellent fighting knife but it was too big and heavy for convenient use when skinning game such as beaver or deer. For these tasks and for general use around the camp, mountain men preferred a smaller, lighter, butcher-skinning knife made by John Russell & Company at a factory on the Green River in Massachusetts. Halfway to the hilt, the blade of each knife was stamped:

> J. Russell & Co.
> Green River Works

The Green River knife was a great success. It became so popular that Russell was shipping 60,000 of them to the West each year and cutlers in Sheffield, England, were imitating it. This knife was responsible for the exhortation, "Give it

to him up to the Green River," which has passed into frontier folklore.

We saw in Chapter IV, for example, that when "Long" Hatcher is trying to recover his stolen rife, he cheerfully says he "socks my big knife up to the Green River, first dig" when he kills an Indian. After the brawl at the Taos fandango, the mountain men left the dance floor strewn with wounded Mexicans, "many most dangerously; for, as may be imagined, a thrust from the keen scalp-knife by the nervous arm of a mountaineer was no baby blow, and seldom failed to

This skinning knife is similar to the Green River knives used by mountain men (Photograph by the author). It was thrown at a pistol target tacked to a tree 15 feet away. The bulls-eye of the target measures 2⅓-inches in diameter.

strike home — up to the 'Green River' on the blade."[249]

Throwing a Knife

Films and television programs notwithstanding, knives were never thrown in combat because the chances of killing or incapacitating an opponent in such a way were not very high. But mountain men almost certainly threw knives for recreation. They definitely competed with each other in throwing tomahawks at targets tacked to trees, during rendezvous and perhaps to wile away the long hours of a winter camp. Knife throwing, or "blade flinging," is a challenging pastime and with a little practice it is not hard to hit a target at close range.

Chapter X

The West of Our Imagination

The man who summed up the lure of the West most succinctly was one who never went there. The 19th century essayist, poet and practical philosopher Henry David Thoreau never strayed far from his native New England, but of the many lapidary sentences in *Walden* (1854), one stands out above the others: "Eastward I go only by force, but westward I go free."

Here Thoreau speaks for all those who have worked in the realm of the imagination and who have tried, ever since the days of the old trans–Appalachian frontier, to lift daily life in the historic West out of its muddy ruts and put it onto a higher, more adventuresome and altogether more romantic plane. These workers in the realm of the imagination are the writers, artists, illustrators, storytellers, musicians, film directors, television producers, sculptors and choreographers who have canonized the frontier by selecting as their subject matter only the most colorful and most dramatic moments of Western life. Their goal has been to astound, or at least to impress, their audiences by presenting a cavalcade of remarkable characters and stirring events, even if these had only a tenuous grounding in historical reality.

Three Faces of the West

It was not difficult to astound or to impress audiences because the frontier did wear so many different faces. Three of them can be discussed here: the West as a Garden of Eden, the importance of anonymity, and the opportunity for self-government.

In the 19th century the West was seen as a magic place where there was no class structure, no established traditions and no social restrictions monitored by prim Victorians or by finger-wagging clergymen. The land itself was held to be a veritable Garden of Eden, a belief spelled out most explicitly by Thomas James in *Three Years Among the Indians and Mexicans* (1846):

> On the third day we issued from very high and desolate mountains on both sides of us, whose tops are covered with snow throughout the year, and came upon a scene of beauty and magnificence combined, unequaled by any other view of nature that I ever beheld. It really realized all my conceptions of the Garden of Eden.... [The plains] and the mountain sides were dark with buffaloes, elk, deer, moose, wild goats,

and wild sheep ... all enjoying a perfect millennium of peace and quiet.... The whole landscape was that of the most splendid English park.[250]

The most important thing about this Garden of Eden was that all its animal and mineral resources were free for the taking: the man who got there first got the most. This fact encouraged other beliefs. In the West, a man could be in charge of his own destiny, free to take up any job he could get and free to move on whenever he liked. There were no family attachments on the frontier to hold a man down. Perhaps most important for many men, there were also unlimited opportunities for adventure and excitement.

The anonymous quality of the frontier was very appealing, too. According to a frontier anecdote, on one occasion a lone rider dismounted to help a Westering family which was stranded on the prairie because their wagon had a broken wheel. The owner of the wagon and the lone rider worked together, side-by-side, for several hours to repair the wheel, discussing at length the details of what had to be done. When the wagon was finally ready to roll again, the owner wanted to thank the stranger, so he asked him, "What did you say your name was?" The lone rider replied: "I didn't say."

Because there was no effective government and no record-keeping on the frontier, a man's past did not follow him around. He could shuck off an old identity and assume a new one as often as he liked. Indeed, men put such a high value on anonymity that it was considered impolite and could even be dangerous to ask someone, "What was your name in the States?" But regardless of what name he chose to use, a man in the West could

help create new democratic institutions tailored to the conditions of the frontier. California is a good case in point.

California had always been governed at long range, first by Spain and then by Mexico. In 1835 General Mariano Guadalupe Vallejo had founded the town of Sonoma (about 40 miles northeast of San Francisco). But Mexican rule ended abruptly on 14 June 1846, when a small band of American settlers invaded Sonoma, captured Vallejo and his garrison, raised an improvised Bear Flag in the town square and proclaimed California a republic. The next month in the port of Monterey, Commodore John Drake Sloat, the captain of the American sloop of war *Portsmouth*, took formal possession of California on behalf of the U.S. Government.

By the time the Forty-niners reached the mines, however, virtually no American institutions of law and order were in place there. It was thus entirely up to the miners to define not only who they were but also how they should defend themselves and their property, punish wrongdoers, reward men of merit and deal with the rest of the world. Indeed, until the 1860s there were no Federal laws governing the ownership of private mining claims on public lands. The miners therefore made up their own unofficial regulations, which became known as the "Miner's Code."[251] Californian miners had, in short, the unique opportunity of creating a brand-new society in the wilderness.

The Mythic West

Once audiences had been sufficiently astounded or impressed by these different faces of the West and as time passed, the next step was an easy one: reality was elevated into myth. Let us see if we can retrace the process by which the usually monotonous and sweat-stained daily life of the 19th century West has become the stuff of legends. But first we need to define what we are talking about. What do we mean by "the mythic West"?

This phrase is used here to highlight the fact that the frontier, which the U.S. Census Bureau said had disappeared by 1890, was not just a matter of geography and population density, but, as the Western historian Robert Athearn put it, this frontier was also

> the West of the mind, of the spirit, a concept that for generations had reassured Americans of a future, a place to go, even though most of them would not choose to move. Somewhere out there in the general direction of the Pacific Ocean lay a depository of unending resources, imperfectly described or understood, and a source of Lebensraum that was *often more of imagery than substance, yet dreamers thought of it as being real.*[252]

Marketing the Mythic West

Athearn's comments help us answer one fundamental question: why are we so willing, even now, to suspend our belief in the facts of frontier history? Why, for example, do we persist in thinking of the rugged Marlboro Man in his thirties or forties, or older, as the typical cowboy? Portraits of the *real* cowboys of the 19th century — taken at their own expense and for their own use at photographic studios in frontier towns across the West — show that many of them were little more than innocent 18-year-olds dressed up for the occasion, trying hard to project a masculine image by prominently displaying Colt Single Action Army revolvers borrowed from the photographer's selection of props.

We build and rebuild the mythic West on three concepts which have a national, an international and, one might even say, a universal appeal: the spirit of adventure, our hopes for a new start in life, and the dream of unbounded personal freedom. The appeal of these concepts is so great that we are willing to suspend our belief in the well-documented but often inconvenient facts of frontier history. Moreover, these concepts are very marketable commodities, so they help explain why from its very beginnings the West has never lacked for promoters and publicists.

Media enthusiasm for the West began in the 1820s, when the first major American novelist, James Fenimore Cooper (1789–1851), wrote adventure stories about frontier life known as the Leatherstocking Tales. In *The Pioneers* (1823), *The Last of the Mohicans* (1826), *The Prairie* (1827) and in other books, Cooper peopled the old trans–Appalachian frontier with heroic and memorable characters such as the backwoodsman Natty Bumpo, who was known as Hawkeye because he was such a superb shot.

Not long thereafter, in 1832, the novelist Washington Irving set out across the wide Missouri to observe and write about the Indian tribes, which he foresaw were destined to disappear as, to use his term, "independent nations." After Irving, there was an even greater demand for factual as well as fictional accounts of the West. In addition to Horace Greeley, many other newsmen crossed the Missouri in the coming decades — for instance, Samuel Bowles of the *Springfield Republican*, a Massachusetts newspaper. Artists, illustrators and photographers went west as well to give "the folks back home" a graphic rather than a merely literary idea of what the frontier was all about.

The mythic West really began in earnest, however, during the last half of the 19th century when the publishers of dime novels began to entertain their readers with an endless series of improbable stories about the frontier. These cheap paperbacks became so popular that cowboys read them in their bunkhouses. To the consternation of their employers (ranch owners who wanted their men to pay attention to cows), some cowboys even tried to model their own behavior on that of their fictional heroes.

The greatest merchandiser of the "real" West was William F. "Buffalo Bill" Cody (1846–1917), who earned his nickname because he killed 4,280 buffalo in 17 months when supplying meat to the crews building the Union Pacific Railroad. Cody had been a Pony Express rider, an Army scout and an Indian fighter. He was also a tireless self-promoter whose exploits were exaggerated in more than 120 dime novels, often written by E.Z.C. Judson, who used the pseudonym of Ned Buntline. Beginning in 1882, Cody, who was a gifted and irrepressible showman, organized a series of live-action Wild West shows which were an instant success, not only in the United States but also in Europe.

These featured real cowboys and real Indians demonstrating their riding, roping skills and shooting skills. Urban audiences were thrilled by the mock battles in Buffalo Bill's shows but they were even more impressed by the exploits an

Ohio cowgirl named Phoebe "Annie Oakley" Moses (1860–1926). Billed as "The Peerless Wing [shotgun] and Rifle Shot," Annie Oakley was nicknamed "Little Sure Shot" by an Indian chief and performed near miracles with shotgun, rifle and pistol alike.

- She could hit targets while standing on the back of a moving horse or while riding a bicycle. When afoot, she could shatter five glass balls — launched into the air simultaneously by spring-powered traps — before any of them hit the ground.
- Waiting until the traps threw two clay pigeons into the air, she would jump over a table, grab her gun off the table-top, and hit both targets in the air.
- Tying up her skirt at the knees and taking off her hat, she would stand on her head and shoot upside down.
- She could shoot a cigarette out of her husband's mouth, hit a dime held between his fingers, and, using a mirror and firing over her shoulder, cut a playing card in two edgewise.
- She would shoot an apple off the head of her little poodle, who would catch one of the pieces in his mouth and eat it.[253] This act was her biggest crowd-pleaser.

The most lasting tribute to Annie Oakley came 20 years after her death. In 1946, Irving Berlin produced his highly successful musical based on her life: *Annie Get Your Gun*. It was turned into a film in 1950.

The Turner Hypothesis

The frontier experience stimulated not only popular culture but academic life as well. The 1890 announcement of the U.S. Census Bureau that the frontier was closed led Professor Frederick Jackson Turner to present a paper in 1893 on the "Significance of the Frontier in American History" at a meeting of the American Historical Association. Turner claimed that the Census Bureau's statement marked the end of a great historic movement. He argued that, "Up to our own day [1893] American history has been in a large degree the history of the colonization of the Great West." Turner's frontier hypothesis was, in short, that the "existence of an area of free land, its continuous recession, and the advance of American settlement westward, explain American development."[254]

Later scholars would criticize the Turner hypothesis as being too simplistic. Today most students of the subject would agree that Turner did not give enough weight to the contributions of other nations and of ethnic minorities in the settlement of the West, nor did he call attention to some of the negative aspects of frontier development. These include the destruction of the culture of the Plains and other Indians, labor exploitation of whites and minorities, racial discrimination, especially against blacks and Chinese, and a cavalier disregard for the environment.

Still, there can be no doubt that Turner was right in pointing to the West as a decisive factor in forming the American character. Indeed, many of the traits that the Western historian Ray Allen Billington detected in what he called the "composite frontiersman" are still evident in American culture today, to the extent that foreigners usually think of them as being typically American. The 19th century frontiersman was materialistic, mobile, versatile, inventive, wasteful, optimistic, and nationalistic.... He scorned precedent and tradition. He was individualistic to the extent that he resented governmental interference in his own economic affairs, but he was willing to cooperate with his neighbors for the public good. Above all, the frontiersman was a practical opportunist, little concerned with the past or with theory, and concerned primarily with devising habits and institutions that would allow him to utilize most efficiently the abundant resources amidst which he lived.[255]

Owen Wister and His Successors

It remained for Owen Wister, an early 20th century novelist, to give the West that "quiet-but-forceful-real-man" image which has become such a permanent part of the mythic West and which has figured in so many books, illustrations, films and television programs. In a culminating point of his famous novel, *The Virginian* (1902), Wister puts his protagonist, whose name is never given (he is referred to only as "the Virginian"), into a card game with a bully and desperado named Trampas, who taunts and insults him. Here is a famous exchange between the two men:

Therefore Trampas spoke, "Your bet, you son-of-a-----."

> The Virginian's pistol came out, and his hand lay on the table, holding it unaimed. And with a voice as gentle as ever, the voice that sounded only like a caress, but drawling a very little more than usual, so that there was almost a space between each word, he issued his orders to the man Trampas: "When you call me that, *smile!*"[256]

The Virginian was praised by literary critics. Other novels and short stories about the West have earned applause, too, for their authenticity, their literary quality, their popular appeal, or for all three qualities. Examples include Andy Adams, *Log of a Cowboy* (1903); Zane Grey, *Riders of the Purple Sage* (1912); Walter van Tilberg Clark, *The Ox-Bow Incident* (1940); A.B. Guthrie, Jr., *The Big Sky* (1947); Thomas Berger, *Little Big Man* (1964); and Larry McMurtry, *Lonesome Dove* (1985).

The Western, however, found its most dramatic medium not in the printed page but on the silver screen. *The Great Train Robbery* (1903) was the first of a long series of Western films which were later — between the 1920s and 1940s — produced in enormous numbers but with only slight variations in their plots. Among the better-made "epics" we can list the following: *The Covered Wagon* (1923); *The Iron Horse* (1924); *The Big Trail* (1930), the first epic Western to use talking in its soundtrack; *Cimarron* (1931); *Destry Rides Again* (1939); *Stagecoach* (1939), one of John Wayne's best films; *My Darling Clementine* (1946); *Red River* (1948); *Winchester 73* (1950); *High Noon* (1952); *Shane* (1953); *Rio Bravo* (1959); *The Man Who Shot Liberty Valance* (1962); *The Wild Bunch* (1969); and *Little Big Man* (1970).

Westerns such as "The Lone Ranger" and "Death Valley Days" were also serialized on radio programs in the 1930s and 1940s. Some of the least-memorable films of the 1930s, '40s and '50s starred "singing cowboys" such as Gene Autry, Tex Ritter and Roy Rogers. Later on, Westerns were remarkably popular on television, where "Gunsmoke," "Bonanza," "Have Gun Will Travel" and "Maverick" drew big audiences.

By the 1960s, the epic Western was near the end of its life-span. A host of light-hearted Western films appeared in its place: *Cat Ballou* (1965), *Butch Cassidy and the Sundance Kid* (1969) and *Blazing Saddles* (1974). Low-budget Westerns, made by Italian or Spanish producers and showing the seamier side of frontier life, such as *A Fistful of Dollars* (1964) and *Pale Rider* (1986), achieved a modest notoriety, too.

Ultimately, though, parody and grimness proved to be dead-ends; soon there was nothing new left to say. One of the few successful Westerns made in the last decade of the 20th century was *Dances with the Wolves* (1990). It was a sign of the times that this film dealt sympathetically with the culture of the Plains Indians, rather than extolling the cowboy virtues immortalized by John Wayne.

By the late 1970s, the space epic began to replace the Western in terms of box-office appeal. The first and most famous film of this genre was *Star Wars* (1977), which used computer-based special effects to achieve spectacular results. The producer, George Lucas, clearly had Westerns in mind when he made it: "I wanted to create a modern myth," he said in an interview in 1999, "but I wanted there to be an action-adventure, Saturday morning serial kind of motif to it."[257] Some of the classic Western themes lived on in this new guise. Like so many Westerns, space epics often pitted a handsome man and a pretty woman against evil forces. The outcome was never in doubt: in the end the "good guys," after enduring many vicissitudes, were sure to triumph over the "bad guys."[258]

Fort Bridger and the Mythic West

Today the mythic West is alive and well at Fort Bridger, not only in the physical layout of the post but also because of the Fort Bridger Annual Mountain Man Rendezvous.

The U.S. Army abandoned Fort Bridger on two occasions (first during the Civil War and then again in 1878) but it was reactivated in the early 1880s. There was a last flurry of building activity at that time which continued up to 1889, but with the end of the Indian wars it was clear there was no further need for a military post in southwestern Wyoming. Fort Bridger was closed for the third and last time in 1890. Many of the buildings constructed by the Army were sold at public auction and moved elsewhere for a new lease of life as private homes, barns or bunkhouses. Most of the structures that remained on the site were allowed to fall into a state of disrepair. But after a long period of neglect, public-spirited groups and individuals in Wy-

oming began to take an interest in restoring what remained of old Fort Bridger. Their efforts bore fruit: in 1920 the State of Wyoming acquired the site, and in 1933 it was dedicated as a Wyoming Historical Landmark and Museum. The survival of Fort Bridger is thus assured.

Most of the buildings at Fort Bridger today date from its years as an Army post. Historically, however, the most interesting exhibit is a replica stockade which closely follows the plan of Jim Bridger's original fort. According to archaeological evidence, this replica is situated precisely on the Oregon Trail and is located about 60 yards northwest of Old Gabe's trading post.

The original Fort Bridger consisted of two stockades made of poles set into the ground. The first stockade, which has been reconstructed, measured 100 feet by 100 feet and contained two log cabins

Log cabin at Fort Bridger (Photograph by the author)

at right angles to one another. Each cabin was divided into two rooms. The proprietors — Bridger and Vasquez — and their families each had half of one cabin; the other cabin housed the blacksmith/carpenter shop and the traderoom. The second stockade, which has not been rebuilt, measured 100 feet by 80 feet and was used to corral the livestock at night to guard them against theft.

Because of their courage, endurance and unique manner of speech and dress, the mountain men have passed into American folklore. Southwestern Wyoming is a good stage for the Fort Bridger Annual Mountain Man Rendezvous, which was first held in 1972. This four-day event is scheduled for the Labor Day weekend and now attracts up to 25,000 people each year. Over 200 lodges and teepees are set up for the Rendezvous, which features men, women and children dressed in period costumes and demonstrating such 1840-era skills as shooting black powder firearms, throwing tomahawks and performing Indian dances.

The Future of the Past

Fort Bridger is only one of the historic monuments or institutions in the United States and Canada which help assure that even as the real West fades away into a fuzzy past, the mythic West will be with us for many years to come. Because the mythic West has a universal appeal, it has achieved a certain immortality. The historic West can never be re-created but the mythic West is always a work in progress, with people constantly building new castles in the air on the gritty foundations of the past.

Nostalgia is indeed a powerful cement. The myth-building process has been going on for a long time, especially since the frontier itself closed down in 1890. To make this clear, let us end our survey of the frontier West with this true story.

An old man who had been a cowboy in Wyoming in the days of his youth went back to Cheyenne in about 1926, after having been away for many decades. Looking around at all the trappings of modern life which had appeared there since the late 19th century, he said to a friend, "Yes, the cowboy is gone. The old range life has disappeared and will never return." Then he added wistfully, "*If I knew a country where it would, I'd go there if I had to go in a canoe.*"[259]

Appendix I

Gender in Frontier History

Women played an essential role in the West, not only as child-bearers but also as culture-bearers. In the 18th century the American population grew rapidly because of a high birthrate and relatively low infant mortality: Daniel and Rebecca Boone were not unusual in having 10 children. Such education as frontier children received was invariably due to their mothers. Moreover, as soon as some degree of law and order was established in a region, it was the women who were quick to encourage the development of schools, churches and other institutions of settled life.[260]

They also exerted a subtle but important civilizing influence on the rough-and-ready mining camps of California and the Rockies and on the shoot-'em-up cow towns of the Great Plains. The American writer Stephen Crane (1870–1900) is best known for *The Red Badge of Courage*, his novel about the American Civil War, but after visiting west Texas he wrote a comic short story, "The Bride Comes to Yellow Sky" (1898).

In this tale, Jack Potter, the marshal of the mythical Texas town of Yellow Sky, arrives on the afternoon train, unexpectedly bringing home a bride. While waiting for Potter to appear, his archenemy, "Scratchy" Wilson, has shot up the town. The two men confront each other on the main street. Wilson, who is carrying two pistols, wants to fight, but Potter tells him he is unarmed: "I ain't got a gun because I've just come from San Anton' [San Antonio] with my wife. I'm married ... This is the lady."

"Married!" exclaims Wilson, quite unable to fathom this new state of affairs. Slowly the light dawns on him that the presence of a woman means there can be no more gunplay in Yellow Sky. This is how Crane ends the story:

> "Well, I 'low [allow] it's off, Jack," said Wilson. He was looking at the ground. "Married!" He was not a student of chivalry; it was merely that in the presence of this foreign condition he was a simple child of the earlier plains. He picked up his starboard revolver, and, placing both weapons in their holsters, he went away. His feet made funnel-shaped tracks in the heavy sand.[261]

Notwithstanding the importance of women on the frontier, *Fort Bridger, Wyoming* has an inherent and unapologetic bias toward the male point of view. There are two reasons for this. The first is that Westering was in essence a masculine enterprise: the fantasy of unbounded personal freedom probably appealed more to men more than to women.

The second reason is that men on the frontier loved to talk or write about their own exploits; other men loved to hear or read about them. Jim Bridger, for example, was such a great raconteur that he was widely quoted by newspapers and books in his own time. Biographies about another famous mountain man, Christopher (Kit) Carson (1809–68), began to appear while he was still alive. Indeed, in his autobiography, Carson tells us that after his failed attempt to rescue some captives being held by the Indians, he found among the captives' possessions a dime novel "in which I was represented as a great hero, slaying Indians by the hundreds."[262]

Before he became the 26th President of the United States, Teddy Roosevelt was a rancher in the Dakota Territory in the mid–1880s and took great pride in his custom-made weapons. Indeed, his favorite pistol (an engraved, nickel-plated Colt .44-40 caliber Single Action Army revolver with the monogram TR carved into its ivory grip) and its hand-tooled holster still survive.[263] Roosevelt, who knew, loved and wrote about the West, used no less than 30 different phrases to describe the starkly masculine qualities he saw in the cowboys.[264]

This combination of male authorship and a male audience meant that it was the testosterone-filled story, not the estrogen account, which was likely to be perpetuated and pass into the folklore and libraries about the West. As Sandra Myers explains in her book *Westering Women* (1982), during the great overland migrations of 1840 to 1860,

> …women's diaries included more details of family life, care of children, and their own camp work. Men's accounts more frequently concentrated on their trail labor, details of [wagon]-train organization, and disputes over decisions made by the captain or other leaders. Men were also more likely to discuss fights and violence, hunting, defense, and possible attacks by Indians or outlaws.[265]

As recorded by most of its participants, then, the history of the West was unabashedly masculine. Indeed, even its humor was masculine. Who can resist the true story of Alfred E. Packer, who guided five prospectors into the San Juan mountains in southwestern Colorado during the winter of 1875? Trapped by a snow storm, the party ran out of food. Packer was the only survivor and was later convicted of murdering the prospectors and eating them.

As soon as Judge M.B. Gerry passed sentence on Packer, an alcoholic named James Dolan, who had been a witness for the prosecution, rushed back to his favorite bar. Dolan breathlessly told the other patrons that this is what the judge, who was a Democrat, said to Packer:

> Stand-up, ye son-of-a-bitch and receive your sentence. You voracious, man-eating son-of-a-bitch, there were only six Democrats in Hinsdale County [Colorado] and you et five of them. I'm going to hang you on Friday and this should teach you a lesson not to reduce the Democratic population of the state.[266]

Packer was subsequently pardoned, however, and died peacefully in Denver in 1906. He was not a learned man and even had trouble spelling his own first name. For this reason, the cafeteria at the student union at the University of Colorado is now officially known as the *Alferd* E. Packer Memorial Dining Room.

Appendix II

"The Snake [Shoshoni] Indians"— Excerpts from Osborne Russell's *Journal of a Trapper* (1914)

These excerpts are from pages 144–148 of Russell's handwritten *Journal*, which was not published until 1914. They have been broken into paragraphs here for easier reading.

The appellation [Snake Indians] by which this nation is distinguished is derived from the Crows, but from what reason I have never been able to determine. They call themselves Sho-sho-nies, but during an acquaintance of nine years [1834–1843], during which time I made further progress in their language than any white man had done before me, I never saw one of the nation who could give me either the derivation or definition of the word "Sho-sho-nie."

Their country comprises all the regions drained by the head branches of Green and Bear Rivers [these headwaters are near the Wind River mountains, about 200 miles northeast of Fort Bridger] and the east and southern branches of the Snake River [in southeastern Idaho]. They are kind and hospitable to whites, thankful for favors, indignant at injuries and but little addicted to theft in their large villages. I have seldom heard them accused of inhospitality; on the contrary I have found it to be a general feature of their character to divide the last morsel of food with the hungry stranger, let their means be what it might for obtaining the next meal.

The Snakes, and in fact most of the Rocky Mountain Indians, believe in a Supreme Deity who resides in the sun and in infernal deities residing in the moon and stars, but all subject to the supreme control of the one residing in the sun. They believe that the spirits of the departed are permitted to watch over the actions of the living and every warrior is protected by a guardian angel in all his actions so long as he obeys [the angel's] rules, a violation of which subjects the offender to misfortunes and disasters during the displeasure of the offended deity.

Their prophets, judges or medicine men are supposed to be guided by deities differing from the others, inasmuch as [such a deity] is continually attendant upon the devotee from birth, gradually instituting into his mind the mysteries of his profession, which cannot be transmitted from one mortal to another. The prophet ... converses freely with his supernatural director, who guides him up from childhood in his manner of eating, drinking and smoking, particularly the latter, for every prophet has a different mode of handling, filling, lighting and smoking the big pipe [which the whites referred to as a "peace pipe"] — such as profound silence in the circle while the piper [smoker] is lighting the pipe, turned around three times in the direction of the sun by the next person on the right previous to giving it to him, or smoking with the feet uncovered. Some cannot smoke in the presence of a female or a dog, and a hundred other movements equally vague and superstitious which would be too tedious to mention here.

A plurality of wives is very common among the Snakes and the marriage contract is dissolved only by the consent of the husband, after which the wife is at liberty to marry again. Prostitution among the women is very rare and fornication whilst living with the husband is punished with the utmost severity. The women perform all the labor about the lodge except the care of the horses.

They are cheerful and affectionate to their husbands and remarkably fond and careful of their children.

The government is a democracy. Deeds of valor promote the chief to the highest points attained, from which he is at any time liable to fall for misdemeanor in office. The population amounts to between 5,000 and 6,000, about half of which live in large villages and range with the buffalo [these Indians would later be known as the Eastern or Wind River Shoshoni]; the remainder [the tribes of the Great Basin] live in small detached companies comprised of two to ten families, who subsist upon roots, fish, seeds and berries. They have but few horses and are much addicted to thieving. From their manner of living they have received the appellation of "Root Diggers."

... The Snakes who live upon buffalo and live in large villages seldom use poison on the arrows [as the "Diggers" were said to have done], either in hunting or war. They are well armed with fusees [muskets] and well supplied with horses. They seldom stop more than eight or ten days in one place, which prevents the accumulation of filth which is so common among Indians that are stationary.... Their lodges [teepees] are spacious, made of dressed [tanned] buffalo skins sewed together and set upon eleven or thirteen long smooth poles to each lodge, which are dragged along [by horses] for that purpose.

Appendix III

How to Butcher a Buffalo: Captain Howard Stansbury's Account (1850)

This is adapted from Stansbury's *Exploration of the Great Salt Lake Valley*, cited by Utley, *Life*, pp. 268–269.

Using ropes and horses if necessary, the mountain men began the butchering process by rolling the dead buffalo over so that its stomach was on the ground and its back was in the air. Then, as Stansbury explains in graphic detail,

… the skinning process commences by making an incision along the top of the backbone, and separating the hide downward, so as to get the more quickly at what are considered the choice parts of the animal. These are the "bass," a hump projecting from the back of the neck just before the shoulders, and which is generally removed with the skin attached; it is about the size of a man's head, and when boiled, resembles marrow, being exceedingly tender, rich, and nutritious.

Next comes the "hump," and the "hump ribs," projections of the vertebrae just behind the shoulders, some of which are a foot in length. These are generally broken off with a mallet made of the lower joint of one of the forelegs, cut off for this purpose.

After these come the "fleece," portions of flesh covering the ribs; the "depuis," a broad, fat part extending from the shoulders to the tail; the "belly fleece;" some of the ribs, called "side ribs," to distinguish them from the hump ribs; the thigh or marrow-bones, and the tongue.

155

"Taking the 'Hump Rib'" (Alfred Jacob Miller, pen and ink, ink wash and graphite on gray card, c. 1837; Amon Carter Museum, Fort Worth, Texas; accession no. 1966.28). The hump rib was a prime cut of buffalo meat. The man negligently resting his hands on the muzzle of his rifle is the English hunter Sir William Drummond Stewart, who was the artist's employer.

Generally the animal is opened and the tenderloin and tallow secured. All the rest, including the hams and shoulders — indeed by far the greater portion of the animal — is left on the ground. When buffalo are plenty, the hump, bass, and tongue — very frequently only the latter — are taken, and occasionally a marrow-bone for a tit-bit.

Appendix IV

A Western Mining Engineer:
Henry Janin (1838–1911)

At the time of the Great Diamond Hoax (1872), Henry Janin was 34 years old. His father, a naturalist by inclination and a lawyer by profession, had emigrated from France to New Orleans, Louisiana, in 1828 and become a U.S. citizen in 1835. Henry Janin himself was born in New Orleans in 1838. He entered Yale University in 1854 and after two years there continued his studies in Germany and France, attending the Royal Saxon Mining Academy in Freiburg and the School of Mines in Paris.

Having completed his studies, Janin returned to the United States in 1861, where he found that "the great development of mining on the Pacific coast, beginning with the discovery of gold and continued by the opening of great quicksilver-and-silver mines … was filling the world with its dazzling promise." He therefore moved to the West, working at first in Santa Clara, California, where his brother Louis was the manager of the Enriquita mercury mine. He then went to Mexico to get some experience with silver mining. By 1864 Janin was back in California and helping Louis develop a new refining process for the Gould & Curry mine on the Comstock Lode in Nevada. Returning to San Francisco that same year, he established himself as a consulting mining engineer and acquired a large practice and a good reputation as a judge of the value of mining properties.

The following account, which is lightly edited, was written about eight years after the Great Diamond Hoax. It is taken from "Mines, Men, Money, Stocks," in the *Pacific Coast Mining Review* of 1878–79, p. 50:

> Henry Janin is well known all over the Pacific Coast as a mining engineer of repute, and a mining operator who has been reasonably successful in his ventures. The Janin family is quite numerous — there being four brothers, all mining engineers — Louis and Alexis being specially known. All are graduates of the German schools, and each enjoys all the confidence of those who most deal in mines.
>
> As a mining engineer, Henry Janin has made large fees in reporting on various properties. Cool as a cucumber, with a temper that could not

be ruffled by almost any breeze; self-reliant; determined and confident, it only requires a little more energy to develop an infallible judgment. His favorable report on the well-remembered "diamond job," put up by those princes of scoundrels, Arnold and Slack, was the result of his too confident nature. Instead of digging himself for the precious stones, he allowed the frauds to do the digging, and it was a success.

This failure was a mortifying one to Mr. Janin, and since then he has been less inclined to follow the business of experting. When he goes anywhere, it is always with the understanding that the mine must be a d----d good one on merit; and the regular fee for examination must be a large one, or the contingent fee sufficient to make him a handsome return. Of recent mines approved by Mr. Janin, and placed at handsome figures, were the Home Stake and Golden Terra mines of the Black Hills [South Dakota].

As an operator, Mr. Janin is very conservative. He always wants to get in at bed-rock [that is, early in the game]; and when a good profit stares him in the face, he cannot resist the temptation [to sell out]. He is not a stayer, but, having realized [a profit] on one [mine], he is ready for another venture. As a result of his operations, he can draw his check to a comfortable degree.

He accommodates himself gracefully to a given situation; lives well, on the best of the land; drinks only the best of wines, and smokes only the best of cigars. Aristocratic in his tastes, gentlemanly in demeanor, and careless of the opinions of those he does not esteem, Mr. Janin enjoys the confidence of those who appreciate merit and worth. The ranks of mining engineers are graced by such gentlemen as A.J. Bowie, William Ashburner, Louis Janin, King — last but not least is Henry Janin. Mr. Janin bears his 38 years with

becoming youth. He is a native of *La Belle Louisiane* [Louisiana], and proud of the land of his birth.

The Great Diamond Hoax humiliated Janin deeply, but it is noteworthy that his professional reputation did not suffer at all as a result of it. The reason was that as soon as the fraud was uncovered, he put into escrow all the money he had earned from his role in this affair; it was all distributed to those who had lost money by following his favorable recommendation. Even Asbury Harpending, a shady character who was a firm believer in the diamond fields himself, did not think Janin had been guilty of any wrongdoing. Harpending wrote:

> To do justice to Henry Janin, I think it was this valuation [Tiffany's assessment that the diamonds were worth $150,000] that disarmed his suspicions and made him less eager to search for traces of chicane.... Perhaps had he remained at the discovery claim instead of exploring the country in the neighborhood, he might have detected traces of fraud. But he considered the most essential thing was an examination to determine the diamondiferous [sic] area, so his employers might ultimately get it all.[267]

Janin did not marry until 1886, when he was 47 years old; His bride, Mary Smith, was only 26. A column in the Weddings section of the *Washington Post* said at that time:

> Mr. Janin, who is a man of great wealth, gave his bride numerous presents, among the most valuable of which was a magnificent pearl necklace, valued at $3,000; a pair of diamond-studded bracelets, pins for the hair, solitaire earrings, dressing cases, the large of which is worth several thousand dollars, each article being of

solid silver, gold or ivory wrought in curious fashion.

The Janins were later divorced and Henry settled down in London. It is said that no man is a hero to his valet, but Janin may have been an exception. After Janin died in London in 1911, his valet sent his cufflinks to his son, Henry Covington Janin, in San Francisco. An attached note, read in part, "a better gentleman never lived."

The editor of the American Institute of Mining and Metallurgical Engineers, who knew Henry Janin well, wrote a long obituary in 1911 in which he evaluated the engineer's life.

> I am qualified by personal observation to say that Henry Janin was one of the best — and perhaps the very best — of those who followed the [mining] business at that time.... Henry Janin preferred the roving life of a consulting expert for others, and a mining ad-venturer on his own account. This career presented the alternation of intensive activity in the field with the social pleasures of San Francisco....
>
> Unlike [the geologist Clarence] King, however, Janin disliked to write, and cared little for public appreciation of his work. His genial temperament and brilliant wit made him the "spoiled child" of many a social circle, while his business clients and associates alone realized what acute, comprehensive, and vigilant sagacity lay beneath that gay, careless exterior....
>
> I have forborne, however, to enter into many personal and domestic details of his life which, if fully stated, might explain its vicissitudes and apparent eccentricities — and, above all, its comparative lack of adequate result. For I have never met a man more wonderfully endowed with intellectual gifts and social charms.... With his extraordinary talents and accomplishments, he might have been great; but at least he remained always dear![268]

Appendix V

Ballad of the Outlaw Sam Bass

This ballad was popular on the Western range in the late 19th century and was often sung around cowboy camp-fires. The version given here appeared at about that time in the Dallas *Semi-Weekly Farm News.*

Sam Bass was born in Indiana,
It was his native home;
And at the age of seventeen
Young Sam began to roam.

He first came out to Texas,
A cowboy for to be;
A kinder gentler fellow
You hardly ever see.

Sam used to deal in race stock.
One called "the Denton Mare."
He matched her in the scrub races
And took her to the fair.

Sam always coined the money
And spent it mighty free:
He always drank good liquor
Wherever he might be.

Sam Bass had four companions,
Four bold and daring lads:
Jim Murphy, Jackson, Underwood,
Joel Collins and "Old Dad."

Four bolder, reckless cowboys
The Wild West never knew;
They whipped the Texas Rangers
And chased the boys in blue.

Sam left the old Joel Collins ranch
In the merry month of May,
With a herd of Texas cattle
The Black Hills for to see.

They sold out at Kansas City
And then got on a spree.
A tougher lot of cowboys
You seldom ever see.

They started back to Texas
And robbed the U.P. train.
Then split up into couples
And started out again.

Joel Collins and his partner
Were overtaken soon,
And with all their hard-earned money
They had to meet their doom.

Sam Bass got back to Texas
All "right side up with care,"
He rode right into Denton,
His old friends met him there.

Sam's life was short in Texas —
Three robberies he did do.
He robbed the Longview passenger
The mail and express, too.

Sam had another comrade,
Called "Arkansas" for short,
He was killed by a Texas Ranger
Who thought it was great sport.

Jim Murphy was arrested,
And then, released on bail,
He jumped his bond at Tyler
And hit the Terrell trail.

But Mayor Jones had posted him,
And that was all a stall —
It was a plan to capture Sam
Before the coming fall.

Sam met his fate at Round Rock,
July the twenty-first,
They filled poor Sam with bullets
And emptied out his purse.

Now Sam is a decaying corpse
Down in the Round Rock clay,
While Jackson's on the border
A-trying to get away.

Jim Murphy borrowed Sam's good money,
And did not want to pay.
So he set out the game to win
By giving Sam away.

He sold poor Sam and also Barnes
And left their friends to mourn.
Jim Murphy will a roasting get
When Gabriel blows his horn.

Some think he'll go to heaven,
For none can surely tell.
But if I'm right in my surmise
No doubt he'll go … the other way.

Selected Chronology

1598	Spanish bring horses to the upper Rio Grande
c. 1700	Plains Indians master the horse and become mounted hunters and warriors
1775	Daniel Boone blazes the Wilderness Road to Kentucky, opening up the trans–Appalachian frontier
1800	Buffalo herds on the Great Plains are estimated to comprise 30 to 50 million animals
1803	President Thomas Jefferson doubles the size of the U.S. by the Louisiana Purchase
1804	Jim Bridger is born in Richmond, Virginia
1804–06	Lewis and Clark explore the unknown lands west of the Mississippi River
1808	Manuel Lisa sets up the Missouri Fur Company, the first frontier firm organized to supply beaver pelts to the hatting trade
1820s	High point of nomadic Shoshoni culture
1821	The Santa Fe Trail opens up the first commercial route to northern Mexico
1822	Rocky Mountain Fur Company founded in Missouri by William H. Ashley. Jim Bridger joins the Ashley-Henry expedition to explore and trap the upper reaches of the Missouri River
1824	Mountain man Jedediah Smith discovers South Pass, a relatively easy passageway for wagons crossing the Rockies
1825	First mountain man rendezvous is held at Henry's Fork in southwestern Wyoming. Subsequently, rendezvous are held almost every year until 1840

c. 1830	Fur traders blaze the Oregon Trail, by which 350,000 people will ultimately travel to Oregon and California, and by which 40,000 Mormons will go to Salt Lake
1832–34	Prussian naturalist Prince Maximilian and Swiss artist Karl Bodmer depict in words and pictures the Indian tribes living near the headwaters of the Missouri River
1836	Battle of the Alamo in Texas
1843	Jim Bridger and Louis Vasquez build Fort Bridger
1844	Mountain man Elisha Stevens and Paiute Indian Truckee pioneer the first wagon trail over the Sierra Nevada mountains
1846	Bear Flag revolt: California declares its independence from Mexico
1847	Brigham Young leads the Mormons to Salt Lake
1847	Francis Parkman's *The Oregon Trail*
1848	War with Mexico adds the American Southwest to the possessions of the U.S.
1849–52	California gold rush
1850	Peak of the great westward migrations
1851	New York editor Horace Greeley's famous advice, "Go West, young man, go West"
1852	Wells, Fargo & Co. founded in New York
1854	Freighting firm of Russell, Majors & Waddell is established
1857–58	Mormon War
1858	Butterfield's Overland Mail route is established
1859	Captain Randolph B. Marcy's *The Prairie Traveler*
1859	Comstock Lode is discovered in Nevada
1860	First Pony Express rider carries mail between St. Joseph, Missouri, and Sacramento, California
1861	Transcontinental telegraph service begins, effectively ending the Pony Express
1863	Beginnings of the University of California's Bancroft Library
1866	First practical repeating rifle, the Winchester "Yellowboy," is invented
1866	Texas cattlemen begin to trail cattle north to railheads in Kansas City and elsewhere
1867	Gold rush near South Pass, Wyoming

1868	The buffalo herds of the Great Plains are estimated to comprise 13 million animals
1869	Transcontinental railroad is completed
1872	Mark Twain's *Roughing It*
1872	Great Diamond Hoax
1873	Colt introduces the Single Action Army revolver
1874	Invention of barbed wire spells the beginning of the end of the open range
1876	Sioux Indians overrun and kill Col. George Armstong Custer and his men at the Battle of the Little Bighorn River in Montana
1878	Texas outlaw Sam Bass is mortally wounded in a gunfight with a Texas Ranger
1879	A typical cattle drive: 15 cowboys trail 2,500 cattle from Corpus Christi, Texas, to Cheyenne, Wyoming — a distance of 1,200 miles
1881	Jim Bridger dies near Westport, Missouri
1881	Gunfight at the O.K. Corral in Tombstone, Arizona: the Earp brothers and "Doc" Holliday vs. the Clanton and McLaury brothers
1886–87	Winter of "The Great Die-Up" kills large numbers of cattle on the northern range
1889	Only 835 buffalo are left alive in the United States
1890	U.S. Census Bureau proclaims the closing of the trans–Mississippi frontier
1890	The Indian wars come to an end
1890	U.S. Army closes Fort Bridger permanently
1933	Fort Bridger becomes a Wyoming Historical Landmark and Museum
1972	Fort Bridger Annual Mountain Man Rendezvous is held for the first time

Bibliography

Aldrich, Lanning (ed). *The Western Art of Charles M. Russell*. New York: Ballantine, 1975.

Alter, J. Cecil. *Jim Bridger*. Norman: University of Oklahoma Press, 1962.

Ambrose, Stephen E. *Undoubted Courage: Meriwether Lewis, Thomas Jefferson, and the Opening of the American West*. New York: Simon and Schuster, 1996.

American Institute of Mining and Metallurgical Engineers. "Henry Janin," an obituary which appeared in the Monthly Bulletin, xxviii, No. 53, May 1911.

Athearn, Robert G. *The Mythic West in Twentieth-Century America*. Lawrence: University of Kansas Press, 1996.

Bartlett, Richard A. *Great Surveys of the American West*. Norman: University of Oklahoma Press, 1962.

Beck, Warren A., and Ynez D. Haase. *Historical Atlas of the American West*. Norman: University of Oklahoma Press, 1989.

Berger, Thomas. *Little Big Man*. New York: Dell, 1964.

_____. *The Return of Little Big Man*. New York: Little, Brown, 1999.

Billington, Ray Allen. *Land of Savagery, Land of Promise: The European Image of the American Frontier in the Nineteenth Century*. Norman: University of Oklahoma Press, 1981.

_____. *The Far Western Frontier 1830–1860*. New York: Harper, 1956.

_____. *Westward Expansion: A History of the American Frontier*. 4th ed. New York: Macmillan, 1974.

Bradbury, John. *Travels in the Interior of America*. London: Sherwood, Neely and Jones, 1817.

Bruff, Joseph Goldsborough. *Gold Rush: The Journals, Drawings and Other Papers of J. Goldsborough Bruff, Captain, Washington City and California Mining Association, April 2, 1849–July 20, 1851*. New York: Columbia University Press, 1949.

Buffalo Bill Historical Center. *American Frontier Life: Early Western Paintings and Prints from the Amon Carter Museum, Fort Worth, Texas*. New York: Abbeville, 1987.

Burroughs, John Rolfe. *Where the Old West Stayed Young*. New York: Morrow, 1962.

Burton, Richard F. *The City of the Saints and Across the Rocky Mountains to California*. London: Eyre and Spottiswoode, 1964.

Cavan, Seamus. *Daniel Boone and the Opening of the Ohio Country*. New York: Chelsea, 1991.

Charlier, Jean-Michel, and Jean Giraud. *Ombres sur Tombstone*. Paris: Dargaud, 1997.

Connell, Evan S. *Son of the Morning Star: Custer and the Little Bighorn*. New York: Harper & Row, 1984.

Cook, James H. *Fifty Years on the Old Frontier as Cowboy, Hunter, Guide, Scout and Ranchman*. New Haven CT: Yale University Press, 1923.

Cook, John R. *The Border and the Buffalo: An Untold Story of the Southwest Plains.* Topeka KS: Crane, 1907.

Crane, Stephen. *The Red Badge of Courage.* New York: Bantam, 1983.

Cunningham, Eugene. *Triggernometry: A Gallery of Gunfighters, with Technical Notes, too, on Leather Slapping as a Fine Art, gathered from many a Loose Holstered Expert over the years.* Norman: University of Oklahoma Press, 1996.

Dallas Commercial Steam Press. *Life and Adventures of Sam Bass.* Dallas: Dallas Commercial Steam Press, 1878.

DeVoto, Bernard. *Across the Wide Missouri.* London: Eyre and Spottiswoode, 1948.

Dynes, Robert J. *The Lee: British Service Rifle from 1888 to 1950.* Bloomfield NJ: Museum Restoration Service, 1979.

Ellison, Robert S. *Fort Bridger, Wyoming: A Brief History.* Casper: Wyoming Historical Landmark Commission, 1931.

Encyclopædia Britannica Online. "Western," on Website http://www.members.eb.com/bol/topic?eu=78685&sctn=1, accessed 29 August 1999.

Erb, Louise Bruning, Anne Bruning Brown, and Gilberta Bruning Hughes. *The Bridger Pass Overland Trail 1862–1869.* Littleton CO: ERBGEM, 1989.

Fadala, Sam. *Black Powder Handbook.* Northbrook IL: DBI Books, 1990.

Fleming, Paula Richardson, and Judith Luskey. *The North American Indians in Early Photographs.* Oxford: Phaidon, 1986.

Flint, Timothy. *Biographical Memoire of Daniel Boone.* Schenectady NY: New College and University Press, 1967.

Forest Service. "Historic Overland Emigrant Trail." U.S. Department of Agriculture, no date.

Garrard, Lewis H. *Wah-To-Yah and the Taos Trail.* Norman: University of Oklahoma Press, 1955.

Goetzmann, William H. *The Mountain Man.* Cody WY: Buffalo Bill Historical Center, 1978.

_____ and Goetzmann, William N. *The West of the Imagination.* New York: Norton, 1986.

Goodwin, Doris Kearns. *No Ordinary Time.* New York: Simon & Schuster, 1994.

Gowans, Fred R., and Eugene E. Campbell. *Fort Bridger: Island in the Wilderness.* Provo UT: Brigham Young University Press, 1975.

Greeley, Horace. *An Overland Journey from New York to San Francisco in the Summer of 1859.* London: Macmillan, 1965.

Gregg, Josiah. *The Commerce of the Prairies.* Chicago: Donnelley, 1926.

Harpending, Asbury. *The Great Diamond Hoax and Other Stirring Incidents in the Life of Asbury Harpending.* Norman: University of Oklahoma Press, 1958.

Harris, Burton. *John Colter: His Years in the Rockies.* Lincoln: University of Nebraska Press, 1993.

Heard, J. Norman. *Handbook of the American Frontier.* Vol. IV: *The Far West.* Lanham MD: Scarecrow, 1997.

Hebard, Grace Raymond. *Washakie: An Account of the Indian Resistance of the Covered Wagon and Union Pacific Railroad Invasions of Their Territory.* Cleveland: Clark, 1930.

Hillerman, Tony (ed). *The Best of the West: An Anthology of Classic Writings from the American West.* New York: HarperPerennial, 1991.

Holling, Holling Clancy. *Tree in the Trail.* Boston: Houghton Mifflin, 1970.

Homsher, Lola M. (ed). *South Pass, 1868: James Chisholm's Journal of the Wyoming Gold Rush.* Lincoln: University of Nebraska Press, 1960.

Howell, Carol (ed). *Cannibalism Is an Acquired Taste, and Other Notes: From Conversations with Anthropologist Omer C. Stewart.* Niwot: University Press of Colorado, 1998.

Hultkrantz, Ake. "The Shoshones in the Rocky Mt. Area" in *Shoshone Indians.* New York: Garland, 1974.

Humfreville, J. Lee. *Twenty Years among Our Savage Indians.* Hartford CT: Worthington, 1901.

James, General Thomas. *Three Years Among the Indians and Mexicans.* St. Louis: Missouri Historical Society, 1916.

Janin, Henry Covington. *Days of Diamonds and Silver and Music.* San Francisco: privately published, 1973.

Janin, Hunt, and Nicki Faircloth. "A Sense of

Wonder: The Engravings of Karl Bodmer." *Persimmon Hill*, Volume 21, Number 4, Winter 1993, pp. 5–13.

_____. "The Earliest Cowboys: Scottish Cattle Drovers." *Persimmon Hill*, Volume 23, Number 1, Spring 1995, pp. 55–60.

Joslyn Art Museum and Editions Alecto. *Bodmer's America: Karl Bodmer's Illustrations to Prince Maximilian of Wied-Neuwied's Travels in the Interior of North America 1832–1834*. London: Editions Alecto, 1991.

Korns, J. Roderic. *West from Fort Bridger: The Pioneering of Immigrant Trails across Utah, 1846–1850*. Salt Lake City: Utah State Historical Society, Volume 19, Nos. 1–4 (January, April, July, October), 1951.

Leonard, Zenas. *Adventures of Zenas Leonard, Fur Trader*. (Ewers, John C. ed). Norman: University of Oklahoma Press, 1959.

Liebling, A.J. "The American Golconda," The *New Yorker*, Vol. XVI (November 16, 1940), pp. 40–48.

Ludlow, Daniel H. (ed). *The Church and Society: Selections from the Encyclopedia of Mormonism*. Salt Lake City: Deseret, 1995.

Maguire, James H., Peter Wild, and Donald A. Barclay (eds). *A Rendezvous Reader: Tall, Tangled, and True Tales of the Mountain Men, 1805–1850*. Salt Lake City: University of Utah Press, 1997.

Majors, Alexander. *Seventy Years on the Frontier*. Chicago: Rand McNally, 1893.

Marcy, Randolph B. *The Prairie Traveler*. Old Saybrook: Globe Pequot Press, no date (reprint of original 1859 edition).

_____. *Thirty Years of Army Life on the Border*. New York: Harper, 1866.

Maximilian, Prince of Wied (H. Evans trans.). *Travels in the Interior of North America*. London: Ackerman, 1843.

McBride, Herbert W. *A Rifleman Went to War*. Mt Ida: Lancer, 1987.

McChristian, Douglas C. *The U.S. Army in the West, 1870–1880: Uniforms, Weapons, and Equipment*. Norman: University of Oklahoma Press, 1995.

Morgan, Dale L. *Overland in 1846: Diaries and Letters of the California-Oregon Trail*. Vol. II. Georgetown DC: Talisman, 1963.

_____ and Harris, Eleanor Towles (eds). *The Rocky Mountain Journals of William Marshall Anderson: The West in 1834*. San Marino: Huntington Library, 1967.

Murdoch, David. *Cowboy*. London: Dorling Kindersley, 1993.

Myres, Sandra L. *Westering Women and the Frontier Experience 1800–1915*. Albuquerque: University of New Mexico Press, 1982.

Parkman, Francis. *The Oregon Trail*. New York: Airmont, 1964.

Pelzer, Louis. *The Cattlemen's Frontier: A record of the trans–Mississippi cattle industry from oxen trains to pooling companies, 1850–1890*. Glendale AZ: Clark, 1936.

Peters, Arthur King. *Seven Trails West*. New York: Abbeville, 1996.

Porter, Mae Reed, and Odessa Davenport. *Scotsman in Buckskin: Sir William Drummond Stewart and the Rocky Mountain Fur Trade*. New York: Hastings, 1963.

Roberts, Robert B. *Encyclopedia of Historic Forts*. New York: Macmillan, 1988.

Rosa, Joseph G. *Age of the Gunfighter: Men and Weapons of the Frontier 1840–1900*. London: Salamander, 1993.

Russell, Carl P. *Firearms, Traps, & Tools of the Mountain Men*. New York: Knopf, 1967.

Russell, Osborne. *Journal of a Trapper, or, Nine Years in the Rocky Mountains 1834–1843*. Boisie ID: Syms-York, 1914.

Ruth, Kent. *Great Day in the West: Forts, Posts, and Rendezvous Beyond the Mississippi*. Norman: University of Oklahoma Press, 1963.

Slatta, Richard W. *Cowboys of the Americas*. New Haven CT: Yale University Press, 1990.

Smith, Grant H. "The History of the Comstock Lode, 1850–1920," *University of Nevada Bulletin*, Vol. XXXVII, No. 3, 1 July 1943.

Smith, Walter H.B. *The N.R.A. Book of Small Arms. Vol. 1, Pistols and Revolvers*. Washington DC: National Rifle Association, 1946.

Stansbury, Howard. *Exploration of the Valley of the Great Salt Lake*. Washington DC: Smithsonian Institution Press, 1988.

Stebbins, Theodore E., Jr., Carol Troyen, and Trevor J. Fairbrother. *A New World: Masterpieces of American Painting 1760–1910*. Boston: Museum of Fine Arts, 1983.

Steedman, Scott, and Mark Bergin. *Un Fort du Far West*. (F. Rose trans. of English original, *A 19th Century Frontier Fort*.) Paris: Hachette, 1995.

Steinbeck, John. *The Red Pony*. New York: Covici-Friede, 1937.

Stevens, William K. "Indian Warfare and Ecology," *International Herald Tribune*, 5 April 1999, p. 11.

Stewart, George R. *The California Trail: An Epic with Many Heroes*. London: Eyre and Spottiswoode, 1964.

Stewart, Omer C. *Peyote Religion: A History*. Norman: University of Oklahoma Press, 1987.

Stone, Elizabeth Arnold. *Uinta County: Its Place in History*. Glendale: Clark, 1924.

Thompson, Robert Luther. *Wiring a Continent: The History of the Telegraph Industry in the United States 1832–1866*. Princeton: Princeton University Press, 1947.

Time-Life Books. *The Canadians*. Alexandria: Time-Life, 1977.

_____. *The Chroniclers*. Alexandria: Time-Life, 1976.

_____. *The Cowboys*. Alexandria: Time-Life, 1973.

_____. *The Expressmen*. Alexandria: Time-Life, 1974.

_____. *The Gamblers*. Alexandria: Time-Life, 1978.

_____. *The Forty-Niners*. New York: Time-Life, 1974.

_____. *The Frontiersmen*. Alexandria: Time-Life, 1977.

_____. *The Great Chiefs*. Alexandria: Time-Life, 1974.

_____. *The Gunfighters*. Alexandria: Time-Life, 1974.

_____. *The Indians*. Alexandria: Time-Life, 1973.

_____. *The Old West*. New York: Prentice Hall, 1990.

_____. *The Ranchers*. Alexandria: Time-Life, 1977.

_____. *The Rivermen*. New York: Time-Life, 1975.

_____. *The Scouts*. Alexandria: Time-Life, 1978.

_____. *The Soldiers*. New York: Time-Life, 1973.

_____. *The Pioneers*. New York: Time-Life, 1974.

_____. *The Trailblazers*. New York: Time-Life, 1973.

_____. *The Women*. Alexandria: Time-Life, 1979.

Trenholm, Virginia Cole, and Maurine Carley. *The Shoshonis: Sentinels of the Rockies*. Norman: University of Oklahoma Press, 1964.

Turner, Frederick Jackson. *The Frontier in American History*. New York: Dover, 1996.

Twain, Mark. *Roughing It*. Berkeley: University of California Press, 1993.

U.S. Fish and Wildlife Service, "Seedskadee National Wildlife Refuge and Vicinity, Green River, Wyoming: A Historical Perspective," on Internet Website http://www.r6.fws.gov/REFUGES/seedskad/index.html, accessed 29 August 1999.

_____. "Seedskadee National Wildlife Refuge," May 1997.

_____. "Seedskadee National Wildlife Refuge: Wildlife Observation Guide," September 1995.

Utley, Robert M. *A Life Wild and Perilous: Mountain Men and the Paths to the Pacific*. New York: Holt, 1997.

Ward, Artemus. *Among the Mormons*. London: Ward, Lock, 1865.

Wentworth, Edward Norris. *America's Sheep Trails*. Ames: Iowa State College Press, 1948.

Wheeler, Sessions S. *Tahoe Heritage: The Bliss Family of Glenbrook, Nevada*. Reno: University of Nevada Press, 1992.

Wilkins, Thurman. *Clarence King*. New York: Macmillan, 1958.

Wilson. R.L. *Colt: An American Legend*. New York: Abbeville, 1985.

Wishart, David J. *The Fur Trade of the Amer-*

ican West 1807–1840: A Geographical Synthesis. Lincoln: University of Nebraska Press, 1979.

Wister, Owen. *The Virginian: A Horseman of the Plains.* New York: Macmillan, 1902.

Woodard, Bruce A. *Diamonds in the Salt.* Boulder: Pruett, 1967.

Endnotes

1. In the mid–19th century there was a spirited debate over whether mules or oxen made the best teams for hauling wagons in the West. Those who favored mules argued that on shorter trips (not over 1,000 miles), when the roads were good and grain could be bought or where grass was abundant, mules were better because they traveled faster and tolerated the summer heat better than oxen.

The advocates of oxen claimed that on a long (greater than 2,000 miles) trip over sandy or muddy roads, oxen had greater endurance than mules, cost less, were less likely to be stampeded by Indians, could be pursued and recaptured more easily by men on horseback if they were driven off, and, finally, they made good eating in case of need. (Mules could be eaten, too, but their flesh was so unpalatable that in the absence of salt and pepper it had to be charred on the outside and have gunpowder sprinkled over it before some men would eat it.)

The outcome of this debate in practical terms was that mules were used for short-haul freight trips and oxen for the long westward pull from the Missouri River. See Marcy, *Traveler*, pp. 27–28.

2. By 1870 the buffalo population of the Great Plains had been split into two parts by the Union Pacific Railroad line. The herd located south of the line was referred to as the southern herd; professional buffalo hunters had wiped this out by 1875. The buffalo north of the line, known as the northern herd, was killed off by 1885. The result of this slaughter was that by 1889 there were only 835 buffalo left alive in the United States. Thanks to conservation efforts, however, there are now about 200,000 buffalo in the country.

3. The beginnings of the Bancroft Library were in 1863, when Hubert Howe Bancroft, the owner of a San Francisco bookstore, was helping an editor write a guide book on the Western states. Bancroft discovered on the shelves of his own store 75 books pertaining to California and the West. This spurred him to collect other books on Western subjects and to summarize them in 39 magisterial volumes, which he wrote himself with the aid of a staff of interviewers, transcribers and writers. Bancroft also collected original documents and interviewed historical figures who were still alive.

4. Berger's 1999 sequel to this masterful work, entitled *The Return of Little Big Man*, was unfortunately not as good.

5. Greeley, *Journey*, p. 167.

6. Cited by Utley, *Life*, p. 178.

7. This account of the Seedskadee National Wildlife Refuge is drawn from my visit there in April 1999; from two descriptive brochures, dated 1997 and 1995, published by the U.S. Department of the Interior's Fish and Wildlife Service; and from the Seedskadee National Wildlife Refuge's Website.

8. In addition to the American frontier, there were Spanish and Canadian frontiers.

These are important, too, but are beyond the scope of this book. Brief summaries of them may be useful, however.

The Spanish Frontier in the Southwest. In 1540–1542 Francisco Vasquez de Coronado led an expedition north from Mexico into central Kansas, looking for the gold-rich Indian cities said to flourish there. The Spanish settled in Santa Fe in 1610 and continued to explore the Southwest thereafter. Father Eusebio Francisco Kino, a Jesuit missionary, personally founded 29 missions and led more then 50 overland expeditions. In 1706 Juan de Urribarri was sent from Santa Fe to rescue Christian Indians held captive by a tribe in the Great Plains. Fray Silvestre Vélez de Escalante failed in his effort in 1776 to find a northern route linking Santa Fe with Monterey, California, in 1776 but crossed Colorado, reached central Utah and returned to Santa Fe with first-hand knowledge of the deserts there.

The French-Canadian Frontier. A French adventurer, Samuel de Champlain, arrived in Montreal, Canada, in 1603. Under his leadership, French-Canadian *voyageurs* headed west and by 1650 were exploring the Great Lakes. ("Voyageurs" is French for "travelers" but in this context it refers to the intrepid brigades of fur trappers who set out in canoes along Canada's rivers and lakes.) In 1788 the North West Company chose Lake Athabasca in Alberta as its northernmost post. The Hudson's Bay Company also flung its posts across Canada. Later on, the North West Mounted Police took over many of these fur-trading forts and began to bring law and order to the Canadian West. This was an easier task than keeping the peace in the American West, basically because there was a lower toleration of violence in Canadian society. Moreover, Canadian men were less inclined to carry pistols than their American counterparts, so injuries and deaths from handguns were much less common.

9. For a good introduction to the settlement of Kentucky, see the chapter on "The Dark and Bloody Ground" in Craven, *Boone*, pp. 51–63.

10. Today the degree of interest in the West is quite extraordinary. For example, a quick check of the World Wide Web on 20 June 1999 using the search engine Yahoo! revealed the following:

Subject Searched	Number of Web sites
American Indians	734
American West	666
Cowboys	556
Mountain men	43
Covered wagons	23

These sites almost certainly overlap so there is some double-counting here, but it is evident that a great many Americans are still interested in the West. The West appeals to foreigners, too. In France at least 36 comic-strip books have chronicled the exploits of "Mr. Blueberry," a fictional character modeled on the archetypal Western gunfighter. See Charlier and Giraud, *Ombres sur Tombstone* [Shadows over Tombstone]. The cowboy "Lucky Luke" is another popular cartoon character in France.

11. Hebard, *Washakie*, p. 25.

12. Edwin C. Bryant, *What I Saw in California; Or Rocky Mountain Adventures*, cited in Utah Historical Quarterly, *West From Fort Bridger*, p. 51. In the mid–19th century, the terms "Shoshoni," "Bannock" and "Snake" were used more or less interchangeably.

13. As Samuel Parker, a missionary, put it, "all restraint was cast aside" by the mountain men at a rendezvous. Parker recounts "as a specimen of mountain life" how, at the 1835 rendezvous, "the great bully of the mountains" (whose name is not given) mounted his horse and, carrying a rifle, challenged any man at the rendezvous to meet him in single combat.

Kit Carson, one of the most famous mountain men, accepted this challenge. Carson mounted his own horse, carrying two single-shot pistols. The two men rode directly at each other. When they were close together, they fired at almost the same time. The bully's rifle bullet went high, over Carson's head. Carson's pistol bullet, however, hit the bully's hand, came out at the wrist and then went through his arm just above the elbow. Carson reached for his other pistol but the bully begged him to spare his life, which Carson magnanimously did.

Watching other mountain men at the rendezvous, Parker was moved to comment:

> Such scenes, some times from passion, and some times for amusement, make the pastime of their wild and wandering life.... Their demoralizing influence with the Indians has been lamentable, in all the ways that sinful propensities dictate. It is said that they have sold [the Indians] packs of cards at high prices, calling them the bible.... The most of them squander away their wages in ornaments for their women and children. [Cited in Maguire, *Reader*, pp. 158–159.]

14. Cited by Morgan, *Journals*, p. 262.

15. The single best account of Bridger's life and times is Morgan's "Galaxy of Mountain Men," in his *Journals*, pp. 259–270. I have drawn heavily on it here. J. Cecil Alter's *Jim Bridger* has been used more sparingly because though much longer and more detailed it is probably not as reliable. See also Marcy, *Thirty Years*, pp. 400–404.

16. William H. Ashley, *The West of William H. Ashley*, cited by Maguire, *Rendezvous*, p. 65.

17. Morgan, *Journals*, p. 260, citing Frederick S. Dellenbaugh, *Frémont and '49*, p. 135. Another mountain man, Etienne Provost, may possibly have seen the Great Salt Lake some weeks or months before Bridger but credit for this discovery is usually given to Bridger.

18. Cited by Morgan, *Journals*, p. 264.

19. After Maguire, *Reader*, pp. 147–148.

20. A brief introduction to Mormonism can be found in Chapter V.

21. Dodge was the chief engineer for the Union Pacific Railroad. Paying tribute to Bridger and his fellow scouts, Dodge wrote:

> In a few hours they would put together a bull boat [a small, round, skin-covered boat] and put us across any stream. Nothing escaped their vision. The dropping of a stick or breaking of a twig, the turning of the growing grass all brought knowledge to them, and they could tell who or what had done it. A single horse or Indian could not cross the trail but that they discovered it, and could tell how long since they had passed. Their methods of hunting game were perfect, and we were

never out of meat. Herbs, roots, berries, bark of trees and everything that was edible they knew. They could minister to the sick, dress wounds — in fact in all my experience I never saw Bridger or the other voyagers of the plains and mountains meet any obstacle they could not over come. [Cited in Time-Life, *Scouts*, p. 15.]

22. Both citations are from Marcy, *Thirty Years*, p. 400.

23. See Time-Life, *Old West*, p. 257, and Mary Ella Inderwick, "Letter to Alice, May 13, 1884, from North Fork Ranch, Alberta," cited by Slatta, *Cowboys*, pp. 60–61.

24. Stone, *Uinta*, p. 54.

25. Flint, *Memoire*, p. 42.

26. See Cavan, *Daniel Boone*.

27. Cited by Flint, *Memoire*, p. 183.

28. Time-Life, *Trailblazers*, p. 85.

29. After Goetzmann, *Imagination*, p. xi.

30. Ambrose, *Courage*, p. 474.

31. For a detailed account, see Ambrose, *Courage*, pp. 377–383.

32. Cited in Time-Life, *Trailblazers*, p. 33.

33. Russell, *Journal*, p. 47.

34. Cited by Time-Life, *Great Chiefs*, p. 139.

35. In this book I have used illustrations by Bodmer and Miller but none by Catlin. The reason is that Catlin's work has always seemed to me to suffer in comparison with these two artists.

36. After Time-Life, *Great Chiefs*, p. 16, and *Indians*, p. 32.

37. The great Shoshoni chief Washakie (discussed in Chapter III) invariably tried to help the whites himself, but not all the Shoshoni warriors were under his control. It was these men who were responsible for the violent incidents involving the Shoshoni. In the autumn of 1862, for example, Washakie could not prevent many of his men from joining the Bannocks, who were attacking and plundering the white settlements. As a first step, he took the loyal members of his band with him back to Fort Bridger. Later, after the U.S. Army had defeated the Bannocks in 1863 at the battle of Bear River (in northern Utah, just south of the Idaho border),

Washakie welcomed the surviving Shoshonis back into to his band.

38. Much of this information is taken from Time-Life, *Indians*, p. 51.

39. Tribes of the Northern Rockies, such as the Shoshonis and the Nez Percé, often rode east in the summer to hunt buffalo on the grasslands of the Great Plains. The nomadic warrior tribes of the Great Plains themselves included the Tonkawa, Comanche, Kiowa, Kiowa-Apache, Western Sioux, Plains Ojibwa, Plains Cree, Gros Ventre (*"big belly"* in French), Blackfoot, Crow, Arapaho, Cheyenne and Assiniboin. After Time-Life, *Old West*, pp. 214–215.

40. Marcy, *Traveler*, pp. 174–175.

41. Marcy, *Traveler*, pp. 174–175.

42. Lt. John Gregory Bourke, cited by Trenholm, *Shoshonis*, p. 250.

43. Hultkrantz, *Shoshones*, pp. 25–27.

44. In 1833 Maximilian and Bodmer traveled up the Missouri on the keelboat *Flora*. Although steamboats began to navigate that river in 1819, they were at first confined to deeper parts of the lower Missouri because they drew six feet of water and had low-powered engines. Thus until the 1850s, unpowered shallow-draft keelboats had to be used in the upper section of the river. These craft could be rowed, sailed and poled upstream. If this proved to be impossible, the crew went ashore and towed the keelboat by means of a long rope known as a cordelle, which was attached to the top of the mast. When all else failed, the men resorted to "warping": they tied the cordelle to a tree, then used the capstan on the boat to pull the vessel upstream by reeling in the cordelle. See Time-Life, *Rivermen*, pp. 20–21, 44–45, 64–65.

45. See Janin, "Wonder," p. 6, and Joslyn, *Bodmer's America*.

46. Cited in Maguire, *Reader*, p. 227.

47. Parkman, *Trail*, p. 160.

48. H.M Chittenden, cited in Bruff, *Journals*, p. 617.

49. Russell, *Journal*, pp. 62–63.

50. Marcy, *Traveler*, pp. 208–211.

51. Marcy, *Traveler*, pp. 211–212.

52. From Frances Fuller Victor, *River of the West*, in Maguire, *Reader*, pp. 234–237.

53. Heard, *Far West*, pp. 281–282.

54. Stewart, *Peyote*, p. 265.

55. Leonard, *Adventures*, p. 48.

56. Bruff's accounts of the Indians are in *Gold Rush*, pp. 86 and 124. The "Digger" Indian was almost certainly a Western Shoshoni.

57. Cited in Time-Life, *Great Chiefs*, p. 142.

58. Parkman, *Oregon Trail*, p. 149.

59. Russell, *Journal*, p. 138.

60. Maximilian, *Travels*, p. 303.

61. Parkman, *Oregon Trail*, p. 151.

62. Marcy, *Traveler*, pp. 220–221.

63. Russell, *Journal*, p. 140.

64. Parkman, *Oregon Trail*, p. 150.

65. Cited in Time-Life, *Great Chiefs*, p. 130.

66. Cited by Time-Life, *Great Chiefs*, p. 146.

67. Lieutenant Bourke, cited in Time-Life, *Great Chiefs*, p. 156.

68. Cited by Time-Life, *Great Chiefs*, p. 159.

69. Time-Life, *Trailblazers*, p. 62.

70. There are two contemporary accounts of Colter's run, which agree on all essential points: Bradbury, *Travels*, pp. 17–21, and James, *Three Years*, pp. 57–63. Both these men knew Colter personally and got the story from him. Bradbury tells us that Colter "came to St. Louis in May, 1810, in a small canoe, from the head waters of the Missouri, a distance of three thousand miles, which he had traversed in thirty days; I saw him on his arrival and received from him an account of his adventures after he had separated from Lewis and Clark's party." James says of Colter: "His veracity was never questioned among us and his character was that of a true American back-woodsman. He was about thirty-five years of age, five feet ten inches in height and wore an open, ingenious, and pleasing countenance of the Daniel Boone stamp. Nature had formed him, like Boone, for hardy indurance [sic] of fatigue, privations and perils."

71. Ruxton, *Adventures in Mexico and the Rocky Mountains*, from Maguire, *Reader*, pp. 95–96.

72. Goetzmann, "The Mountain Man as Jacksonian Man," cited by Wishart, *Fur Trade*, p. 206.

73. Dodge, *Biographical Sketch of Jim Bridger*, cited by Utley, *Life*, p. 45.

74. Ewers, *Five Indian Tribes*, cited by Wishart, *Fur Trade*, p. 206.

75. White, "Animals and Enterprise" in *The Oxford History of the American West*, cited by Wishart, *Fur Trade*, p. 85.

76. This quote and other information in this section are from Russell, *Journal*, pp. 141–144.

77. Russell, *Journal*, p. 142.

78. Time-Life, *Trailblazers*, p. 77.

79. After Chittenden, *The American Fur Trade of the Far West*, cited by Wishart, *Fur Trade*, p. 207.

80. Maguire, *Rendezvous*, p. 165.

81. Maguire, *Reader*, p. 139.

82. Russell, *Journal*, p. 137.

83. A frontier anecdote uses the "possibles" sack to show how utterly independent the mountain men were:

An English visitor joined a group of mountain men sitting around a campfire on the last day of a rendezvous. One of these men mounted his horse and set off for another 11 months in the wilderness. As he did so, however, his "possibles" sack came loose and fell into the dust. The mountain man himself did not see this happen, but the other trappers did. Still, they said nothing. Not wanting to interfere, the Englishman waited until the man had ridden out of sight. Then he asked the remaining trappers, "Why didn't you tell him he has lost his "possibles" sack?" Their laconic answer was, "He'll find out soon enough."

84. Maguire, *Reader*, pp. 46–47. Unless otherwise attributed, the conversations of the mountain men used here come from Garrard, *Wah-To-Yah*, pp. 161–163, and have been lightly edited.

85. There is a technical distinction between pistols and revolvers but these terms are often used interchangeably, as they are in this book. The technical difference is that a pistol has a chamber which is integral with or permanently aligned with the bore. A revolver has a series of chambers in a cylinder; a mechanism revolves the cylinder so that each chamber is successively aligned with the bore.

86. J. Lee Humfreville, *Twenty Years among Our Savage Indians*, from Maguire, *Reader*, pp. 148–151.

87. "Cavyard" comes from the Spanish *caballada*, a band of saddle horses.

88. Improbable as it may seem, this story rings true. For example, another mountainman, "Old Bill" Williams had a similar experience. While trapping by himself near the headwaters of the Yellowstone River, he was attacked by three Blackfoot Indians, whose arrows wounded him in the shoulder and leg. Old Bill managed to escape. The Indians took his rifle, mule and pelts but he still had his Green River knife. He rested for two days and then began to follow the Indians' trail. Four days later he found them and crept into their camp at night. He killed and scalped two of the Indians without waking the third. Old Bill then woke up the remaining Indian and showed him the two bloody scalps. Terrified, the Blackfoot sprinted out of the camp and got away. Later, when asked why he had let the last Indian escape, Old Bill said: "Ef I'd akilt that Injun, thyar wouldn't a been nobody left ter tell them Blackfeet how them bucks had gone under nor who'd a rubbed 'em out." (Cited in Time-Life, *Scouts*, pp. 16–17.)

89. Ruxton, *Adventures in Mexico and the Rocky Mountains*, from Maguire, *Reader*, p. 96.

90. Ferris, *Life in the Rocky Mountains*, from Maguire, *Reader*, pp. 176–177.

91. Ferris, *Life in the Rocky Mountains*, cited by Maguire, *Reader*, p. 176.

92. Morgan, *Journals*, p. 265.

93. Townsend, *Narrative of a Journey across the Rocky Mountains to the Columbia River*, cited by Maguire, *Reader*, p. 14.

94. Wislizenus' *A Journey to the Rocky Mountains in 1839* is cited both by Maguire, *Reader*, p. 175, and by Trenholm, *Shoshonis*, pp. 91–93.

95. Time-Life, *Trailblazers*, pp. 77, 80.

96. George Frederick Ruxton, *Blackwood's* magazine c. 1846, cited by Hillerman, *Best*, pp. 114–115.

97. Leonard, *Adventures*, p. 11.

98. The two sources of Hugh Glass's story are Alfred Jacob Miller, *The West of Alfred Jacob Miller*, and George C. Yount, *George C. Yount and His Chronicles of the*

West. Both are cited by Maguire, *Reader*, pp. 29–35.

99. Utley, *Life*, p. 57.

100. Utley, *Life*, pp. 58, 63.

101. Gregg, *Commerce*, pp. 47–49.

102. George C. Yount, *George C. Yount and His Chronicles of the West*, cited by Maguire, *Reader*, pp. 139–141. Emphasis in original.

103. The beaver is a resilient animal and can recolonize its territories quickly once trapping stops. Today beavers are common in the Fort Bridger area, where they cause problems for the local ranchers because their dams flood the hayfields. Ranchers used to dynamite the dams but this is now illegal. Today beavers are sometimes shot, even though this, too, is illegal. A few ranchers, however, still believe that the best policy is, as an ex-cowboy in the town of Fort Bridger told me, "shoot, shovel, and shut up."

104. Victor, *River of the West*, cited by Wishart, *Fur Trade*, p. 209. Wishart goes on to say that these two ex-mountain men went on to have successful second careers in Oregon. Meek was elected as Oregon's first sheriff in 1843 and five years later was appointed as the first U.S. marshall of the Territory. Newell was elected to Oregon's first territorial legislature in 1849 and that same year was appointed as one of the U.S. officials responsible for Indian affairs in the Oregon Territory.

105. See Morgan, *Journals*, p. 267, and Gowans, *Fort Bridger*, p. 11.

106. For details on the precursors to Fort Bridger, see Gowans, *Fort Bridger*.

107. Anderson, *Journals*, pp. 267–268.

108. Cited by Gowans, *Fort Bridger*, p. 12.

109. Cited by Gowans, *Fort Bridger*, p. 13.

110. J.M. Shively, *Route and Distances to Oregon and California*, in Morgan, *Overland in 1846*, p. 738.

111. Utah Historical Quarterly, *West From Fort Bridger*, pp. 51–52.

112. Marcy, *Prairie Traveler*, p. 20.

113. Bruff, *Gold Rush*, p. 68.

114. Both quotes are from Goodwin, *No Ordinary Time*, p. 332.

115. E-mail of 10 June 1999 from Mrs. Kris Hall.

116. John Steinbeck, *The Red Pony*.

117. For a well-written account of the Whitman party, see DeVoto, *Across the Wide Missouri*. This book won the Pulitzer Prize for history in 1947 and DeVoto's description of southwestern Wyoming is worth quoting here.

> From that impalpable divide [South Pass], looking southward for eight or ten miles across a seemingly unbroken level of sage, one's gaze rested at last on a low ridge, a little greener than the aching plain, a fragmented prolongation of the Antelope Hills…. At the utmost extent of one's vision southwestward, a slate-blue vagueness which seemed to float above the earth meant mountain peaks that were in neither the United States nor Oregon but Mexico. In this vast emptiness the sage and greasewood seemed level as a surveyor's bench but that was another illusion of thin air, for actually the plain undulated and thrust up sizeable buttes. Actually, also the baked, heat-quivering surface was not so dry as it seemed; there were gullies with snow water in them and even an occasional, incredible small patch of marsh.

DeVoto's chapter on the Whitmans' crossing of South Pass is reprinted in Hillerman, *Best*, pp. 369–372.

118. Russell, *Journal*, p. 46. It was not only the "rude savages" who wanted to stare at white women. Just before the 1838 rendezvous, held that year at the junction of the Pope Agie (often spelled Popeasia) and Wind Rivers in central-west Wyoming, Jim Bridger is said to have had a sign put up on the door of an old schoolhouse. "Come to Popeasia"; it said, "plenty of whiskey and white women." Cited by Time-Life, *Women*, p. 30.

119. Marcy, *Traveler*, pp. 24–25.

120. Marcy, *Traveler*, pp. 35–36.

121. Marcy, *Traveler*, p. 39.

122. Jesse Applegate, *A Day with the Cow Column in 1843*, cited in Time-Life, *Pioneers*, pp. 90–91.

123. Marcy, *Traveler*, pp. 221–222.

124. Ludlow, *Church*, pp. 333–334.

125. William Richards, "History of

Brigham Young," Latter-day Saints Church Historian's Office, p. 95, cited by Trenholm, *Shoshonis*, p. 108.

126. Trenholm, *Shoshonis*, p. 108.

127. Gowans, *Fort Bridger*, p. 31.

128. Gowans, *Fort Bridger*, p. 31.

129. Gowans, *Fort Bridger*, p. 31.

130. Marcy, *Traveler*, p. 36. Emphasis in original.

131. Stone, *Uinta*, p. 53.

132. Cited by Stone, *Uinta*, p. 53.

133. Cited in Time-Life, *Forty-niners*, p. 17.

134. Homsher, *South Pass*, p. 215.

135. One of these aspiring miners was mountain man Osborne Russell. He had moved to Oregon after his years in the Rockies (1834–43) and in 1848 came to California to look for gold. In a letter of 10 November 1849, written from "Gallowstown" (i.e., Hangtown, later renamed Placerville), addressed to his sister in Maine, Russell wrote that, "The most [gold] I have ever dug in a day was $100, but have frequently obtained $40 to $60 per day."

Having done so well at mining, Russell then branched out into merchandising, selling supplies and room and board to Placerville miners. Together with a partner, he also bought two cargo boats to carry goods and passengers between Sacramento and Portland. This venture was a disaster, however, because his partner absconded with all their money, sold one of the boats and pocketed the proceeds. Russell spent the rest of his days trying to repay his creditors. Finally hospitalized in Placerville with "Miner's Rheumatism" (he was paralyzed from the waist down), he died there in 1892 at the age of 78. See Russell's *Journal* for details of his long and adventuresome life.

136. Details on the gold rush fleet were provided by the San Francisco Maritime Museum, which cites Stillman, *Seeking the Golden Fleece: A Record of Pioneer Life in California*. San Francisco: Roman, 1877, as the source of this information.

137. Cited by Time-Life, *Old West*, p. 140.

138. Bruff, *Journals*, p. 65.

139. Bruff, *Journals*, p. 77.

140. Bruff, *Journals*, p. 81.

141. Tahoe National Forest, *Emigrant Trail*.

142. From Hillerman, *Best*, pp. 379–384.

143. Tahoe National Forest, *Emigrant Trail*.

144. Joseph E. Ware, *The Emigrants' Guide to California*, cited by Time-Life, *The Old West*, p. 130.

145. Tahoe National Forest, *Emigrant Trails*.

146. This account is taken from "Goodbye, Death Valley" in Hillerman, *Best*, pp. 385–390.

147. Stansbury, *Exploration*, p. 74.

148. Utley, *Life*, pp. 269–271.

149. Utley, *Life*, pp. 267–268.

150. Marcy, *Thirty Years*, pp. 401–404.

151. Utley, *Life*, p. 277.

152. Marcy, *Thirty Years*, p. 401.

153. Ruth, *Great Day*, p. 290.

154. Peters, *Seven Trails*, p. 120.

155. Cited by Ruth, *Great Day*, p. 292.

156. Cited by Time-Life, *Pioneers*, p. 181.

157. Roberts, *Encyclopedia*, p. 856.

158. Lander's report is cited by Hebard, *Washakie*, pp. 94–95.

159. Roberts, *Encyclopedia*, p. 856.

160. Cited by Marianne Babal, Wells Fargo Bank Historical Services, "Wells Fargo in Wyoming," 9 February 1996, p. 1.

161. After Time-Life, *Expressmen*, pp. 191, 224.

162. Time-Life, *Expressmen*, pp. 20, 33, 68, 127.

163. This description comes from a personal inspection of the Wells Fargo coach in Wells Fargo's main office in San Francisco and from Time-Life, *Expressmen*, pp. 134–137.

164. Greeley, *Overland Journey*, pp. 167–170.

165. See Ward, *Among the Mormons*, pp. 29–34.

166. See Burton, *City of the Saints*, pp. 196–198, and "A revolver is an admirable tool," an excerpt from the same book, which is reprinted in Hillerman, *Best*, pp. 409–412.

167. Taken from Hillerman, *Best*, pp. 391–393.

168. An excellent primary source on

the Pony Express is Majors, *Seventy Years*. For a useful secondary source, see "The fabled Pony Express" in Time-Life's *Expressmen*, pp. 88–121. I have drawn freely on both sources for my account.

169. One of my prized possessions as a young boy was a dramatic account, recorded on a 78-rpm record, of Haslam's famous ride.

170. See Majors, *Seventy Years*, p. 180. Other Pony Express riders claimed to have chalked up even more impressive mileage. Jack Keetley said he had once ridden 340 miles nonstop in about 24 hours. William F. "Buffalo Bill" Cody asserted that he had gone 384 miles nonstop. Haslam's record, however, is the one most often cited by histories of the West. After the Pony Express ceased its operations, Haslam became a rider for Wells, Fargo & Co.

171. Twain, *Roughing It*, pp. 51–52.

172. For a discussion of the telegraph industry in the United States, see Thompson, *Wiring a Continent*. My account here is also drawn from Time-Life, *Expressmen*, pp. 112–113.

173. Ruth, *Great Day*, p. 291.

174. Time-Life, *Old West*, p. 195.

175. Cited by Hillerman, *Best*, pp. 425–426.

176. Time-Life, *Expressmen*, p. 221.

177. Both accounts are from Time-Life, *Old West*, pp. 198–199.

178. Ellison, *Fort Bridger*, p. 51.

179. This and other treaties involving the Shoshonis are discussed in Hebard, *Washakie*.

180. Time-Life, *Old West*, p. 199.

181. Tahoe, *Trail*.

182. It is still possible to pan for gold in the California mountains today. Local stores will happily sell you a pan of the proper size and will point you toward the nearest creek. Much of the land in the Sierras is National Forest, open to the public, so trespassing on private property is not a problem. Only the most dedicated enthusiast, however, is likely to get a show of "color," that is, a tiny trace of gold dust.

183. Cited by Wheeler, *Tahoe*, pp. 9, 11.

184. Homsher, *South Pass*, pp. 215–223.

185. Sources on the Great Diamond

Hoax include Bartlett, *Surveys*, which is based on Emmons' own Field Notes, entitled "The Diamond Discovery of 1872"; Wilkins, *King*; Harpending, *Hoax*; Liebling, *Golconda*; an excerpt from Randall Henderson's *On Desert Trails*, cited by Hillerman, *Best*, pp 289–291; and my own records of the Janin family.

186. Cited by Bartlett, *Surveys*, p. 196.

187. Cited by Bartlett, *Surveys*, p. 198.

188. New York *Times*, 5 December 1872, cited by Bartlett, *Surveys*, p. 201.

189. Liebling, *Golconda*, p. 48.

190. Crane, *Badge*, p. 3.

191. Enlisted men assigned to frontier posts had to put up with low pay, bad living conditions, harsh discipline, loneliness, monotony, and the threat of being killed or captured by Indians. Not surprisingly, about one-third of them deserted during their first year of service. See Time-Life, *Soldiers*, pp. 68–69.

192. Cited by Time-Life, *Soldiers*, p. 162.

193. The Springfield Armory in Springfield, Massachusetts, was established by Congress in 1794 to make rifles for the U.S. Army.

194. In 1877, Turkish soldiers armed with lever action Winchester rifles used them in battle "with such striking effect ... that the attention of all the great powers was drawn towards the advisability of adopting some form of repeating or magazine rifle." (See Dynes, *The Lee*, p. 3.) The inherent weaknesses of the lever action could not be overcome, however, and in 1880 Germany took the lead in introducing a bolt action rifle for military use. This was the .43 caliber Model 71 Mauser, which held eight cartridges in a tubular magazine. The U.S. Army continued to use its single-shot Springfields until 1892, when it adopted the bolt action, Norwegian-designed, Krag-Jorgensen rifle. Later, by modifying the Mauser the Springfield Armory produced in 1906 one of the best and most accurate military rifles of all time — the bolt action .30-06 Springfield.

195. Ellison, *Fort Bridger*, p. 52.

196. This account is drawn from Burroughs, *Old West*, p. 8 ff, and from Slatta, *Cowboys*, pp. 24–25.

197. This quote and other details of

Hoy's life are from the Hoy Manuscript, Colorado State University, cited by Burroughs, *Old West*, p. 10.

198. William Thomas Hamilton, *My Sixty Years on the Plains*, cited by Maguire, *Reader*, pp. 87, 175.

199. Slatta, *Cowboys*, p. 221.

200. Slatta, *Cowboys*, p. 102.

201. Joseph G. McCoy, *Cattle Trade of the West and Southwest*, p. 10. McCoy is cited both by Pelzer, *Frontier*, p. 245, and by Slatta, *Cowboys*, p. 48. The cowboy's love of tobacco was one of the two reasons why he often wore a leather vest, even in the hottest weather. It is difficult for a man on horseback to reach into the pockets of his jeans. The side pockets of a vest, however, are easy to reach and are admirably suited for carrying the "makins" for a smoke, i.e., cigarette papers and a small cloth bag full of Bull Durham tobacco. The second reason for the vest is that the other pocket could hold a notebook called a "tally book," which was used to record brands and other details about ranch livestock.

202. Time-Life, *Cowboys*, p. 49.

203. Murdock, *Cowboy*, p. 7.

204. See Janin and Faircloth, "The Earliest Cowboys," p. 55.

205. Slatta, *Cowboys*, p. 72.

206. Charles M. MacInnes, *In the Shadow of the Rockies*. London: Rivingtons, 1930, p. 217, cited by Slatta, *Cowboys*, p. 73.

207. This account is taken from the Dodge City *Times* of 10 July 1880, reprinted in Hillerman, *Best*, pp. 169–170.

208. Florence B. Hughes, "Listening-in at the Old Timer's Hut," *Canadian Cattlemen*, June 1941, cited in Slatta, *Cowboys*, p. 50.

209. Slatta, *Cowboys*, p. 187.

210. Cited by Pelzer, *Frontier*, p. 248.

211. This account is drawn from Cunningham, *Triggernometry*, pp. 274–297.

212. The telegram to President Harrison was sent from Cheyenne after dark on 12 April 1892. Before sunrise the next day, three troops of cavalry had arrived to quell the Johnson County War.

213. See the extract from T.A. Larsen's *Wyoming*, reprinted as "The Johnson County War" in Hillerman, *Best*, pp. 365–366; and Time-Life, *Gunfighters*, pp. 206–223.

214. Time-Life, *Gunfighters*, p. 223.

215. See Time-Life, *Gunfighters*, pp. 201–204, 207; and Cunningham, *Triggernometry*, pp. xxviii–xxix.

216. Wentworth, *Sheep Trails*, pp. 308–316.

217. Wentworth, *Sheep Trails*, p. vii.

218. See Burroughs, *Old West*, p. 67.

219. "Diamondfield Jack's" real name was Jackson Lee Davis. He earned his nickname through repeated allusions to his brief career as a diamond-hunter in southwestern Idaho near Silver City. Although the case against him was weak, he was convicted of killing the two sheepmen and spent more than five years in Idaho jails before finally being granted a full pardon. See Time-Life, *Ranchers*, pp. 121–124.

220. After Burroughs, *Old West*, pp. 525–543.

221. Cited by Time-Life, *Old West*, p. 223.

222. Cook, *Border*, p. 121–122.

223. Cook, *Border*, p. 126.

224. Cook, *Border*, pp. 175–176.

225. Marcy, *Traveler*, p. 237.

226. Cook, *Border*, p. 411.

227. Cunningham, *Triggernometry*, p. 7.

228. Russell, *Firearms*, pp. 60–62, 87.

229. Parkman, *Oregon Trail*, p. 229.

230. Parkman, *Oregon Trail*, p. 56.

231. Twain, *Roughing It*, p. 5.

232. After McBride, *Rifleman*, p. 172.

233. Marcy, *Traveler*, pp. 41–43.

234. Cited by Wilson, *Colt*, p. 18.

235. It should be noted that Colt also made rifles and shotguns in addition to the many different kinds of pistols it offered for sale. A standard reference is Wilson, *Colt*, which is the official history of Colt firearms from 1836 to 1978.

236. Marcy, *Thirty Years*, cited by Wilson, *Colt*, pp. 52–54.

237. Although not as popular as the Colt .36 Navy and .44 Army revolvers, the 1858 Remington New Army revolver, also made in both calibers, was a much better pistol. Esthetically, the Colt may have been more handsome than the Remington and it may have had a slightly better balance in the hand. Because of its open-top design the Colt was also easier to take apart for cleaning.

(The simple act of driving out the barrel wedge broke the Colt down into its three major parts — barrel, cylinder and grip.) The Remington, however, had a solid frame, which made it much stronger and therefore more durable in combat. It is said that, during the Civil War, soldiers would trade a handful of Colts for one Remington New Army; after the war, surplus Remingtons sold much better than surplus Colts.

238. Cook, James H., *Fifty Years*, p. 183.

239. Wentworth, *Sheep Trails*, p. 282.

240. Cited by Wilson, *Colt*, p. 58.

241. Both these accounts are cited by Joseph G. Rosa in his Introduction to Cunningham, *Triggernometry*, p. xx–xxi.

242. McBride, *Rifleman*, pp. 176–177.

243. George W. Romspert, *The Western Echo: a Description of the Western States and Territories of the United States as Gathered in a Tour by Wagon*, cited by Pelzer, *Cattlemen's Frontier*, p. 245.

244. Elfego Baca, *The Political Record of Elfego Baca*, reprinted in Hillerman, *Best*, pp. 335–338. Another source — James H. Cook, *Fifty Years*, p. 260 — confirms that about 4,000 shots were fired. At first this seems hard to believe, but if each of the 80 cowboys fired 50 times over the 36-hour period, the total would indeed be 4,000 rounds. A cowboy carried about 30 cartridges on his gunbelt. Colleagues could have brought him more from camp or from town.

245. Burton, *City of the Saints*, cited by Hillerman, *Best*, p. 410.

246. Cited by Joseph G. Rosa in his Introduction to Cunningham, *Triggernometry*, p. xx. Italics in original.

247. This quote and much of following account are taken from Time-Life, *The Old West*, p. 78.

248. Johnson's exploits were so notorious that they have been the subject of at least two books — Thorp's and Bunker's *Crow Killer* (1958) and Fisher's novel *Mountain Man* (1965) — and one movie — Pollack's *Jeremiah Johnson* (1972), starring Robert Redford. The account used here is taken from the excerpt from *Crow Killer* reprinted in Maguire, *Reader*, pp. 232–233. Johnson's contemporaries disagreed about whether he actually ate the livers of the Indians he killed: some claimed he did but others said he only made gobbling sounds while rubbing the liver against his whiskers. Johnson later became a "wood-hawk" (a supplier of firewood for steamboats) in the 1870s. Even in his old age he was still vigorous. One observer said of him: "His matted hair and bushy beard fluttered in the breeze and his giant frame and limbs … formed an exceedingly impressive picture." (Cited in Time-Life, *Rivermen*, p. 180.)

249. This quote and the description of Green River knives is taken from Russell, *Firearms, Traps, & Tools*, pp. 199–202.

250. Cited by Maguire, *Reader*, p. 82.

251. Holliday, *The World Rushed In*, p. 400, cited by Wheeler, *Tahoe*, pp. 8, 142.

252. The German word "Lebensraum" refers to the extra land wanted by a nation for expansion of trade or for reasons of national prestige. The citation is from Athearn, *Mythic West*, pp. 10–11. Emphasis has been added.

253. See Berger, *Return*, pp. 215–216, for these accounts of Annie Oakley's shooting.

254. Turner, *Frontier*, p. 1.

255. Billington, *Expansion*, p. 655.

256. Wister, *Virginian*, p. 29.

257. Lucas was interviewed by the British weekly magazine *Time Out* for its July 14–21, 1999 issue; see pp. 18–19.

258. Much of this information comes from the Encyclopedia Britannica's Internet article on Westerns.

259. Cited by Pelzer, *Cattlemen's Frontier*, p. 248. Emphasis added.

260. For a good selection of contemporary illustrations of women in the West, see Time-Life, *The Women*.

261. Stephen Crane, "The Bride Comes to Yellow Sky," reprinted in Hillerman, *Best*, pp. 496–505.

262. Kit Carson, *Autobiography*, cited in Maguire, *Rendezvous*, pp. 162–163.

263. Wilson, *Colt*, p. 182.

264. Fron Branch, *The Cowboy and His Interpreters*, cited by Pelzer, *Frontier*, p. 244.

265. Myers, *Women*, p. 99.

266. Walker Dixon Grissom, cited by Hillerman, *Best*, pp. 463–465. As reported by the *Denver Post*, what the judge really said was hardly less florid than Dolan's own

account. The judge was not a man of few words and his statement was too long to reproduce here, but this excerpt gives its flavor:

In 1874 you [Packer], in company with five companions, passed through the beautiful mountain valley where stands the town of Lake City. At that time the hand of man had not marred the beauties of nature. The picture was fresh from the hand of the Great Artist who created it. You and your companions camped at the base of a grand old mountain, in sight of the place you now stand, on the banks of a stream as pure and beautiful as ever traced by the finger of God upon the bosom of earth.... In this goodly favored spot you conceived your murderous designs.... No eye saw the bloody deed performed; no ear, save your own, caught the groans of your dying victims.... You, Alfred Packer, sowed the wind; you must now reap the whirlwind.... I [the judge] am but the instrument of society to impose the punishment which the law provides.... Close your ears to the blandishments of hope.... But prepare to meet the spirits of thy murdered victims. Prepare for the dread certainty of death....

267. Harpending, *Hoax*, pp. 153, 180.

268. Reprinted in Janin, *Days*.

Index